SportingNews

SELECTS

PRO FOOTBALL'S
GREATEST
QUARTERBACKS

Edited by Barry Reeves and Ron Smith
Designed by Bill Wilson
Photos edited by Albert Dickson

CONTRIBUTING WRITERS

Paul Attner/TSN senior writer: Introduction (14), Fran Tarkenton (90), Troy Aikman (92), Peyton Manning (98), Bobby Layne (106), Norm Van Brocklin (108), Tom Brady (110), Sonny Jurgensen (116), Jim Kelly (118), Bob Griese (122), Joe Namath (123), Warren Moon (124) and Archie Manning family (148).

Mike Kilduff/Free-lance writer: The perfect quarterback (20), Sid Luckman (96), Tom Brady-Joe Montana (115), Y.A. Tittle (120) and Len Dawson (121).

Michael Olesker/Baltimore Sun: Johnny Unitas (28).

Bill Plaschke/Los Angeles Times: Joe Montana (38).

Alan Ross/Historian and author: Otto Graham (46), John Hadl (136), Jim Hart (140) and team-by-team rankings (168).

Joe Hoppel/TSN senior editor: John Elway introduction (52).

Dennis Tuttle/Free-lance writer: Sammy Baugh (60).

Steve Harrison/Miami Herald: Dan Marino (66).

Tom Silverstein/Milwaukee Journal Sentinel: Brett Favre (72).

Gerry Dulac/Pittsburgh Post-Gazette: Terry Bradshaw (78).

Matt Crossman/TSN associate editor: Roger Staubach (82).

David Claerbaut/Author: Bart Starr, excerpted from the book, When Leadership Mattered (86).

Dan Pompei/TSN senior writer: Peyton Manning-Marvin Harrison (101) and Donovan McNabb (138).

Phil Barber/Santa Rosa (Calif.) Press Democrat: Greatest passes (154).

Vinnie Iyer/TSN projects editor: Phil Simms (126), Bob Waterfield (127), Randall Cunningham (131), John Brodie (139), Steve McNair (145), Jack Kemp (146) and Running quarterbacks (160).

Other contributors: George Winkler (Steve Young, page 94); Jessica Daues (Dan Fouts, 104); Ron Smith (George Blanda, 125; Ace Parker, 128); Katie Koss (Ken Stabler, 129; Joe Theismann, 130; Daryle Lamonica, 132; Charlie Conerly, 141; Paddy Driscoll, 142; Dutch Clark, 144); Barry Reeves (Boomer Esiason, 133; Ken Anderson, 134; Benny Friedman, 147); Dave Sloan (Arnie Herber, 135; Jim Plunkett, 137); Dennis Dillon (Raymond Berry on Unitas, 36; Daunte Culpepper, 143).

Copy editors: Barry Reeves, Dave Sloan, Ron Smith

Cover design: Michael Behrens

Page design: Chris Callan, Russ Carr, Jack Kruyne, Chad Painter, Bob Parajon and Bill Wilson

Prepress specialists: Vern Kasal, Steve Romer, Pamela Speh

PHOTO CREDITS

T – top, B – bottom, L – left, R – right, M – middle

Malcolm Emmons – Unitas cover, Staubach cover, inside front cover, 8-9, 12-13, 23(3), 24T, 26B, 28-29, 30, 31, 32, 33, 34, 37, 38, 39, 40, 41, 42, 44TL, 78(2), 79, 80, 81, 82(2), 84(2), 85, 86TR, 87, 88, 89, 90, 91(3),104, 105, 116, 117, 121(2), 122(2), 123B, 125(2), 129T, 130, 132, 134R, 136, 137B, 139, 140, 148, 164L, 166, 170, 172, 175

Sporting News Archives – Montana cover, 7, 16TL, 16 BL, 21(2), 22T, 24B, 25B, 28R, 35, 38L, 43, 44BR, 45, 46, 50(2),51, 52, 53, 55, 60-61, 62, 63, 64(2), 65, 68T, 70(2), 71, 74, 75, 86BL, 92B, 94T, 96, 97(2), 100R, 106, 107, 108, 109, 118, 119(2), 120B, 124(2), 126(2), 127(2), 131, 133, 134L, 137T, 141(2), 143, 144(2), 146(2), 156R, 162, 163T, 164B, 168L, 168M

Corbis – 46-47

Pro Football Hall of Fame – 135, 142, 147

Indianapolis Colts – 36

Jill Oulette – 115

Cleveland Press Collection of Cleveland State University – 49

Wide World Photos – 10-11, 15, 21(3), 48, 56-57, 123T, 128, 147, 154, 155, 156L, 157R, 158T, 160

Dozier Mobley/Wide World Photos – 2-3, 120T

Albert Dickson/Sporting News – 4-5, 14, 17, 26T, 27(2), 54L, 59, 66(2), 68B, 72-73, 76, 77, 93, 94B, 95, 98, 99, 100L, 101, 102, 110, 113, 114, 150-151, 157L, 159, 161L, 163B, 167R, 169, 174

Bob Leverone/Sporting News – Favre cover, inside back cover, 16 TR, 69, 111, 138, 145B, 149, 158B, 161R, 167L, 168R

Robert Seale/Sporting News – 18, 22B, 23TL, 25T, 58, 92T, 112, 145T, 165

Jay Drowns/Sporting News – 152-153

Todd Warshaw for TSN – 54R

Bernie Nunez for TSN – 173

The classic picture of frustration, New York Giants quarterback Y.A. Tittle sitting in disbelief after throwing an interception/touchdown against the Pittsburgh Steelers, was taken in the second week of the 1964 season, Tittle's last in the NFL.

This book was produced with four cover versions—ISBN 10: 0-89204-796-8, ISBN 13: 978-0-8920-4796-3 (Johnny Unitas cover); ISBN 10: 0-89204-818-2, ISBN 13: 978-0-8920-4818-2 (Joe Montana cover); ISBN 10: 0-89204-819-0, ISBN 13: 978-0-8920-4819-9 (Roger Staubach cover); ISBN 10: 0-89204-820-4, ISBN 13: 978-0-8920-4820-5 (Brett Favre cover).

10 9 8 7 6 5 4 3 2 1

CO

Brett Favre

NTENTS

FOREWORD

BY TROY AIKMAN

We have no secret handshake. Few of us know the Greek alphabet. We don't stuff tissue paper in chicken wire and parade a float across campus. But we are a fraternity, this group of men who have played quarterback in the National Football League.

Oh Lord, do I remember my initiation into this fraternity. It was 1989, my rookie year in Dallas, and unless you count training camp, there was no pledge period. Jimmy Johnson tossed me into the fire, making me the starter for the first game. We lost to the Saints, 28-0. I started 10 more games that year—a broken finger kept me out of the other five—and we lost every one of them. I got sacked 19 times, and you'd need a spiral notebook and a couple of sharp pencils to track all the other times I left divots in the turf.

Welcome to the NFL, kid.

David Carr knows what I'm talking about. He got pounded as a rookie quarterback for the Texans in 2002, absorbing 76 sacks. Peyton Manning knows. He threw 28 interceptions while the Colts went 3-13 behind him in 1998. John Elway, Terry Bradshaw, Steve Young, Dan Fouts—it's a distinguished group that can speak to the learning curve required to play quarterback at its highest level.

It never gets easy. Many have said the hardest thing to do in sports is to hit a baseball. I've played enough baseball to know that's probably true. But I believe the hardest position to play in sports is quarterback.

A quarterback takes a beating. Even with five, six, even seven guys trying to keep him on his feet, any quarterback will take some nasty hits. And he usually doesn't see them coming. If a quarterback is doing his job right as he prepares to throw, his eyes are focused downfield, not behind him or off to the side. Defensive ends feast on that. Have you ever felt a 280-pound block of muscle crash into your back at full speed while you're looking the other way? For your sake, I hope not. When I was young, I'd be OK two or three days after a game. But toward the end of my career, the soreness lingered until just before the next game, when I subjected myself to another battering. I can still feel some of those shots.

Lots of guys can absorb hits, but a quarterback must do more. For starters, he must get back up and run the next play within 45 seconds. That's a real motivator for the other guys on the team. They'll play their hearts out for a quarterback if they know he'll scrape himself off the ground and get back in the huddle.

That takes as much mental toughness as physical toughness. In fact, mental toughness might be a quarterback's most important attribute. Has he thrown three interceptions and left his team with a 14-point deficit entering the fourth quarter? He can't even think about his mistakes. It's his job to radiate confidence and lead his team to victory. Is he getting hammered in the papers and on sports talk radio? Hey, it comes with the territory, pal. He's the quarterback, so he gets more than his share of the glory when he's winning. When he's not, he'd better be able to take the heat. Teammates respect that as much as his ability to lay the ball on a receiver's fingertips 50 yards away.

The toughest part of playing quarterback, though, is the amount of information that must be processed in mere seconds while all hell is breaking loose around him. An NFL playbook is about as thick as a Sears catalog. The quarterback must know hundreds of plays, each featuring multiple variations based on the defensive alignment. As he approaches the line, he must see what look the defense is showing and, if necessary, adjust the play. After the snap, he must recognize blitzes, spot changes in coverage, go through his reads to find the best target and then deliver the ball quickly and accurately without being rattled by the pass rush.

Joe Montana was amazing that way. He truly was Joe Cool, the calm in the midst of the storm. He was graceful, almost like a ballerina at quarterback, and his game looked effortless.

I respect Joe so much for that. I know how hard it is to play quarterback, yet he made it look easy. Call it a "quarterback thing," I guess, but you'd have to be a quarterback to truly appreciate the amazing nature of what he did. Even other football players don't really get it. That's why there's a real fraternity among those who have played the position and why quarterbacks typically have so much respect for each other, particularly those who have enjoyed success.

Thank goodness I didn't have to try to rank the great quarterbacks, a task shouldered by the writers and editors at *Sporting News*. It's hard enough to rate players in the same era, such as John Elway and Dan Marino. Elway won a pair of Super Bowls and compiled great numbers, but not like Marino's. Danny set all the records, but he doesn't have a ring. Which

one is better? Beats me. And then you start trying to compare players from different eras, when the rules and strategies were different. What I do know is that all these players were successful within their systems, all were made better by the players around them, and virtually all of them won a lot of football games. If you look at the top 10, from Johnny Unitas through Bart Starr, you can make a case that at least a handful of them deserve top billing. We're talking about degrees of greatness, so the actual ranking next to each guy's name doesn't mean much to me.

What does impress me is

Aikman (8), with the help of such players as Michael Irvin, led the Cowboys to three Super Bowl victories.

cerned, that's what it's all about.

I've heard some people fretting that there aren't any great young quarterbacks to carry the torch for the Montanas and Marinos of the world. Rubbish. Twenty years from now, we'll be talking about Peyton Manning the way we talk about Roger Staubach and Joe Namath now. Shoot, Manning already is on the list, as are Tom Brady, Donovan McNabb and Daunte Culpepper, and if they continue to improve, they'll shoot up the rankings even further.

With such players as Michael Vick and Eli Manning coming along, it's a great time

What impresses me is the way each player put his personal touch on the position I love.

the way each player put his personal touch on the position I love. Elway was a master of the comeback. As much as winning championships, his ability to bring Denver back to win late in games was a huge measuring stick of his greatness. Marino was as intense of a competitor as I've ever watched. The game didn't seem to come as easily to him as it did to Montana, and I always admired the grit with which he played to become the most prolific passer in pro football history. I admire Brett Favre for his recklessness and child-like love of the game.

He'll keep slinging that ball, even if he already has four interceptions and appears headed for eight. Somehow, he gets the job done. Steve Young was a fighter. He never quit, no matter how late in the game and how many points the 49ers were down. When Jim Kelly played, he might have been the toughest guy on the field for either team. And the balls Warren Moon threw were about as pretty as any I've seen.

These guys were my contemporaries, so I can speak more to their greatness than some others in the top 50. I

wish I'd been able to watch players such as Unitas and Otto Graham, Sammy Baugh and Sid Luckman. But considering their high rankings, it's evident the panel that assembled the list was cognizant of more than just stats. The numbers of most of the old-timers don't match up to what guys are doing today. But they were great leaders and they were winners, and as far as I'm con-

to be a fan of quarterbacks. And then there are the guys in college and high school who are patterning their games after Brady and McNabb, working toward their chance to make a name for themselves. I have no doubt that many of these quarterbacks will do just that.

It's a tight-knit group, this fraternity of quarterbacks, but we always have room for more.

POISE

AND LEADERSHIP ...

9

CHAMPIONSHIP EXECUTION ...

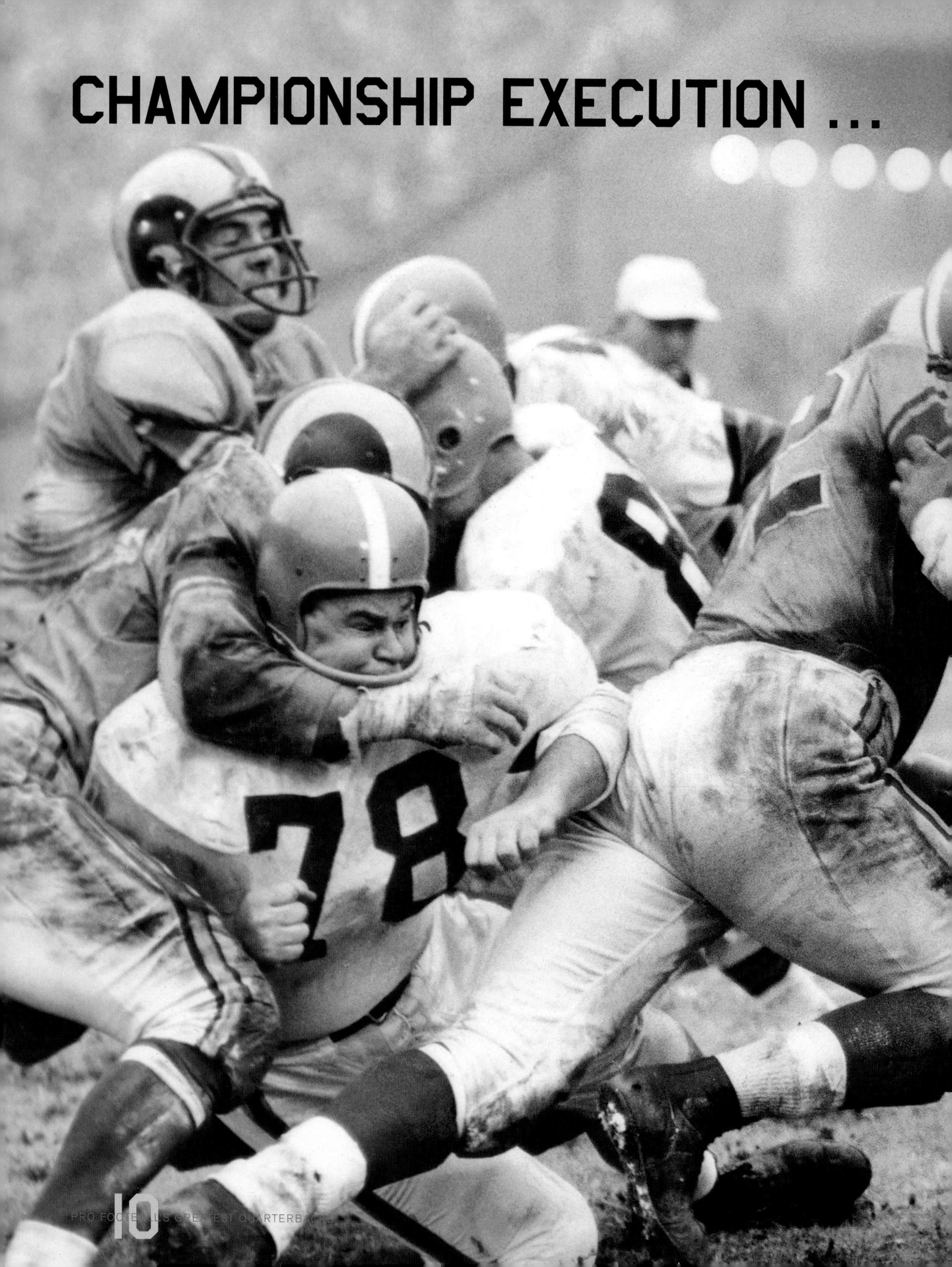

MENTAL AND
PHYSICAL TOUGHNESS ...

GREATEST QUARTERBACKS

13

... DEFINE **GREAT**

PRO FOOTBALL'S GREATEST QUARTERBACKS

'NESS

hese days, they are appraised at $20,000 new. Put one on eBay, and who knows what it would fetch. But for the quarterbacks who possess it, a championship ring has value far more important than dollar signs. They are forever linked—the ring, the position and the role a glittery piece of jewelry can play in determining the real measure of a career's worth of achievement.

Look at the 50 names on our list of greatest NFL quarterbacks. Quick quiz: How many have a ring? Right answer: 32. That is 64 percent of our distinguished group. The ring becomes even more fashionable among the top 10. Of those, just Dan Marino lacks an adornment on his finger. From the top 25, he is joined by Fran Tarkenton, Peyton Manning, Dan Fouts, Jim Kelly and Y.A. Tittle in the championship-less club. Of the top 25, the only ones not in the Hall of Fame are Troy Aikman (three rings), Brett Favre (one ring), Tom Brady (three rings) and Manning. Aikman was awaiting eligibility and the other three still were playing through the 2004 season.

The debate about the worth of a ring is one of the most fascinating in football. It can be the difference between a complete career and a lasting void, between mere acclaim and a proud bust in Canton. Whether fair or not, the ring has come to stand as the symbol of a winner, and those quarterbacks who

have performed admirably in their careers yet lack a championship among their accomplishments face a difficult challenge getting into the Hall of Fame. Certainly, quarterbacks with or without a title aren't readily welcomed into the Hall; with Marino, Steve Young and

Benny Friedman being inducted in 2005, the quarterback total stood at just 29.

Of course, being a quarterback on a winner doesn't automatically mandate Hall of Fame space. There are plenty of Super Bowl quarterbacks who will never have a sniff of immortality, be it Trent Dilfer or Doug Williams or Brad Johnson or Jim McMahon. They all have the ring and the credibility that accompanies directing their team to a championship. But greatness? Not in their futures.

Still, you gaze at our Top 50 list and pick out the names of those not in the Hall and wonder if some of their careers would have been viewed differently with a

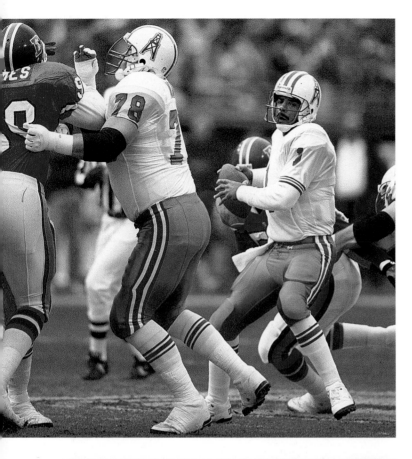

Greatness often is in the eye of the beholder. Moon (top left) and Marino (top right) compiled gaudy statistics without playing on a championship team. Former New Orleans star Archie Manning (8) never even played for a team with a winning record.

championship. Look at No. 50. Peyton Manning's dad, Archie, is considered by experts from his generation an outstanding quarterback and one of the best of his era. Yet he played on rotten teams in New Orleans, and his courage amid chaos received more praise than his abundant skills. Put him on better outfits, give him a ring and he likely would answer the Canton roll call.

"He was an absolutely terrific player who deserved better than he got," said Ron Wolf, the former Packers general manager. "He had much more talent than a lot of the guys he played with who got more recognition. But it is hard to make an argument about his greatness when his teams didn't win. It is just unfair, but it is also reality."

There are others like Archie: Boomer Esiason, Randall Cunningham, Jim Hart and, possibly, Warren Moon, who is eligible for Hall of Fame election in 2006. Moon has career numbers reflecting rare skills; he was a star in Canada, a dominant player in the states. Few have thrown for more yards and touchdowns, completed more passes. Yet he is an outsider looking in the Hall

door, gazing at peers with much less snazzy statistics who best him in one critical area: They have a ring and he doesn't.

This failure didn't prevent Kelly, who suffered four Super Bowl losses, or Tarkenton, who came up short in three championship games, from gaining approval of the Hall selection committee. Maybe Kelly's admission was as much a sympathy vote for heartbreak as it was for career achievement. And Tarkenton, until Marino came along, was holder of all the major career passing records, a body of work that demanded inclusion among the greats. Besides, Tarkenton was so much fun to watch, scrambling as he did long before Michael Vick became fashionable. Now, it will be Moon's turn. Will the lack of a title hold him out– or at least delay–his selection despite first-ballot credentials? It would be unconscionable if he is denied entry into the Hall. Yet, the missing ring could haunt him.

This debate over the ring has a contemporary feel, now that it is enveloping Peyton Manning, who already is carving out a career path unprecedented in league history. Until Manning, no player had ever passed for 4,000 yards in six consecutive years. Only two players–Marino and Favre–had exceeded his string of seven consecutive 20-plus touchdown seasons. Until Peyton, no quarterback had compiled a 121.1 passer rating, which he did in 2004. Until him, no quarterback had thrown for 49 touchdown passes in a season, which he also did in 2004. There were times during that 2004 season that no quarterback had ever played with more skill for a more consistent period. At times, he appeared unstoppable, his work so silky and effortless that he seemed to be toying with defenses, able to complete a pass any time he chose no matter how defenses schemed to stop him.

This debate over the ring has a contemporary feel, now that it is enveloping Peyton Manning, who already is carving out a career path unprecedented in league history.

Yet ... there remains the matter of him winning in the playoffs. In 2003, he put together back-to-back postseason games that left fans breathless with his precision and production. But in the AFC championship game against New England, he emerged a hesitant, stumbling, ineffective player, neutralized by the intricate defenses of the Patriots. So in 2004, he came into a postseason rematch with the Patriots even more honed, more prepared, his offense considered among the best the league had ever seen. But the result was even more devastating. His Colts could muster just a lone field goal against New England. Manning soon was out of sync, flustered, unsure. And once again, his team lost.

So it was the Patriots who went on to win back-to-back Super Bowls while the Colts limped back to Indianapolis, wondering if they ever could figure how to get past this significant obstacle. That burden falls squarely upon Manning, whose control over his offense is unmatched by any current quarterback. He is allowed to audiblize on every play, and it is his reading of defenses that ultimately determines the success of his team. His playoff failures cast a harsh, critical light on his

'That is why we are in the game, to win a Super Bowl and championships.

career achievements. There are loud whispers: Is he this generation's Marino, so prolific, yet unable to win all the games that count?

Marino thought it would never happen as it did for him. In his second season, his Dolphins played the 49ers in Super Bowl 19. They lost, 38-16, but he believed this would be easy, getting to more of these championships. "I had no reason to think otherwise," Marino said. "I was young, we had a good team, I guess I

didn't know any better." Surely, with him at quarterback and Don Shula as coach, this was just the beginning of an illustrious run at more titles. That it didn't work out that way—Marino would play in no more Super Bowls over the remaining 15 years of his career—haunts him even to this day. He even wondered if the lack of a ring would keep him out of the Hall, a question that was answered at Super Bowl 39 when he was elected in the first year of eligibility.

Great players make great plays, as did Denver's Elway (7) when he scrambled for a key first down in the third quarter of Super Bowl 32 against the Packers.

"I wish I had won (a ring)," he said. "I wish I had won. Over 20 years, that's what you think about. Because I never got the opportunity again, and that's the one feeling I'll never have as a player. That's the one thing that a lot of quarterbacks have felt. To walk off the field and say you won a Super Bowl. I've had every other feeling you could possibly have in the league, in the game, and the emotions of it, but that one.

I would trade a lot of what I did accomplish for a ring."

The two—Manning and Marino—are linked, too, by hero worship. Growing up, Manning admired Marino, studied how he played, marveled at his command and his intelligence and his decision-making skills. Like Marino, Peyton's assets dictate that he be a pocket quarterback unlike his dad, who had elusive mobility. And with every failure, just as with

Whether that is fair or not, that is the way greatness is judged.' —Tom Donahoe

Marino, the pressure grows, the comparisons become more locked, the questions more harsh. When Manning's 2004 season went up in flames in the playoff loss to New England, he was just 28 years old. To complicate matters, he then watched his peer, Brady, win his third Super Bowl ring. That makes Brady an almost sure Hall of Fame lock, even though he never will match Manning's career statistics, at least not as long as Bill Belichick is coaching the Patriots. But Brady is linked with winning, and that leads him on a sure path to Canton.

 quarterback plays the most difficult position in sports. He touches the ball on every offensive snap amid a jumble of jargon, schemes and defensive shenanigans. It's not like a pitcher who is isolated one-on-one against a lone batter. There are 21 other bodies in the mix, all scurrying at a breathtaking pace. Study just one play. It is choreographed chaos. And in the middle of it is the quarterback, whose passing success is determined by a combination of precise reading, uncommon coolness and a magnificent ability to somehow slow down the action and sort out the various pieces. Don't ever take for granted how easy the best make this look; it is incredibly hard, and their ease just reflects the brilliance of their abilities.

"There are a lot of quarterbacks out there who have never learned the mental mechanics of playing quarterback," said Aikman, who ought to know. "These are the mechanics of playing with a three-point lead, with a seven-point lead, knowing how to play against a four-point deficit compared to a seven, knowing how much time is on the clock, what to do with third-and-long—do I force it in there or just take what I can get and maintain field position? Lots of things go into running an offense that gives your team a chance to win. That's what eventually separates people at this position."

For the best ones, the financial reward is outlandish. Peyton Manning's $34.5 million signing bonus (before the 2004 season) reflects the importance of the position. And that is the distinguishing element: With only occasional exceptions, a team's long-term success depends ultimately on the ability of its quarterback to not only execute his responsibilities correctly, but also elevate the play of those around him.

That's why the measure of the ring is essential. What better way to decide which quarterback has separated himself and become that special player capable of molding a championship group around him? It's not unfair to place such a burden on the position. For sure, anyone playing the spot understands the responsibilities and the resulting expectation. But tell this to quarterbacks of note and prepare yourself for harsh retorts. Just consider the views of three Super Bowl champions about the ring issue:

"As a quarterback, the Super Bowl is ultimately what I think guys are judged on," said Aikman, winner of three rings with the Cowboys. "That is why we play. But there is so much more than a quarterback that determines if you can achieve a ring. I had a great supporting cast, a great defense. Bradshaw, Montana, they had those things, too. It takes all of that to achieve something so lofty. Look at Marino, Fouts, Kelly, Moon, guys who haven't won a Super Bowl. Does it take away from their greatness? I don't think so. Is there an element of their career that is missing? Absolutely."

Bradshaw, who has four rings, shares that thinking. "Here's the sad thing about it," he said. "People say, 'OK, let's stack all of the quarterbacks side by side and everything is even. He won one and that guy didn't so he ain't as good.' It's not fair. It's not fair. Because it's better defense over here, or better receivers over there or better offense over there, but if that's what you're into, measuring people, there it is. There it is."

Montana, who also can display four rings, claims "a ring is not as necessary as people believe. Look at Danny (Marino). How can you put that kind of damper on the career he enjoyed? He feels his career was not validated because he didn't win a title, but that is just wrong."

But these are quarterbacks, after all, defending their brethren. You'd expect such loyalty. But they also understand they live in a harsh but realistic world. "I think they have to win a championship to be included among the greats," said Bills general manager Tom Donahoe. "That is why we are in the game, to win a Super Bowl and championships. Whether that is fair or not, that is the way greatness is judged. That puts the icing on the cake for someone's career. It just has to be a factor. But we also have to be careful not to judge too quickly. Someone like Peyton, he has many years left in his career and I think it is unfair to say, 'He can't win the big one.' First of all, he can. And second, let's have his career play out first before we pass final verdict on it."

There is another point that must be made. Certain quarterbacks were drafted to win titles. That's why they were chosen early in the first round. Otherwise, why bother spending the time and considerable money it takes to develop a rookie into a player good enough to be the best? Of the current group of dominant quarterbacks, Manning, Donovan McNabb and Daunte Culpepper are in this select bunch, separated from the beginning and loaded with exalted expectations. The same should be expected of David Carr, of Eli Manning, of Philip Rivers, of Carson Palmer, of Byron Leftwich, of Ben Roethlisberger, of Michael Vick, of Joey Harrington, of Aaron Rodgers, of Alex Smith.

"There is always going to be pressure on guys like Donovan and Culpepper and Manning to be a champion," said Aikman. "I learned that even when you win one, the pressure doesn't go away. Then they want another one. But if you haven't won any, it will always be said, 'Hey, he didn't live up to expectations.' "

OK, no one says this job is easy. But the rewards seem so worth the effort—the fame, glamour, riches and, possibly, like a gold-encrusted carrot, that wondrous ring.

IN SEARCH OF THE PERFECT

he perfect quarterback. Was there ever such a person in pro football? Does this individual exist in today's NFL? No and no, but that doesn't mean NFL teams can't dream as they continue a quixotic quest for Mr. Everything.

To understand what makes this ideal so hard to satisfy, consider the following excerpt from the scouting manual produced by Gil Brandt during his time with the Cowboys:

The most important quality is the ability to throw exceptionally well—both long and short. Leadership, intelligence and poise are important to his success. Should be quick away from the center, have quickness of delivery and be confident when rushed or forced out of the pocket. Straightaway speed and running ability is not necessarily important; however, quickness is important. Should be able to throw accurately off-balance.

"Obviously there is no one person who fits that description because some guys can't throw as well as others or with as much velocity," Brandt said. "But that is a description of what you would like to have as your prototype quarterback."

Brandt is one of five current or former personnel decision makers—Ernie Accorsi, Floyd Reese, Carl Peterson and Ron Wolf are the others—who sat with the *Sporting News* to discuss the players who best satisfy each of the qualities required in a modern quarterback.

Little was unanimous, except that even among the all-time best quarterbacks, no one—repeat: no one!—was the best at everything. From the analysis and anecdotes of our panel of football experts, we piece together a perfect quarterback, if only in our dreams.

Five longtime personnel men discuss the NFL's legendary QBs
and provide a blueprint for the ultimate field general

QUARTERBACK

The experts

Carl Peterson, president/general manager of the Chiefs, has overseen football operations for the team since December of 1988. In Peterson's front-office roles with the Eagles, Philadelphia Stars (USFL) and the Chiefs through 2004, his teams posted a .619 winning percentage (239-147-2), including 18 winning records and 15 playoff teams.

Ron Wolf is a retired scout and personnel director, most notably when he was the general manager of the Packers. From 1991-2001, Wolf directed a revival of Packer tradition, including back-to-back NFC championships ('96, '97) and Green Bay's first NFL title in 29 years (Super Bowl 31). Wolf is most appreciated by Packers fans for trading a first-round draft pick to Atlanta for Brett Favre, who at that point was a raw, underachieving talent.

Gil Brandt, a senior analyst for NFL.com, is a retired vice president of player personnel with the Cowboys, for whom he directed football operations from 1960 until 1989. Brandt is best known for his innovative scouting, talent evaluation and management practices while building the franchise into a perennial championship contender.

Floyd Reese, who has almost three decades of NFL experience, has been general manager of the Titans/Oilers since 1994. The winningest general manager in franchise history, he has assembled a consistently successful roster and helped choreograph the team's first Super Bowl appearance after the 1999 season.

Ernie Accorsi joined the Giants as an assistant to legendary general manager George Young in 1994 and has been general manager since 1998. Accorsi ran the football operation of two other NFL franchises as G.M. of the Colts (1982-83) and the Browns (1985-1992). Accorsi is best known for engineering trades to acquire the draft rights to a pair of collegiate quarterbacks–Bernie Kosar in the 1985 supplemental draft and Eli Manning in the 2004 NFL draft.

As is the case with any major construction project, we build up from ground level. Starting with the area of the body and the skills least-often associated with a pro football quarterback, we examine legs. Who is the best runner?

Peterson: I'd have to say Michael Vick and Steve Young.

Reese: Vick is a great combination of both running and passing skills, but as a runner, he's got paralyzing speed for a quarterback.

Accorsi: I didn't go back into ancient times for most of these; mine are fairly modern, although Otto Graham was a great runner and a great athlete. He was drafted by the NBA out of Northwestern. He was as good—if not better—a runner as he was a passer. He was a legitimate runner, not a scrambler, a runner. He called his own number a lot. He played pro football for 10 years and played in 10 championship games.

Wolf: Roger Staubach's ability to avoid (tackles) and make positive yardage made him a great runner. Another guy who pops into my head is Bobby Douglass. He was a very, very powerful runner.

Reese: Douglass was a fullback with a quarterback's number. He was a big, giant guy and others were afraid to tackle him because he would hurt you.

Brandt: Douglass was a lefthanded quarterback who came into the league as

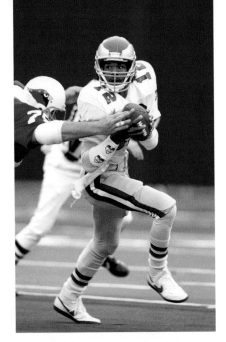

'Cunningham changed the face of the game because he was a superb runner.'

a rollout quarterback with a strong arm. He loved to roll out … then run.

Wolf: You know who was really good? Terry Bradshaw. And another guy you can't forget in all these running things is Randall Cunningham. What he did was incredible.

Brandt: Cunningham was probably the best as a runner. He had speed, and he was probably a player who was really a runner first and a passer second.

Wolf: I think Cunningham changed the face of the game because he was a superb runner. And Bradshaw because of his ability to run, although he was schooled not to run. But his ability to run made him a remarkable player, and he made himself into one heck of a quarterback.

Brandt: As these players come into the league and after they are there for a while, they probably don't want to run but pass. Roger Staubach, when he came to us in Dallas, wanted to run. That was what he did in college. Gradually, those quarterbacks like Cunningham, Douglass and Staubach, who come in wanting to run, what happens is the coaches finally get to them as well as the opposing players finally get to them. They find out it is a little different when you were running in college than when you are running in the NFL—because of the speed of the players you are playing against.

'Vick is a great combination of both running and passing skills, but as a runner, he's got paralyzing speed for a quarterback.'

Most agree that a runner is not the same thing as a scrambler, although the legs are the main cog in both cases. Who is the best at scrambling?

Accorsi: I scouted Ben Roethlisberger in the Mobile Alabama GMAC Bowl because we obviously were interested in a quarterback (for the 2004 draft). He made a scramble play right at the end of the half where he threw a touchdown pass to the tight end. As I sat there, you know what went through my mind? Roger Staubach. The only difference was that two defenders in this incredible scramble hit Roethlisberger and bounced off him. You didn't see that as much with Staubach. Roethlisberger is bigger. But a lot of times with Staubach, even if it was a one-handed touch, you wouldn't have got him. He just had an ability to be slippery and squirm away from people.

Reese: In modern day, talking about the ability to get free to throw the ball or to gain yardage and get the one or two first downs you need to win a game, I'd have to put our guy, Steve McNair, right up at the top of that list.

Brandt: I think Donovan McNabb is pretty good right now. I think Cunningham was pretty good and Staubach, but nobody was a scrambler like (Fran) Tarkenton. He was unbelievable. We played him one time in

Let's create some leg room by moving to the arm and going up top to stretch the field. When throwing the deep pass, who comes to mind?

Wolf: I don't think I saw anybody throw the ball deep any better than Joe Namath. There are other people who threw a great deep ball. Certainly in the modern era you have Elway and (Dan) Marino and before that John Unitas, Norm Van Brocklin, Y.A. Tittle and Sonny Jurgensen. But when I think of the deep pass, I think of Joe Namath, and here's why: The ball came out quickly. The ball went downfield quickly. He was generally on target with his deep balls.

Accorsi: A tough decision for me. I narrowed it to Namath and (Terry) Bradshaw. And I eventually picked Namath. They both could just throw the ball. I saw Namath in the famous shootout with Unitas in 1972, where (Namath) just was throwing the ball off his back foot 60 or 70 yards downfield. In that game, he threw two hellacious bombs to

1964 in Dallas, where we used to conveniently let the visiting team and their dark uniforms sit on the sunny side of the field. It was probably 105 degrees. Tarkenton scrambled around for nine seconds, which doesn't seem like a lot, but boy I tell you what, all you saw were defensive linemen chasing and falling.

Reese: Tarkenton wasn't a real by-the-book guy, but he was very elusive and had incredible instincts. He had the ability to make up plays or change plays and be effective. You'd see time and again, where a backside rusher had a free shot at his back. Literally, a step or a half step before the collision, he was able to scramble out and usually in the direction of the rush, which is really incredible. He just had a knack for it.

Wolf: (Tarkenton) was absolutely no threat as a runner. He ran around, bought time and with his style, more or less, truly changed the game when he played. The difference between those two is also that Staubach won a few Super Bowls and

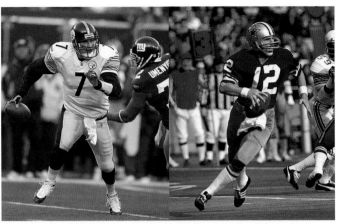

'As I watched Ben Roethlisberger, you know what went though my mind? Roger Staubach.'

'Nobody was a scrambler like Tarkenton.'

Tarkenton never did.

Accorsi: Staubach had eyes in the back of his head. He had this ability to escape. Most of these (scrambling) guys are not great pure pocket passers. Even though he threw for a billion yards, I didn't think Tarkenton was a great pocket passer because he ran all over the place. But Staubach was also a great pocket passer. He had a great sense of presence where he could feel somebody converging on him and avoid that (defender) without actually seeing him.

Peterson: I'll give this to John Elway; he had a patent on the ability to feel a guy coming from his left or blind side and do the famous pivot to his right and get outside the guy and buy some more time.

Brandt: I'll tell you, Elway was a great scrambler—although he was tackled for a loss more than any other quarterback in history. He was not fast. He was kind of a pigeon-toed guy but had tremendous quickness and athletic ability. He was a scrambler with great arm strength. He could scramble and as he was about to be forced out of bounds on one side of the field, then he'd throw the ball to a receiver across the field on the other side.

(Richard) Caster that he threw off his back foot. It was just amazing. It's a flip of the coin. The only reason I picked Namath over Bradshaw, I thought Namath had the ability to throw it farther when he wasn't even set. Now Bradshaw seemed to be bigger and stronger and more muscular. Namath had more of a whip to his arm. It's a close call. The two of them were incredible throwing the ball deep. If you were to make an argument for Bradshaw, I wouldn't argue with you. I thought Namath was a little more accurate deep.

Brandt: Deep passer? … Bradshaw. (Brandt is laughing a little as he answers, perhaps recalling a couple Super Bowls from the 1970s.)

Wolf: And I proba-

'Namath had the ability to throw it farther when he wasn't even set.'

bly think (about Namath) that way because of all those years while I was with the Raiders, we were playing them all the time.

Brandt: We probably played against Bradshaw 10 or 12 times, but I also remember him in college at Louisiana Tech. At one time, he had the world record or something for under-21 as a javelin thrower. So the guy had a strong arm.

Peterson: We played against Elway enough times, I remember vividly when he'd scramble to get himself out of trouble and buy a second chance, and by this time his receivers were 80 yards downfield. Our defensive backs, Kevin Ross on one play in particular, didn't think Elway

could throw it that far. (Ross) was wrong. Elway threw it that far and scored a touchdown. That's a powerful deep thrower.

Reese: I remember when Jeff Blake was at Cincinnati with (Carl) Pickens and Darnay Scott, he had an uncanny ability with the long ball. Over the years, the Raider quarterbacks like Snake (Ken Stabler), (Jim) Plunkett or Daryle Lamonica, they always threw the long ball very well. Today, I would have to say Peyton Manning throws a long ball as well as anybody, although he has a receiver (Marvin Harrison) with uncanny ability, and that makes it a little bit easier. It's hard to throw the long ball if you've got big, slow receivers.

Accorsi: I thought that for Bradshaw a lot of times (his receivers) made some incredible catches for him. Namath had good receivers, but he didn't have Hall of Fame receivers like Bradshaw had with Lynn Swann and John Stallworth. That's probably where I cut the mustard on that.

It's one thing to heave the ball with all your might, but what about precision? Who comes to mind when you hear the words accuracy and touch?

Brandt: I think accuracy is one of the most important categories in the success of a quarterback. And when I think about accuracy, two guys come to mind: Troy Aikman and Len Dawson. Len didn't have a great arm. He wasn't tall in stature. But the guy had the ability to put the ball where they could catch it. As for Aikman, we went to work him out before we drafted him. We went out to UCLA, and we had him throw more than 100 passes—all different routes. There wasn't one uncatchable ball. If you look at Aikman during his career with the Cowboys, you very seldom see him overthrow a receiver … if the guy ran the right route. You seldom see where he bounced one in front of the receiver. He just had the ability to lay the ball in there very, very accurately, which he did many times to Michael Irvin.

Wolf: If you're talking about just pure touch, then I think of Lenny Dawson. That offense they ran in Kansas City, he was the guy who made that go. He was just superb. And I guess you'd have to say Joe Montana because of the incredible ability he had.

Accorsi: Montana because I thought he played with the best rhythm. He didn't have a great arm. Yet, you saw him play games where every pass was exactly where it was supposed to be.

Peterson: Although he liked to criticize himself and say, "I threw a tight wobble," Montana had phenomenal anticipation and knew where to throw it and where the receiver was going to be. I think you can call that touch.

Accorsi: Accuracy and touch, but he did not have a cannon. Of all (the great quarterbacks), Montana is the only one who didn't have a strong arm. And he was able to throw the ball down the field because he had the touch. Something I learned

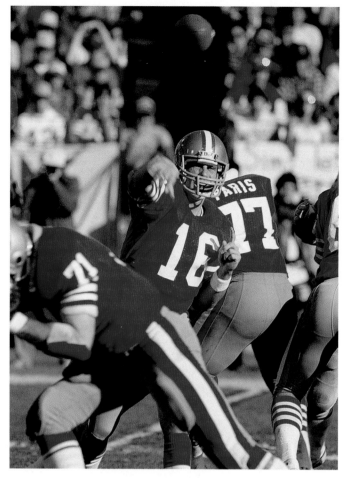

'Of all the great quarterbacks, Montana is the only one who didn't have a strong arm.'

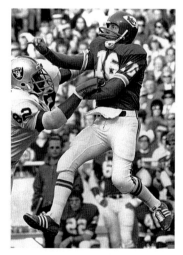

'If you're talking about just pure touch, then I think of Lenny Dawson.'

from a coach, who said, "You don't have to have a long arm to throw deep; you have to throw early." A lot of times you have to have the guts that this guy is going to break deep, so you throw it early and let him run under it. Instead of waiting until he's 45 yards down the field, you throw when he's 25 yards down the field and let him break and he makes the long play. Instead of throw long and run short, Montana was the master of throw short and run long. He was able to hit (Jerry) Rice on the break when Rice was at full speed. You don't see that much. On those slants, the ball was delivered at exactly the right time as Rice was at full speed.

Peterson: I would stand behind Joe in practice at field level, and he'd throw the ball, and I would think: "Where is he throwing that?" Then all of a sudden the receiver is there. Time and time and time again. He knew where to throw it and with what speed, accuracy and touch.

Wolf: If Dawson were quarterbacking today and in that same system as Joe (had with the 49ers), that would be interesting to hear what people would say about who is better. I am probably committing a heresy there but …

Brandt: Bart Starr could throw the ball in there to those crossing routes if he had to, and he could also do it with touch. I think Dan Marino had the humility to take something off the ball and throw it with good touch.

Peterson: Marino had very good touch. I've always believed it starts with accuracy. You've got to get the ball from Point A to Point B. You got to get it to, as we always say, the open receiver. It doesn't have to be the tightest spiral or be the prettiest pass. But it has got to be there and be in a position where a receiver can catch it.

Brandt: Initially, I did not think Elway knew how to throw the ball with touch. But toward the end of his career, if (the throw) needed to be there fast, then it was there fast. When it needed to be lobbed there, it was done that way.

Reese: The one young guy I've been impressed with is the (Chad) Pennington kid of the Jets. The things that impress you with him are his touch and accuracy.

Brandt: Peyton Manning, if you notice how he throws the ball to (Edgerrin) James on the swings and conversely how he throws it to (Marvin) Harrison when he runs that slant route. I think Peyton has very good touch on the ball. … This is probably one thing that will keep Michael Vick from being a great quarterback. He will beat you, and then he will have another chance to beat you but not do it simply because he will miss a wide-open guy. And that is one area that I think you either have it or you don't have it.

It's late, who's great? The best quarterback for the two-minute drill is …

Wolf: Both Elway and Ken Stabler were superb in those situations. The biggest one for Snake (Stabler) was against Miami in a playoff game, although he did that quite a bit. I watched Elway on television and also on tapes and film; he did some marvelous things, particularly against Cleveland a couple of times bringing that team back from disaster and winning.

Accorsi: Now, you're talking to the former general manager of the Cleveland Browns, so you realize Elway changed my life with one of his (last-minute drives). He was one of those guys—you couldn't stop him. And he made so many comebacks. I don't know if anybody brought back more teams in crucial situations with playoff games or playoff berths on the line. A lot of times in those comebacks, you are in a prevent defense. He'd roll, and now he was big and pretty fast, particularly when he was young, so you had to come up and contain him because he might run for 30 yards. So if you came up and left your man, you'd be completely out of position, and with all arm Elway would zing it down the

'I don't know if anybody brought back more teams in crucial situations with playoff games or playoff berths on the line than Elway.'

field 60 or 70 yards—complete. The complete package for leading comebacks.

Peterson: I like Kurt Warner, when he was really at the top of his game and not injured because he seemed to do it so many times. And I would put Dan Marino in there because he did it so well. Certainly one of the best, and one I was able to observe closely, was Joe Montana. He had such knowledge of the

whole field coupled with the clock in his head, knowing when to get rid of it, when to down it and when to use timeouts. That's a big part of a two-minute drill, the field generalship.

Accorsi: If you have a separate category for field general, I would put Unitas in that and keep Elway as the best in the 2-minute drill. If you don't have that category, I'd put Unitas here (in the two-minute drill) ahead of Elway because (Unitas) called all his own plays. He was a coach on the field. We don't have that as much now because they call these damn plays with that damn thing in the helmet. There was a great play in the 1958 sudden-death game (against the Giants). Unitas is running out of time, and he has no

timeouts left. You can't spike the ball in those days because it was intentional grounding. You had to actually try to complete a pass, or they'd call the penalty. He couldn't stop the clock, yet Unitas ran a trap draw to Alan Ameche for about 35 or 40 yards. I asked John about that play call. He said, "I heard the defensive cornerback tell (Sam) Huff: 'I need help on (Ray) Berry.' Huff took one step to the right to just cheat over and try to confront Berry, so I changed the play. I knew we could trap Huff because he was one step to the right instead of right in front of me." It's stuff like that that he was the best at.

Brandt: Staubach, Elway, Marino. Staubach's greatest one was when we played at Minnesota (in a 1975 divisional playoff game). He hit a fourth-and-15 pass to Drew Pearson that was just an unbelievable throw. Then he hit another pass to Drew for a touchdown. We didn't play Elway as much as we played Marino, who beat us 28-21 in Miami and knocked us out of a chance to go to the playoffs. Marino hit big plays right at the end of the game to beat us.

'Steve DeBerg was a magician with the ball.'

Some say play-action fakes and passes are art form. If so, who is Michelangelo?

Peterson: Currently, I think of (Tom) Brady, but the best I was ever around was Steve DeBerg. He was a magician with the ball. He would really carry out the fake tremendously with the run and end up with the ball and freeze linebackers and defensive backs.

Brandt: We used to call it the "fire pass," rather than play-action pass. To give you an answer, I think you have to go to the teams that like to run a lot of play-action, like Buffalo with Jim Kelly. And the year that Dick Vermeil won it with Warner at quarterback, Warner was very good.

Accorsi: I'd say Bart Starr because the Packers won five world championships in the '60s and

Unitas won none because (Vince) Lombardi knew he didn't have Unitas, so he play-actioned himself to five titles. Yes, Starr had those two big horses behind him with (Jim) Taylor and (Paul) Hornung that enabled him to do that. There have been other good ones, and Boomer Esiason was great, but he didn't win a championship, so I'd say Bart Starr.

Brandt: Yes, Boomer was a flash-and-pass guy. He was especially good when he did it at Cincinnati, where they would throw a lot of times to the tight end in the middle of the field.

Wolf: I think the first and the foremost in that area would be Montana. By actually studying him all those years, I could see that he bought time by his ability to play fake. Another person who did a superb job of that was John Unitas.

'It appears that the really great ones

'**Peyton Manning** is more of a student of the game than anybody I've seen in years and years and years.'

What about skills that won't show on the film or measure in the statistics. For example, who reads a defense the best?

Accorsi: Unitas.

Brandt: I would imagine that Unitas was pretty good at reading the defense because he called his own plays.

Accorsi: I'll tell you a great story about his play-calling and Unitas. He wins a championship in 1958, and the offensive coach leaves to take another job as a head coach. So Unitas gets a new offensive coach in '59, Don McCafferty, who later won a Super Bowl as a coach. Before the first preseason game, McCafferty says to Unitas, "Do you want me to help you at all?" Unitas says, "If you think they're going to blitz, let me know. Otherwise sit back, relax and enjoy the game."

Reese: Peyton Manning is more of a student of the game than anybody I've seen

Another intangible to consider: toughness. Who tops the chart for quarterbacks?

Wolf: Most anybody who played this game, and anybody who has ever played quarterback is tough—Favre, Marino, Elway, Aikman, Namath and Unitas. Since I'm living down here near Baltimore now, that's all they talk about around here is how tough Unitas was.

Accorsi: When you hear those guys talking about the 1960 Bears game where Unitas was hit in the mouth. It was bleeding so bad they reached down and got mud and packed the cut on his face to stop the bleeding. (Coach Weeb Ewbank) comes out with 20 or something seconds to go and says, "You got to come out, John." Unitas says, "If you try to take me out, I'll kill you." Then he threw a touchdown pass to Lenny Moore to win the game. I don't know how you can be any tougher than that.

Physically and mentally, he was just so tough. And there wasn't any phony about it. His body, during the late part of his career, was basically deformed. His rib cage was all out of whack. He had taken such a beating, especially after he got rid of the ball, because he held the ball until the last second. Dick Lynch was a killer (defensive player for the Giants). During the 1959 championship game, Lynch came on

'**Unitas** says, "If you try to take me out, I'll kill you." ... I don't know how you can be any tougher than that.'

a corner blitz. Later, Lynch says, "I am coming full speed. Unitas saw me. No one is blocking me. He looked at me and stared me right down and knew I was going to knock the hell out of him. At the last second, he zinged the ball down the field as I

could do more than one thing.'

in years and years and years. Not only does he study his opponent's defense, but he's a bright kid. He doesn't do it to catch up; he does it to be perfect.

Brandt: Marino, Montana and Peyton. The thing about reading defenses isn't that a player has intelligence or lacks intelligence. Roger was very smart, but he didn't have the ability to read a defense the way Danny White did.

'I never saw Rich (Gannon) back away.'

Brandt: I've seen Don Meredith play with broken ribs and injuries where he should have been in the hospital. As far as I'm concerned, every one of the quarterbacks is tough, but I just think that Meredith was the physically toughest one I've seen play.

Peterson: Most of them, just to play the position, are tough, but Rich Gannon is exceedingly tough. He is also great on his feet. He always finds a way to complete third down. When he was healthy the year he took (the Raiders) to the Super Bowl, he was phenomenal. He knew sometimes he was going to take it himself and take a shot, but if they needed 3 yards he'd get 4 yards. There are so many tough players at that position because you have to have no regard for getting hit as you throw the ball. It's always the defensive coordinator's delight to try to get a guy to start hearing footsteps. I never saw Rich back away.

Earlier, the phrase "field general" was suggested. And the quarterback who best handles the duties of leadership is …

Wolf: Certainly Bart Starr because he won five titles in seven years. I don't think you can attribute all that to Lombardi. I think somebody had to do it on the field. He did it on the field. Aikman, Elway and obviously Joe Montana. I was associated for almost 10 years with Brett Favre, and there was a lot of leadership there.

Peterson: Again, I say Montana because of his demeanor on the field. Not a real vocal guy, but I think every guy who played with him or against him really felt that until the game was over, he could move a football team, score points and beat you.

Reese: The No. 1 objective of every quarterback is to win games, so I have to consider the guys who have won a lot of games or championships: Steve Young, Brett Favre and John Elway.

Brandt: I think a present-day quarterback who has great leadership (skills) is Tom Brady. I think Bart Starr was a leader in a different way. And Staubach, too. … You can have the greatest work ethic in the world and do all the running, weightlifting and whatever, but if a quarterback doesn't win, then all of the sudden the guy isn't such a great leader. I'm not sure that if you talked to the Denver players after their first three Super Bowl losses with Elway that he would not have been as great a leader in their eyes as he was after the Broncos won their two Super Bowls.

Accorsi: Unitas would cut your heart out. I used to hear Sam Huff or Ray Nitschke say, "(Unitas) would be looking around. When you are playing the middle linebacker against him, the more he looked at you the more you knew he was figuring out how to beat you."

Brandt: Unitas would have been an interesting player in today's game. It would have been interesting because he was a guy who was strictly a dropback passer. He was

not known for his fleetness of foot. But he did have tremendous accuracy; just go back to the '58 championship game and see some of the sideline routes he threw to Raymond Berry when he caught 13 passes in that game. I just don't see Unitas in today's mix. I think he was great, but this is a different era, and I'm not sure just how good he would be. Yet, in saying that, it seems that the great ones find a way to be successful no matter what era they're in.

Wolf: I don't know what all this tells us, but it appears that the really great ones could do more than one thing. I'm talking about Sammy Baugh, Otto Graham and Sid Luckman. Aikman, Elway, Favre, Young, Montana and Staubach. The guy you probably can't question is the one from my era,

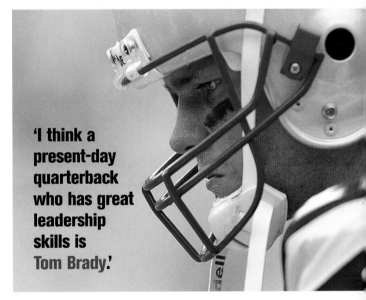

'I think a present-day quarterback who has great leadership skills is Tom Brady.'

the '60s and '70s—I would be hard-pressed to find anybody any better than John Unitas was. But don't forget Otto Graham. What he did was incredible.

Unitas led us on a two-minute drill in 1970 against Houston. He threw a corner pattern to (Roy) Jefferson. He threw the ball perfectly and turned around and walked off the field without seeing Jefferson catch the ball. On the airplane coming back, I ask him: "Did you see Jefferson catch the ball?"

He says, "Nope."

I say, "Why?"

He answers, "I knew I threw it perfectly. Nothing more I could do about it. My job was done."

1

JOHNNY UNITAS

U

JOHNNY NITAS

As we all live in the fleeting instant and cannot remember the history of the past 20 minutes, the greatest quarterback of all-time is imagined to be Peyton Manning on sheer skills or Tom Brady, who wins Super Bowls. This will pass soon enough. If our recollections go back a little longer, we point to Joe Montana, John Elway or maybe even Troy Aikman. All were wonderful in their time, and all come up short when memory reaches back to John Constantine Unitas of the Baltimore Colts.

nitas beat you long and short. He beat you the first moment he leaned over center or the last second of play. He practically invented the 2-minute drill and then turned it into an art form. He threw touchdowns in consecutive games from the end of the first Eisenhower administration to the dawning of the Kennedy years. He retired owning 22 different passing records. He called all of his own plays and much of the time ad-libbed when he reached the line of scrimmage. In the frigid dusk at Yankee Stadium, he dominated the famous sudden-death championship contest called *The Greatest Game Ever Played*, which changed a nation's sporting culture forever. It did not matter that linemen with blood in their eyes clutched at him; Unitas waited and waited before throwing the football. He was so tough that stories about him, all true, would be unbelievable if history did not bear them out.

John Mackey, the Hall of Fame tight end, once said, "Being in the huddle with John was like being in the huddle with God."

At Unitas' last game in Baltimore, a plane pulling a banner that read "Unitas We Stand" flew over the stadium. Moments later, on his final pass as a Colt, Unitas threw a 63-yard touchdown pass. That was Unitas; he could outperform even the grandest of expectations. Ernie Accorsi, the New York Giants general manager who broke in with the Colts, said, "You want to know what leadership is? All you had to do was watch John Unitas get off the team bus."

Teams, seasons:
Baltimore Colts, 1956-72; San Diego Chargers, 1973
Height: 6-1
Weight: 194
Born: 5-7-33
Died: 9-11-02
College: Louisville
Championship teams:
1958, '59, '70 seasons
Career passing yards/TDs:
40,239/290

A STELLAR RESUME

A few of Johnny Unitas' accomplishments during his career with the Baltimore Colts (1956-1972) and San Diego Chargers (1973):

■ Completed 2,830 passes for 40,239 yards and 290 touchdowns.

■ At retirement, held 22 NFL records, including most passes attempted, most completions, most passing yards, most 300-yard passing games, most touchdown passes and most seasons leading the league in touchdown passes.

■ Threw touchdown passes in 47 consecutive games, still a record.

■ Led the NFL in passing yards four times.

■ Set an NFL championship game record with 349 yards passing against the Giants in 1958. It has since been broken.

■ Quarterbacked the Colts to NFL titles in 1958 and 1959 (he was injured in 1968) and to a Super Bowl 5 win after the 1970 season.

■ TSN's Player of the Year in 1959, 1964 and 1967.

■ Associated Press Player of the Year in 1964 and 1967.

■ Played in 10 Pro Bowls; was MVP three times.

■ Named "Greatest Quarterback of All-Time" during the NFL's 50th anniversary celebration in 1969.

■ Named to the 1960s All-Decade Team.

■ Named to the NFL's 75th Anniversary Team.

■ Inducted into the Pro Football Hall of Fame in 1979.

Too puny

Unitas started his career as a kid nobody wanted and ended his days being lauded at 216 Emory Street, a scruffy alley in southwest Baltimore. The little row house was the birthplace of one George Herman Ruth Jr., later known as Babe. Twenty years ago, the building was converted into a sports museum, The Babe Ruth Birthplace and Museum, and Unitas was there, in March 2002, six months before a fatal heart attack blindsided him.

Unitas was there to donate all of his memorabilia, trophies, sculptures and such, which never impressed him much, anyway. The place was packed with adoring fans. Unitas stood there, shoulders stooped, as though preparing to take a snap from center, his hands huge and his fingers bent at impossible angles. He barely seemed to notice the crowd pressing in on him. He spotted a TV monitor on a distant wall, like a second receiver. As always, he displayed great peripheral vision. On the screen, he saw a grainy black-and-white game film he hadn't seen in half a century.

It was Unitas when it was all beginning for him, back at St. Justin's High School in Pittsburgh. There he was, ducking a linebacker. A coach named Jim Carey hollered from the sideline, and kids named Tom Boyle and Rich Keeling tried to throw protective blocks.

He still remembered their names. It had been a lifetime since he had scrambled out of that tough Pittsburgh youth, with the father who died when Unitas was 5 and the mother who scrubbed office floors at night to support her four children until she found work at a small coal-delivery company.

At 17, Unitas was 6 feet tall and weighed 138 pounds. Stopwatches and scales, though, can't measure a man's heart. He imagined playing big-time college ball but was turned away. Too puny, they said. He settled for the University of Louisville, where football was considered a mere warmup for basketball season.

The Pittsburgh Steelers made him the 102nd pick in the 1955 draft and then cut him without letting him play a single preseason down. Unitas hitchhiked home to save bus fare. He got work on a construction crew and played sandlot ball for $6 a game on a junior-high field strewn with cinders from nearby steel mills. The Colts heard about him and placed an 80-cent phone call offering him a tryout. Unitas hesitated. After all, the construction job paid him $125 a week with overtime. So the Colts offered a few bucks more.

He led the Colts to three championships. Three times, he was honored as the league's MVP. He played in 10 Pro Bowls. He was the first quarterback to throw for 40,000 yards. When he retired in 1973, he owned virtually every important NFL passing record, from most completed passes and most touchdown passes to most 300-yard games and his incredible consecutive-games touchdown streak.

'As long as the Colts have Unitas, they could put nine or 10 girls on the field and still win.' –Jack Christiansen

47 games

Forty-seven consecutive NFL games with a touchdown pass. The Streak–pro football's version of Joe DiMaggio's 56-game hitting streak in baseball–ended in storybook fashion. In Game 43, he completed five passes–four for touchdowns–in the first half. The next week, he threw for four more touchdowns, including three in the first 20 minutes. In Game 45, his nose broken and his face bloodied by the Chicago Bears, his own teammates could not face him in the huddle.

It was late in 1960, at Wrigley Field, with the Colts and Chicago Bears tied for first place. In Baltimore, they still talk about the game. Art Donovan, the Colts Hall of Fame tackle who served with the Marines in the Pacific, said, "The game against the Bears?

That was worse than World War II."

With less than a minute remaining, the Colts trailed by three points. The Bears' Doug Atkins hit Unitas in the backfield and shattered his nose. Atkins stood over Unitas, declaring, "You're finished, Unitas." The Colts called a timeout. They couldn't get his nose to stop bleeding. Jim Parker, the Hall of Fame offensive lineman, said, "It was awful. You couldn't even look at John's face, it was so busted up. And the blood kept coming. Finally, Alex Sandusky reached down and grabbed a clump of mud and shoved it up Unitas' nose."

"Forget it," said Weeb Ewbank, the Colts' coach. "We're taking you out of the game."

"You do," said the dazed Unitas, looking up, "and I'll kill you."

Unitas stayed in the game. With 17 seconds left, Unitas turned in the huddle to Lenny Moore. "I'm looking at him," Hall of Famer Moore remembered four decades later, "and I'm thinking, 'How is this man standing here?' I mean, get him out of the game while he's still conscious. But John's looking at me, and he's remembering a play we had, called '66,' which was me going down about 15 yards and angling in, or I could break it off and do a short post. This time he says, 'I want you to give me that break-in, then plant and break back to the outside.' Now, we hadn't done this before. It was a new play. We hadn't worked on it, and we hadn't timed it. With all the other things going on, he thinks of this new move at this second."

Unitas threw long, and Moore caught it over J.C. Caroline in the end zone. Colts 24, Bears 20.

Baltimore tough

The draw of Unitas wasn't exclusive to the football field. He lifted an entire city on his broad, stooping shoulders. He gave working-class Baltimore a new image to see in its municipal mirror. The town cast off its historic inferiority complex. It was no longer that marble-stoop city stuck somewhere between glittery New York and Washington. It was the place where John Unitas orchestrated miracles. Parents named children after Baltimore players. In public schools, there were teachers who followed the daily *Pledge of Allegiance* with the *Colts Marching Song.*

In Unitas, Baltimore recognized one of its own—an ordinary man who did extraordinary things; the working stiff with a crew cut who put aside a lunch pail and threw footballs across the horizon. Stripped of his uniform, he was a skinny, pale, practically albino scarecrow. But, in high-topped shoes and helmet, the scrawny Ray Bolger became the indomitable Rambo.

"As long as the Colts have Unitas, they could put nine or 10 girls on the field and still win," 49ers coach Jack Christiansen once said.

In 1958, the Green Bay Packers' John Symank hit Unitas so viciously that he broke his ribs and punctured a lung. Air leaked into his chest cavity. Taken to Union Memorial Hospital for emergency surgery, Unitas received last rites.

"The thing that makes Unitas is his physical courage," said Merlin Olsen, a Hall of Fame defensive tackle. "He is the bravest man I've known in football."

Three weeks later, wearing a bulky protective vest, Unitas returned to the lineup against the Los Angeles Rams. On the Colts' first play from scrimmage, he lofted a 58-yard touchdown pass to Moore. In the radio press box, broadcaster Chuck Thompson cried, "How rusty can a guy get?"

The Game

Though it often was called football's greatest game and was listed as the top sports event of the 20th century by one national poll, the 1958 sudden-death championship game ranks as an also-ran in the minds of some old Colts.

They remember, instead, the dramatic regular-season game that clinched the conference title that year. On a freezing day in Baltimore, the Colts trailed San Francisco at half-time, 27-7. Late in the fourth quarter, behind Unitas, they narrowed it to 27-21. Ewbank, always jittery on the sideline, called a fourth-down timeout.

"Let's do this," he told Unitas. Then he changed his mind. "No, let's do this." Then he changed it again. Unitas stared and said nothing. Finally, Ewbank threw up his hands. "John, just get the first down." Unitas immediately hit Raymond Berry for a first down. Then he handed off to Moore, who ran 73 yards for a touchdown. With two minutes remaining, Unitas threw another pass to Berry, this one for an insurance score. Colts 35, Niners 27.

'The thing that makes Unitas is his physical courage. He is the bravest man I've known in football.' –Merlin Olsen

But the sudden-death game a few weeks later changed the nation. Until then, baseball was the undisputed national game. College football was more popular than the pros.

The '58 championship game had everything: A huge national audience, a Yankee Stadium setting, the glamorous Giants and the cool, unconquerable Unitas, oblivious to the clock, impervious to the swirling wind and plunging temperature, with a goal line 86 yards away.

Trailing 17-14, the Colts had the ball at their own 14-yard line with less than two minutes to play. Remember Elway and *The Drive* against Cleveland? This drive was its grandfather. On third-and-10, Unitas hit Moore for 11 yards, then threw incomplete. With barely a minute left, he hit Berry for 25 yards to midfield. Less than a minute remained, and the clock was running. He hit Berry again, for 15. The Colts couldn't stop the clock. Unitas hit Berry for 22. With seven seconds left in the gathering dusk, a Steve Myhra field goal tied the score.

In overtime, Unitas drove the Colts 80 yards in 13 plays. At the Giants' 7, Ewbank called timeout. "Keep the ball on the ground, John."

"OK," Unitas said. Instead, looking over the Giants defense, Unitas checked off and fired a sideline pass to tight end Jim Mutscheller, who fell out of bounds at the 1. It

was precisely the play the Giants had not anticipated. On the next play, Alan Ameche barged into the end zone.

"What if the pass to Mutscheller had been intercepted?" Unitas was asked after the game.

"When you know what you're doing," replied the laconic Unitas, "you don't get intercepted."

A whole country fell in love with a game, and the game had found its guiding light.

'Textbook'

Four decades later, they gathered around Unitas on Emory Street. There were many who had watched him during 17 seasons at Baltimore's Memorial Stadium, the place once dubbed the World's Largest Outdoor Insane Asylum. Now, the Babe Ruth Museum's director, Michael Gibbons, was telling everybody how appropriate it was that Unitas' memorabilia would remain there. Early in the 20th century, it was Ruth more than anyone who had made baseball part of the American experience. And, at mid-century, it

was Unitas more than anyone who made pro football part of that same athletic devotional.

Unitas looked up again at the distant TV monitor showing his old high school film. He seemed lost in that sweet moment. He seemed oblivious to the praise. A guy whispered, "What are you thinking?"

"Boy, I was slow," Unitas laughed. That's all.

"You were never a sentimental type," the guy said. "Does this stuff … ?"

"No, I'm not," Unitas said. "I'm just not that kind of guy."

And therein always lay one of his greatest strengths. Others felt the throb of the moment flood over them. They invested it with great romance or great suffocating pressure. Unitas, whose mother scrubbed office floors when everyone else had gone home, kept a sense of perspective.

With time running out and frenzied crowds screaming for a Colts score—and predators closing in on him—he kept emotional distance. He wanted to win. But a man who had lost his father at age 5 knew there were worse things in life than losing a football game.

At Unitas' death, Hall of Fame Buffalo coach Marv Levy was asked what made Unitas so great. He talked of mechanics. "Magnificent," Levy said. "He was textbook. This is the way to drop back. This is the way to set up. This is the way to direct your eyes and head down the field. This is the way to hold your elbows in."

Big deal.

Unitas' favorite receiver, Berry, remembered the hours and hours of practice when everyone else had gone home, and hours more spent watching game film.

Big deal.

"He had the physical attributes," Accorsi said. "That's sometimes overlooked. But it was his eyes and his stomach. You looked at those steel-gray eyes, and he came to beat your ass."

That's closer to it.

Here's something else. At Unitas' death, Pittsburgh Steelers owner Dan Rooney, whose father Art had drafted Unitas in 1955, said, "Unitas was the guy who really brought the game to modern times."

He was Elvis at the dawn of rock and roll or Jolson at the start of talkies, declaring, "You ain't heard nothin' yet."

Unitas invented the picture of the quarterback that lingers in our minds. The others will come and go. They all play in John Unitas' endless shadow, the outlines still visible in the hazy late afternoon of memory.

An inside slant on Johnny U.

By Raymond Berry

I didn't know anything about Johnny Unitas until I came to the Baltimore Colts' training camp in 1956, my second year in the NFL. I remember standing up at the top of the hill, looking down at the guys on our practice field in Westminster, Md., and somebody told me we had a new quarterback from Louisville.

Unitas had been cut by Pittsburgh two years before and had been playing for a semipro team. He came in as a free agent, hoping he could hang on and get a job. I think the only guy who really knew about him was Weeb Ewbank, our coach.

In the fourth game that season, we played the Bears in Chicago, and George Shaw, our starting quarterback, got his knee severely injured. So John came in. He handed off on his first play, threw an incompletion on his second, then fired a pass out on the right flat. J.C. Caroline, the Bears' corner, picked the ball off and went 59 yards for a touchdown. That was John's first completed pass in the NFL. But as the game went on, he had a pretty good day and put up some decent numbers.

Berry (left) and Unitas (right) were key members of the Colts' 1958 and '59 championship teams that included coach Weeb Ewbank and Lenny Moore (24).

It should have been a huge tipoff for anybody who was really astute. Here's a guy who got hit upside the head with a 2-by-4 very early in his opening opportunity to play in the NFL, and it didn't even faze him. He just kept coming at Chicago. And that was Unitas.

He had that mental toughness, confidence and competitive streak about him, which I think was a catalyst for his great physical skills. Before that 1956 season was over, we combined for a lot of big plays. I finished 10th in the league in catches, and he did real well. It was a launching for both of us.

Football meant everything to John. He and I were on the same page about that. It was, without question, the most important thing in our lives at that time. We worked very, very hard at it and were not content to be half-assed about anything.

John was absolutely locked in on moving the ball any way he could move it, getting it into the end zone and winning. And he couldn't have cared less about hype, publicity or who got the credit. All those things were garbage to him, and everybody on our team knew it. When you have that type of attitude in your leader, it's going to cause the ones behind him to fall into the same pattern. What we had in Baltimore was a totally unified team that didn't think about individuals at all. It was a great place to play because of that, and John set the tone.

John had instinctive abilities to call plays, to be aware of what defenses were doing and to use his players to attack defenses. He was a master at confusing (the defenses) and crossing them up. Delivering the football when he wanted to was his focus.

He was very tough physically in the pocket. I don't think he ever was intimidated by a pass rush. It was a useless effort by the defense to hit him in the pocket or hit him late because it didn't bother him. I remember a game against the Bears in Chicago in 1960. They were the Monsters of the Midway, and they tried to intimidate you. On this particular day, they hit John in the face, and he was bleeding from just below his nose. But he refused to come out of the game. Alex Sandusky picked mud up off the field and packed it on the wound to try to stop the blood. Then John stepped up and fired the game-winning touchdown pass to Lenny Moore.

Unitas had a reputation for being gruff. He could get his message across, you might say. The closest he ever came to criticizing me was when we played the Packers one time in Green Bay. We had a short post pattern called, but when I started to go inside, Jesse Whittenton, one of their corners, must have read my intentions because he jumped inside ahead of me. When he did that, I reacted and went straight ahead. Trouble was, John already had put the ball in the air, so Jesse was the one who got the reception. That was embarrassing. When I came off the field, I said, "Boy, I screwed up." John just shook his head. I went to the other end of the bench because I didn't want to have to look at him.

Most people saw John only on the field, where he was all business. But off the field, it was obvious just watching him around people that he was loose and had a great sense of humor. I think another thing that might surprise people is that John was really a great father to his eight children—a great daddy—and he really had a knack for dealing with little kids.

I think John's best pass was whatever was called for. He didn't have any limitations. He had all the pitches. He could touch-throw it, he could throw it long, short, medium, inside, outside, deep, wherever. But when he really had to put the power behind it, I don't think anyone in the league was better. He could rifle that ball to the outside

set up Steve Myhra's 20-yard field goal that sent the game into overtime, where we won on Alan Ameche's 1-yard touchdown run.

John and I worked together after practice all the time. One of the things we talked about on our list of plays that we rehearsed was what would we do on a 10-yard square-in if a linebacker ever walked right out on me. We concluded that the best thing to do would be to convert it to a slant. If the linebacker came out on me, I'd give him an outside fake coming off the line, try to get him to hit me, and then I'd slant underneath him. The one time it happened was on the first of those three passes in a row in that '58 championship.

When I came to the line of scrimmage, Harland Svare, one of the Giants' outside linebackers, walked right up on me. We had no timeouts left, and the clock was running. We didn't have time to talk. So I looked at John, and he looked at me, and I'm sure we both thought, "I hope he remembers what we both agreed on." The ball was snapped, and the fake worked. John drilled it to me about 6 yards deep, and we picked up 25 yards to midfield. The next play, he hit me on a slant, and we picked up 15 more. The next play was a hook. I faked to the inside, the cornerback went for it, and I spun outside and ran for 22 yards to the Giants' 13.

Over the years, the more I comprehended the significance of that 1958 championship game, the more I got curious about wanting to know John's side. To catch three straight passes during a 2-minute drive just doesn't happen very often. Years

as fast as anybody.

Our favorite play was probably what we called the "Q" pattern. The "Q" pattern was based on our 10-yard square pattern. I'd go down about 10 yards and make my break, like I was squaring inside. Then, when the defensive back made his move and tried to go inside with me, I'd plant my inside foot and head to the corner. The defensive back would overrun me, and I'd have clear sailing to the outside. For a couple of years there, it was like a lethal weapon.

People often ask me what was my greatest catch. I'd have to say there were three of them—the three in a row during the 2-minute drive in the 1958 NFL championship game against the Giants. They helped

later, I asked him, "John, why did you throw three in a row to me in that drive?" And his answer was: "I figured you'd catch it."

When I first heard that John had died, I just felt numb. Then, after I reflected a bit, I was so thankful that in the past year I had been with John in two really quality times. One of those was when John and his wife, Sandy, came out to where we live, in the mountains just west of Denver, and visited with us for a couple of days. It was one of the best visits we've had in years. Sandy and my wife, Sally, just sat there and listened while John and I talked. When we got through, Sandy said, "You two ought to do a book together and call it Unitas to Berry."

Come to think of it, we already did.

2

JOE

If you want to know the real Montana, just ask the men who snapped him the ball

he rest of us have just seen greatness. These dozen men have felt it. The rest of us, even most teammates and friends, have been forced to follow the wonders of Joe Montana from a distance. These dozen men have been close enough to hear them. He has breathed down their shoulder pads. Screamed through their ear holes. Leaned exhaustedly on their hip pads. Dripped blood on their backs.

They caught none of his touchdown passes. They received none of his handoffs. They didn't play starring roles in The Catch or The Drive or the many-sequeled Comeback Kid. But before Joe Montana started anything, it started with them. Brian Phillips. Joe Debranski. Mark Gorscak. Vince Klees. Steve Quehl. Dave Huffman. Fred Quillan. Randy Cross. Chuck Thomas. Walt Downing. Jesse Sapolu. Tim Grunhard.

Meet Joe's centers.

From the Monongahela (Pa.) Wildcats to the Kansas City Chiefs, they etched their names into the footnotes of football history simply by being the ones to give one of its greatest quarterbacks the ball. The men looked back to discover what they shared was far more than pigskin. With Montana they have laughed, celebrated, hurt, fought and experienced a relationship far deeper than the word "Hut."

In celebration of Montana's retirement in 1995, they agreed to share some of these tales. They live in small towns and big cities from the Boston area to San Francisco. They are cement mixers and stockbrokers and TV analysts. Besides all being literally touched by legend, they have

Teams, seasons:
San Francisco 49ers, 1979-92; Kansas City Chiefs, 1993-94
Height: 6-2
Weight: 200
Born: 6-11-56
College: Notre Dame
Championship teams:
1981, '84, '88, '89 seasons
Career passing yards/TDs:
40,551/273

another thing in common. The Question.

"Frankly, even now, everybody wants to know what it was like to have Joe Montana's hands all over your butt," former Notre Dame center Quehl said. Everybody? He paused. "Mostly the girls," he said. The career of Joe Montana, from a different perspective …

The early years

Brian Phillips

I guess I was his first center, huh? Midget league and junior high. I can't believe somebody remembered. I don't even know if Joe remembers. People in this town don't think he remembers any of us. He

MONTANA

> 'Sometimes he would look at linemen and say, "You've got to block that guy." He was so intense, you would look back and say, "OK, OK, OK." ' –Dave Huffman

never comes back and hasn't really left anything behind. So he probably doesn't remember me either. That's OK. I understand. I sure remember him. I remember him for a blue Chevy Caprice. That's the car his dad drove us around in, about eight or nine of us kids. He drove us all over the Pittsburgh area to play basketball. St. Anthony's. The Armory. The Mounds.

Back then, it was obvious his dad was a big reason for Joe's success. His dad would get involved in everything Joe did, go to the practices, the games, all that stuff. His dad sometimes acted like everybody's dad. Another reason for Joe's success was those drives in that Caprice. Because we would go into other neighborhoods, sometimes tough, inner-city neighborhoods, and play kids in basketball. And we would win. Just storm them. That made us tough.

Gosh, Joe was a great basketball player. Better than football, if you ask me. I've seen him play one-on-one, spot some guy eight points and beat him, 10-8. Beat him with his left hand. Unbelievable leaping ability. I'm serious. He could fly. He was also a heck of a punter. Just a great athlete. And a good wide receiver.

Once in high school, Ringgold (of Monongahela) played Brownsville. I lined up in the slot, Joe handed the ball to running back Fidget Corbett, who handed the ball to me. By that time, Joe was running down the left sideline.

I threw him a pass. He caught it. Touchdown. Believe it or not. Has he ever caught a touchdown pass since? I don't think so. I guess maybe that puts us in history together. Also maybe I'm the only center who leaned over a ball one time and noticed that he was not behind me like he was supposed to be. He had lined up over guard. "Hey Joe," I yelled. "Wrong ass."

Montana arrived at Notre Dame with 'good looks, an All-American smile and tons of ability.'

You didn't want to mess too badly with Joe, though. He may be a great practical joker these days, but I was there when it started. We're lying on mats in a school hallway outside the high school cafeteria, resting during three-a-day practices one summer. All of us are eating fruit. You know, dates, apples, pears. Well, our big tackle, Tank

Tabarella, threw an apple core at Joe. He played dead for a second, then rose up and fired an apple core back at Tank. Well, Tank ducked and the core flew into the cafeteria and hit one of the workers. Hit her good. Gave her a hurting. But Joe fell back down so fast, she never knew where it came from.

People talk about that bullet he threw to Dwight Clark in that championship game as being his best pass ever. I know better.

Joe Debranski

When I think about Joe, I think about his hands. It was only at Ringgold High, but already they were the softest, smoothest hands of any quarterback who had ever lined up underneath me. This was also a problem. Because I could never tell when Joe didn't have his hands there. There was nothing to stop him from playing a practical joke by pulling his hands out at the last minute and watching me snap the ball into my crotch. He thought that was funny. Ha-ha. All of us forgave Joe for his stunts, though, because he was even smoother on the field.

I was there on that Friday against Monessen. The game that made Joe Montana. Big rivalry between a couple of steel towns. They were a powerhouse. Supposed to whip us. Nice time for Joe's first game as a starter. We walked on to the field before the game, and I couldn't believe it. Our team was in total silence. Nobody said a word. It was so quiet, nobody even said, "Don't say anything." We thought, "So this is how Montana leads his team before a game." The intensity was incredible. And what happens? What do you think? Joe throws three touchdown

passes, takes us to a 21-7 lead at the end of the first half, and we hang on for a 34-all tie.

That game was so good, I wish I could get the film and send it to you. Apparently the coach sent it to Notre Dame because some say that the Monessen game is what convinced Notre Dame to take Montana. Guys around town still talk about that game.

Mark Gorscak

I only regularly centered for Joe during his senior year at Ringgold High, but even then, I could tell how cool he was. It was his hands. He would always slide them underneath me late. Like, right before the snap. Never worried that he might miss the ball. Just went up there and grabbed it, and that was it. Another thing I remember about Joe was his eyes. When he wanted to get something done, he would give us this look in the huddle. We just knew he was going to do it. I went to the Ringgold campus in Donora while Joe went to the campus in Monongahela, so I never really saw him off the field except during summer workouts. And during that time, I probably saw him more on the basketball court.

Blue and golden years

Vince Klees

Everybody talks so much about Joe Montana being a small-town boy; it has almost become cliche. But I remember when it was true. He came to Notre Dame as a freshman from Monongahela with good looks, an All-American smile and a ton of ability. He could have dated any woman on campus. But you know what? All he talked about was wanting to get married. Back home. To his high school sweetheart.

Joe and I mostly stood on the sideline together those early Notre Dame years. Montana didn't start until the fourth game of his junior year, so we spent a lot of time talking to each other. And sure enough, he was just a sweet small-town kid who couldn't stop talking about his wedding, which we couldn't believe. We would gather around him at night and tell him, "C'mon, man, you're Joe Montana, you look good, you can have anything you want here; forget about marriage!" But he wouldn't. He couldn't. By the next year, he was married. My future wife was friends with his first wife, and a couple of times, my wife would baby-sit for their dog. I forget what kind of dog it was, but I do remember its name—Pupper. I remember thinking, what a ridiculous name for a dog. It was so corny. So small town. But it was perfect.

The only thing that wasn't quaint about Joe was his ability. It was huge. He was destined for greatness. We could see it every day. Not on the practice field because Dan Devine (who coached Montana after his freshman season) wouldn't let him show much. I'm talking about the basketball court. I'll never forget playing intramurals once and looking up and seeing a kid hanging above the rim, waiting for the ball like Michael Jordan or something. Believe it or not, that was Joe.

Devine didn't allow him to show that ability until nearly his senior year. And only Devine could have explained why the man who became one of the greatest quarterbacks ever sat on the bench. To this day, some of us are still wondering.

Steve Quehl

A little story about Joe and a costume party. It was held at Ara Parseghian's house because it involved Ara's daughter. A nice place. All upperclassmen. A big deal. And here comes Joe, just a sophomore, and guess how

he's dressed? Like a bunny rabbit. Seriously. A bunny. We looked at him and thought, that fits this guy exactly. All innocent. All small town.

We learned later that year, in games against North Carolina and Air Force, that looks were deceiving. In my opinion, it was in those two games in 1975 that the Montana legacy started. Joe didn't play as a freshman and was buried on the bench as a sophomore. But

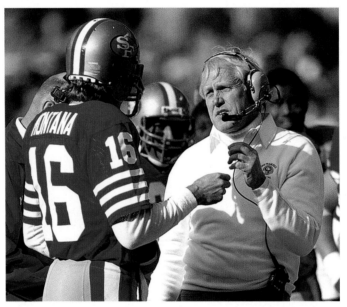

Montana was quiet and reserved, but that didn't stop him from becoming the perfect leader for 49ers coach Walsh's West Coast offense.

we got ourselves in trouble in Chapel Hill against North Carolina that year (down 14-6 with 6:04 left to play), and Joe was brought in. We looked at each other like, "What do we have to lose?" We didn't know anything about this guy. Well, we found out. In those final minutes, he literally won the game with his arm (Montana threw two touchdown passes, including an 80-yard game winner to Ted Burgmeier to lead Notre Dame to a 21-14 victory). I mean, the guy did it all. And in such heat. I'm suffering heat prostration, stripping down between series to take ice baths on the sideline, and Joe

is unbelievably cool.

Later that year, we are playing at Air Force, in a game we always win, but we aren't winning. They get ahead and stay ahead. Nothing we could do. And then Joe came in. He wasn't a great practice player; maybe that's why he didn't play more early in his career. But by then, we knew what he could do under pressure. He could step up, read a defense and put the ball where it

needs to be. Man, you can't practice that. So he walked into that huddle in Colorado Springs (Notre Dame trailing 30-10 with 13 minutes remaining). We looked around at each other and said, "Hey, here's our shot." By then, he was instant credibility. Sure enough, he pulled it out for us (Montana led Notre Dame on three touchdown drives for a 31-30 win). It was incredible. He was passing, running … and finally earned everybody a game ball.

To this day, that is one of only two game balls that I own. The other one is from the infamous Rudy game against Georgia Tech at the end of

Joe's sophomore season. The game they immortalized in the movie, where (walk-on) Rudy (Ruettiger) got to play and was carried off the field by a couple of guys and all that. Yeah, I have the ball from that game. The only ball. I don't think Rudy knows it. And I don't think I want him to know it.

Dave Huffman

What are you talking to me for? I centered for Joe for three years at Notre Dame but never saw one thing he did. I was pointed in the other direction, remember? I can tell you this. In three years, we did not have one fumbled snap. That is not by accident. Joe and I stayed out late every day after practice during our sophomore year and practiced that snap. That's how intense he was. After a while, he was like, "Give it to me, and get out of the way." And so I did. Ah, some of the things I saw …

Everybody has their own favorite Montana game. Mine was against Purdue in Joe's junior year. The last game he didn't start. If you ask me, that is when the real Montana legacy started. Our other quarterbacks blew up in one game, and suddenly we needed Montana (Notre Dame trailed 21-14 with 11 minutes to go). And there he was. Came in and took us down the field and saved us … again (Montana threw two touchdown passes in a 31-24 victory).

What he would do was kneel down in the middle of the huddle, lick his fingers and say, "OK, let's win this game." And that's what would happen. Sometimes he would look at linemen and say, "You've got to block that guy." He was so intense, you would look back and say, "OK, OK, OK." Not that he was always that intense.

I'm sure you've heard the stories. He was always stealing somebody's jockstrap, stuff like that. Once he even walked up to the line and stuck his hands under Teddy Horansky, one of our guards. As a joke. Teddy jumped about 5 feet. One time I got Joe back, or so I thought. I cut out a hole in my football pants so that when he stepped up behind me and put his hands up there, all he felt was skin. He went, "Whoooa." Next thing I know, he drops back to pass and drills me in the back of the head.

The good thing about Joe is, he never forgets you. When he was being courted by the Vikings years ago, back when I was still their center, I remember him telling the press, "I really know just three things about Minnesota. It's cold, you play in a dome, and one of your players is my idiot friend." Touching, huh?

Oh, and about his last Notre Dame game. You know, the famous Cotton Bowl (after the 1978 season, when Montana led Notre Dame to a 35-34 victory over Houston after trailing 34-12). I know everybody talks about Joe drinking chicken soup in the locker room at halftime because he was so cold and sick. Well, it wasn't soup. It was some cheap broth. Some instant stuff you mix in a cup. I don't know how Joe came out in the second half and did what he did. But I know that by then, we weren't surprised.

'He was always ahead of the game, and I think that's what made him the best 2-minute quarterback ever.' –Tim Grunhard

The glory years

Fred Quillan

I centered for Joe from his rookie season with the 49ers in 1979 until I retired after the 1987 season. We won two Super Bowls during that time. Collected all sorts of great memories. But let me tell you about the gas. Joe was always playing tricks on me. Filling up envelopes with shaving cream and sticking them halfway under the door, then stepping on them. Stuff like that.

If he really got me mad, I would make sure I would eat tacos or burritos before practice. That way, by the time practice started, I would be, uh, gassy. I'm not making this up. So one time I was furious with him, and I ate all morning and early afternoon, and during practice it was really bad. Joe would step underneath me to take the snap, and I would, uh, well, you know … I did it so much that day, got it smelling so bad, that Joe finally stepped away from me, stopped practice and shouted, "I cannot play with this guy! I will not take another snap." Bill Walsh, our coach, was over there watching it and couldn't believe it. This was during that 1984 season, when we had one of the best NFL teams ever, and practice has stopped because one of the guys was, uh, breaking wind? Joe starts yelling, I yell back, and Bill just throws up his hands and walks away.

Actually, Joe was a center's best friend. If there was ever a bad snap, Joe took the fall. Every time. One time in practice, we messed up a snap, Walsh was irate, and Joe immediately took the blame. But it was clearly my fault, so I told Walsh that. Joe snapped back that it was his fault, and I yelled back that it was my fault, and here we were arguing again. Walsh couldn't figure it out, and threw up his hands again and walked away. After practice, Joe comes up to me and says, "Fred, don't you ever do that again. You keep your mouth shut, and I'll take the blame. Always." "Why?" I asked. "Because, Fred, I'm a quarterback, and you're a center. You will always get yelled at more than me. If I take the blame, they won't yell so much." Is that class or what?

I remember the worst call of my life was when I told a reporter that Steve DeBerg was better prepared to be our quarterback. Because Joe was so quiet, we just didn't know about his leadership. Midway through his second season, he proved it. He came into the huddle, and it was like a different team. He inspired such respect in us and, more important, trust. That's why one of the low points of my career was missing my guy in New York during the 1986 playoffs and watching Jim Burt knock Joe out of the game. Joe stayed in New York with a

concussion that night while I went crazy on the airplane home. I wanted to jump off the plane. I wanted to get home and jump off a bridge. It wasn't all my fault because a lot of things happened on that play, but I felt really bad. The next year, Joe never said a word to me about it. It was like he would never stop taking up for his linemen, no matter what.

Some people say he is just a great quarterback. I know him as much more.

Chuck Thomas

I guess I'm the answer to a trivia question. Who was Joe Montana's center in the one game where Montana crossed the union picket line? Joe's replacement center. That was me. In 1987. The third and final replacement game. Most people forget that Joe crossed the line. Although maybe some union people remember. Anyway, I don't think Joe was thumbing his nose at anybody; I think he just anticipated the end of the strike and came on in with a bunch of other guys. Am I glad he did. At the time, I had been with the 49ers in training camp, hurt my hamstring, then came back when the strike hit. After the strike, I would be mostly a backup until I left the team after the 1992 season.

But for one game, I was the starter, and Joe was my quarterback. I'll never forget it. In fact, I'm looking at a game ball from that day right now. It was against St. Louis. And the Cardinals were going hard after Joe. They had a heck of a blitz package coming in, throwing everything at him but the kitchen sink. But we hung in there. We protected him. The jewel wasn't damaged. We won. It was great. He didn't say much after that game. But a couple of years later, while I was still on the team as a backup, there was something he did I will never forget.

In the playoffs after the 1989 season, Bubba Paris, one of our tackles, had an agreement with Joe. If our line kept him from getting sacked in the postseason, he would buy us a gift. They shook on it. Well, except for once when he ran out of bounds—which doesn't really count—he was never sacked during the postseason. The capper was, our year ended with our Super Bowl victory over the Broncos. I didn't think anything of their agreement until I came to minicamp in 1990. There, sitting in my locker was a Rolex watch. On the back were these words, "To Chuck, With Much Appreciation, Super Bowl XXIV, Joe Montana." I couldn't believe it. I was a backup. I had been a replacement player. I had worked hard and had contributed a lot, but still … you can imagine how I felt. I walked over to him and said, "Joe, I really, really appreciate this." He looked at me all embarrassed. I guess for him, I overreacted. He just said, "Good work." And that was it.

I have two Super Bowl rings. I have that painted game ball from St. Louis. But this Rolex watch, that is my prize possession.

Walt Downing

I was a center with the 49ers from 1978 to 1983. Backed up a lot of offensive linemen. Started a few games for Fred Quillan. But Joe and I were close for a number of reasons. Like, our birthdays were the same date. Not just day, but date. Both of us were born on June 11, 1956. Both born in Pennsylvania, me outside Philadelphia and Joe, of course, outside Pittsburgh. By sharing a birthday with Joe, I used to have fun at a lot of parties. I remember once we were doing a celebrity thing down in Santa Cruz, they gave us this cake when they found out it was both of our birthdays. So we decided to try to hit each other in the face with this cake. I don't remember the exact results of the fight, but I remember that I at least got a little spot of cream on him. I'm sure I hit his nose. It's so big, it's hard to miss. Those were the days.

Teams were like family back then. We'd all go have dinner after the game, just sit around afterward and talk, that's what Joe loved to do. He was really shy at first. He could have done a ton more commercials back then, but that's not what he wanted. Sometimes when we were going out, Joe didn't even want to drive his Ferrari. So I drove it for him.

Now I'm 6-foot-4, about 275 pounds, so you can imagine how I looked. Ever seen somebody big trying to drive those Malibu Fun Center racecars? That was me. But Joe was comfortable. He was happy. He really felt good around his offensive linemen.

I remember once when Ed ("Too Tall") Jones of Dallas was just about ready to hammer him. Joe stepped around him and threw about a 45-yard bullet to Dwight Clark. Joe jumped up and said something to Too Tall. Then Joe turned the other way and looked for one of us to hide behind. That's the way he was. But that was just fine with us. He took such good care of us, it was the least we could do for him.

Randy Cross

I know you've probably heard this story a lot, but I want to let you know that it is the absolute, gospel truth. The John Candy story. I know it happened because I was there and heard every word of it. It was in the Super Bowl after the 1988 season, against the Bengals. We're deep in our territory late in the game. We're trailing. We need a big drive for the win. Joe steps into the huddle, stops, looks over on the sideline and says, "Hey, isn't that John Candy over there?" Gospel truth. He was doing that sort of thing all the time. And a lot of it was absolutely intentional. He was just trying to make us as relaxed as he was. Of course, everybody knows how he followed up that John Candy line with one of the greatest drives ever to give us the win. And he really was relaxed. That was real.

The one thing that set him apart from many other quarterbacks, and this is something that only a center would know, was the feel of his hands. They were never nervous. They were never rushed. It's hard to explain, but as a center, it's something you feel. And I felt it. The story of his coolness was not in his face, but his hands.

Underneath all that, though, there was an unbelievable competitiveness. You could tell because it was also visible off the field. Especially off the field. I'm beating him in golf, and all of a sudden he gets real quiet. A lot of great athletes meditate, but not many people go into a trance. Joe, he would go into a trance.

Another example of his competitiveness was in New Orleans in 1980. We stayed at some sleazy hotel. It had a big room near the lobby with all of these electronic games. One of those games was that old electric football game where you move your men by rolling a big ball that sticks out at either end of the field. You remember those games? Anyway, Joe and Steve DeBerg (the 49ers' starter at the time) start playing that game. And they keep playing. And playing. For at least a couple of hours, they played that game. By the end of the day, I looked down at their

hands and noticed that they were blue. They had spent the day saying, "You quit … No, you quit … No, you quit." And we were playing a game the next day.

Always cool and controlled, Montana already had achieved legendary status by the time he reached Kansas City.

Jesse Sapolu

I don't know if there has ever been anybody where the final two minutes have been so automatic. In 1988, we won a bunch of games in the last two minutes or so. It was like, 11. Did you know that? With him around, everybody knew that the 49ers were automatic at the end. That's not just the way it looked; that's the way it felt. It was the attitude we had in the huddle. Whether in the Super Bowl or the preseason. With Joe, it was like we were just 11 kids from some park, trying to beat some other park in a game. That's all it was.

I really appreciated Joe when I had to center for someone else. Like Steve Bono. Any mistakes made between the center and the quarterback, Joe would always shout, "My fault, my fault." The minute something went wrong with Steve Bono, though, he would

look at me and say, "What happened?"

The game I remember most is not the great Super Bowl victories but an early-season game in Philadelphia in 1989. Our line made so many mistakes in that game that Joe was sacked or knocked down about six or seven times. I don't know how he survived, but he did and was still able to throw five touchdown passes. The next week, when we watched the film, (offensive line coach) Bobb McKittrick stood up and apologized to the whole team for the poor play of our line. Later that day I'm sitting in front of my locker, real upset, and Joe walks over. Taps me in the ribs. "Shit happens," he said.

To me, that's the true Joe Montana, being able to forget about a bad play or bad day, moving on to the next play or next week, overcoming mistakes and being better for them. To me, that's a man.

The final years
Tim Grunhard

The thing about Joe is that he never gets too high or too low. He's always on an even keel. That's what really helped him do so well in those close games. He was always able to transcend the hype for a particular game or a particular play and just stay within himself. … The best example would probably be from the Denver game from Monday

night (in 1994). We had only 1:22 left. But Joe was always on the same keel, telling guys that we would get it done if we concentrate on doing our jobs. A lot of people get nervous, like, "Oh, no, we've got to make it all up on this one play." He's never that way. There was a game in San Diego his first year here. We're trying to score a touchdown late in the game to win it. He throws incomplete passes on the first three downs. Most quarterbacks I know would have said, "Geez, I've thrown three bad passes, maybe I'm off my game right now." Joe knew if he stayed level and did what he had to do, he would be successful. He completed the fourth-down pass, we got the first down, we scored a touchdown, and we won the game.

He was probably the biggest prankster in the locker room. From putting shaving cream into the guys' helmets to powdering their shoes, it was probably Joe who did it. Everybody was a victim. Nobody was spared. He always found a way to keep that locker room loose. That's the one thing that's so important in this league, and he did it so well.

The one thing that surprised me is that I thought he would be more of a motivator than he really was. I always thought he was one of those guys who was whooping and hollering in the huddle. But he just went about his business. In the 2-minute offense, he would always be thinking two, three, four plays ahead, about what we would do if we got the first down on this play or what we would do if the guy didn't get out of bounds or whatever. He was always ahead of the game, and I think that's what made him the best 2-minute quarterback ever.

3

OTTO

From his Illinois roots to NFL greatness, multi-talented Otto never failed to play sweet music

Picture a football player in uniform, muddied, dripping wet hair plastered against his helmetless head. He's on a high school football field, but it's halftime and he's marching, puffing away on the cornet, not catching his breath in the locker room. As the last note sounds and the players come jogging back on the field, the youngster discards the horn, grabs his helmet and rejoins his teammates for the second half.

Such was the life of Otto Graham at Waukegan (Ill.) High School in the late 1930s. It's tough when you're not only the best athlete in school, but a master of many instruments as well.

Team, seasons:
Cleveland Browns (AAFC/NFL), 1946-49/1950-55

Height: 6-1

Weight: 196

Born: 12-6-21 Died: 12-17-03

College: Northwestern

Championship teams:
1946, '47, '48, '49, '50, '54, '55

Career passing yards/TDs:
13,499/88 (NFL)

"I had the musical background because of my parents," said Graham in an interview before his death in December 2003 at age 82. "My father was head of the music department at Waukegan High School. My mother played the organ at Bob Feller's wedding."

By 16, Otto was Illinois state champion on the French horn. As a senior, he was a member of Waukegan High's national champion brass sextet. "I have to tell you," said Graham, "they didn't win because of me. I helped, but those guys were the real stars. I just went 'ooom-pa-pa.' "

Meanwhile, he was winning all-state honors in basketball and football and earning his first football honor as the state's top drop-kicker. A real conflict developed as his

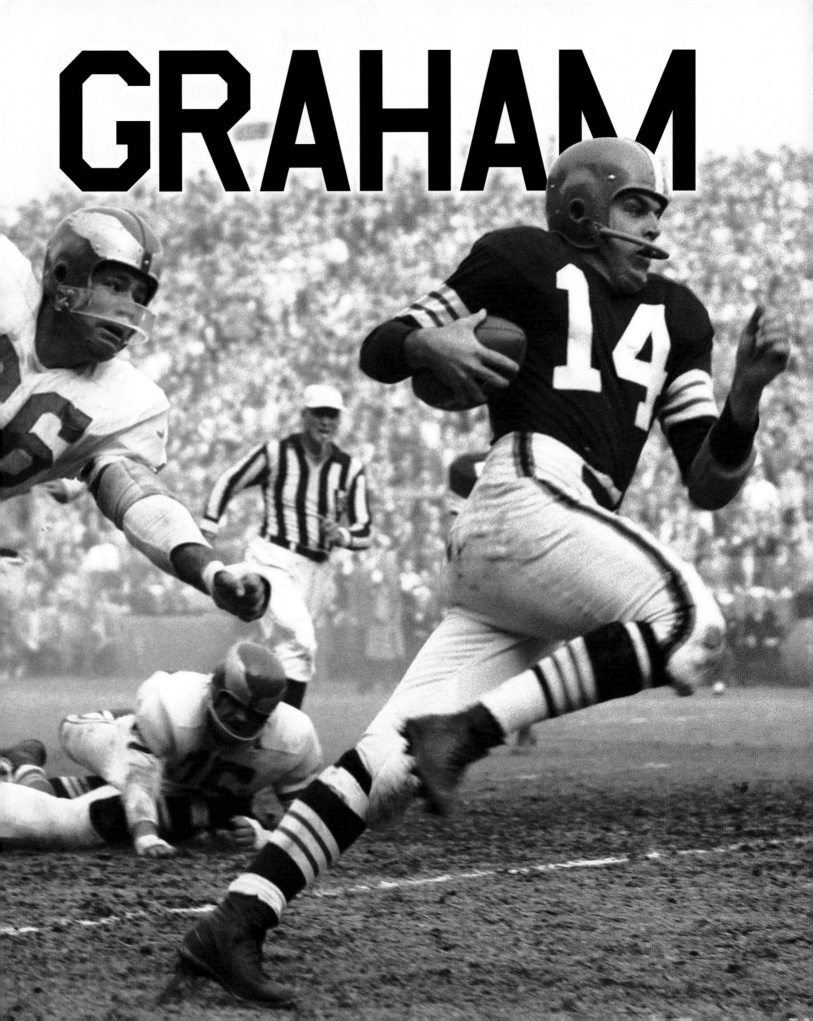

GRAHAM

It is the most important classification of all, number of championships won, that has Graham alone among the game's icons. … **Seven league titles in 10 years**—most observers believe it is a record that will never be approached.

musical and athletic endeavors overlapped after school, a process that slowly exasperated his coaches as well as his father. A showdown loomed.

Credit Otto's father for being alert to the signals of distress coming from his third-oldest son, who favored sports but didn't want to hurt his father's feelings. Otto Sr., a onetime major league baseball prospect, knew that his primary responsibility as a father was to support his son's choice. Sports won out, and Otto Jr. went on to become a Hall of Fame quarterback with the Cleveland Browns and the embodiment of winning on a football field.

Music had something to do with that. Graham had

to learn a position that was taking pro football by storm, the "T-formation" quarterback. That meant a crash course in mastering new mechanics involving timing, cadence and footwork. There were pivots and turns and spins—a virtual traffic circle around which the whole offense revolved, with backs going in motion away from the play and halfbacks and fullbacks crisscrossing diagonally on each side of the pivoted quarterback. Ballhandling and faking with and without the ball became prized skills. That role required a facile dexterity.

"The music definitely was a factor in helping me with timing," said Graham. "Although I didn't anticipate it, I worked at (per-

fecting the mechanics) very hard, and I was having fun. Of course, I think other factors, like natural coordination, play into it as well."

Indeed, Graham was a terrific athlete. He went to Northwestern on a basketball scholarship and twice earned All-American

recognition in that sport. Legendary coach Lynn "Pappy" Waldorf spotted him in a freshman intramural football game and persuaded him to try out for spring football. Graham went on to become one of only a handful of athletes who were a first-team All-American in both football

"I went down and talked with him one day in 1945, and he said they're going to have a new league soon and that he wanted me to be his quarterback. As a show of good faith, he sent me a monthly check for $275 until the war ended, plus, once the new league started, $7,500 a year for the first two seasons. At the time, I was making just $75 a month in the Navy. My answer was, 'Where do I sign?!' When Detroit heard about it, they asked me to send them a copy of the contract to give to their lawyers to see if they could break it. I wrote back, 'What do you mean break it? I signed it, and I'm going to honor it!' "

So Graham became the original Brown—the first player signed by the franchise. But it was basketball that gave him his first taste of pro sports. The Rochester Royals (today's Sacramento Kings) of the National Basketball League (a pre-NBA circuit) signed Graham after he was mustered out of the Navy in 1945. With a season to kill before the advent of the AAFC, Otto turned his attention to basketball.

"We had some great players," said Graham, a guard. "Al Cervi (future Basketball Hall of Famer), Red Holzman (longtime New York Knicks head coach), Chuck Connors (TV's The Rifleman). Yeah, we had a good team. We breezed through it all. It was fun. I'm glad I played pro basketball."

The Royals won the NBL championship in 1946. But the rigors of constant travel quickly wore on Graham

and basketball the same year (1943, his senior season). He also finished third in the Heisman Trophy balloting that year. Then it was time to serve his country in World War II.

Graham was drafted by the Detroit Lions in 1944, while in the Navy. But Paul Brown, who was get-

ting ready to launch a team bearing his name in Cleveland in the fledgling All-America Football Conference, had his eye on Graham, too.

"Paul Brown got in touch with me," Graham recalled. "He was up at Great Lakes Naval Training Station, which was right next to

Waukegan. I had played against him when he was head coach at Ohio State. I guess I impressed him. I remember one time I ran to my left, stopped and threw the ball all the way across the field for a touchdown of about 50 yards. Twice we beat him. So, he remembered that about me.

and his young, pregnant wife, Bev. One year of pro basketball was enough. Then it was on to the AAFC and Cleveland, where he would take this business of winning to an entirely new level.

n 10 years with the Browns, Graham posted a stunning 105-17-4 record.

Otto Graham Sr. (left) and Browns coach Paul Brown (right, below right) celebrate with Otto Jr. in 1954 after a win over the Lions in the NFL championship game.

That's a winning percentage of .849. If you took the 10 best seasons of other great winners Joe Montana, Johnny Unitas, Sid Luckman and Bart Starr from their respective 15-, 18-, 12- and 16-year careers, it would be no contest; Graham's closest pursuer, Luckman, is more than 100 points behind at .748, followed by Starr (.717), Montana (.711) and Unitas (.689).

Graham was all-league in nine of his 10 pro seasons, a five-time league passing champion and a five-time MVP (twice in the AAFC, three times in the NFL). He threw for 23,584 passing yards and 174 touchdowns and rushed for an amazing 44 TDs. Graham displayed all-around athleticism in his early AAFC days, returning 22 punts for 250 yards in 1946 and '47. He also intercepted five passes and returned one for a touchdown as a safety in his first year. He never missed a game in his 10-year pro career.

But it is the most important classification of all, number of championships won, that has Graham alone among the game's icons. No NFL team or quarterback in history can match it.

Graham and his Browns teammates made an unprecedented 10 straight title game appearances, claiming the AAFC crown all four years of that league's existence (1946-49) before turning their attention to the NFL in 1950, where they clicked off another six consecutive championship game appearances, winning three times. Seven league titles in 10 years—most observers believe it is a record that will never be approached.

"Otto was the greatest of all quarterbacks," Brown once said. "For 10 years, he propelled his team to 10 championship games. That's the test of a real quarterback. He was my greatest player. ... I don't discount Marion Motley, Dante Lavelli or Jim Brown. But the guy that was the engineer, the guy with the touch that pulled us out of many situations, was Otto Graham."

Though he could fire a football, he was said to have had the softest touch. Receivers loved his passes—they were on the mark, and the kind you could pluck right out of the air.

Brown said Graham had the best peripheral vision of anybody he ever had seen. When he ran, often on broken plays, Graham displayed an uncanny sixth sense in evading pursuers. He would just barely squirm away from the grasp of pass rushers. With would-be tacklers ready to nail him, Graham would shift gears, gain speed and create separation. More than one

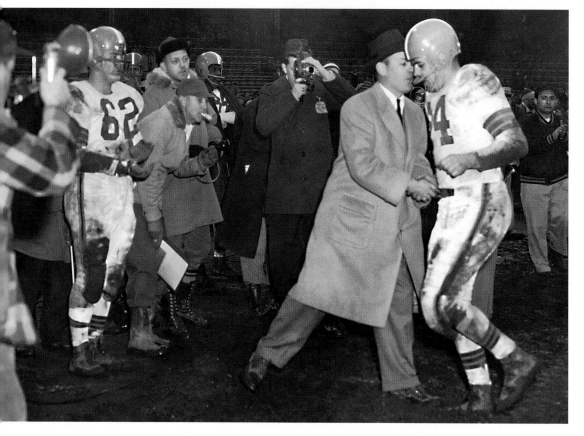

pulled us out of many situations, was Otto Graham." —Paul Brown

defender was burned by his deceptive long-legged stride. "I didn't have blinding speed," Graham said, "but I had good speed, and I wasn't afraid to run. If I saw an opening, I'd take it."

 hough the championships placed him alone among the league's great quarterbacks, Graham savored no victory more than his first in the NFL. The Browns made their NFL debut against the defending two-time NFL champion Eagles on September 16, 1950, in Philadelphia.

"Oh, the derogatory comments that were being made by the NFL owners, players, coaches—you name it!" Graham said five decades later. "They said the worst team in the NFL could beat (the AAFC's) best team. When we went into that game, I can assure you that no team in the entire history of sport was as well-prepared mentally as we were. We couldn't wait to get to them, and we killed them, of course." Final score: Cleveland 35, Philadelphia 10. Graham threw three touchdown passes. By the end of the season the Browns were NFL champs, following a 30-28 win over the Los Angeles Rams. When he called it quits five years later, the Rams were the victims of Cleveland's seventh championship and second in a row. Graham walked out on top.

"Otto could've played

for a couple more years and still been on top," said Lavelli, the Browns' Hall of Fame receiver who pulled down so many of Graham's passes. "But he evidently got tired of traveling and the pressure to keep winning. All the players wanted him to come back, and he finally decided he didn't want to do it. I think we'd have won again (in 1956) if he'd have come back."

Following his wonder years in Cleveland came a 24-year association with the U.S. Coast Guard Academy in New London, Conn., as both head coach (1959-65) and athletic director (1969-85), including coaching that school's only undefeated/untied team, in 1963. In his three years away from the academy (1966-68), he was head coach of the Washington

Redskins, where his teams went 17-22-3. "I always tell people that the thing I should be known for more than anything else is that Vince Lombardi replaced me as head coach of the Washington Redskins," he joked.

Years later, the man who set the standard for winning as an NFL quarterback had some interesting thoughts about his life and career.

"Just last night I was watching The Three Tenors sing," Graham said in a 1995 interview. "I could watch them every day of the year. I get chills listening to those guys. If I could sing like that, my God almighty, you could take all these damn trophies and melt 'em down for all I'd care.

"When I played music, I played because I had to. I wish I'd been smart and kept it up after college. I could still be playing the piano or the violin, the cornet or the French horn. You might laugh, but I would trade every trophy or honor I've ever had if I could still play the piano. You can play the piano until you're 70 or 80 years old and play it beautifully. You can be the life of the party. You can't play football at 70 or 80.

"So, I tell kids: If you have a talent like that, keep it up, and you'll have the last laugh. I could've followed up with those instruments I played, but back then it was, 'I'd rather play football, I'd rather play basketball.' You wake up in life too late, that's all."

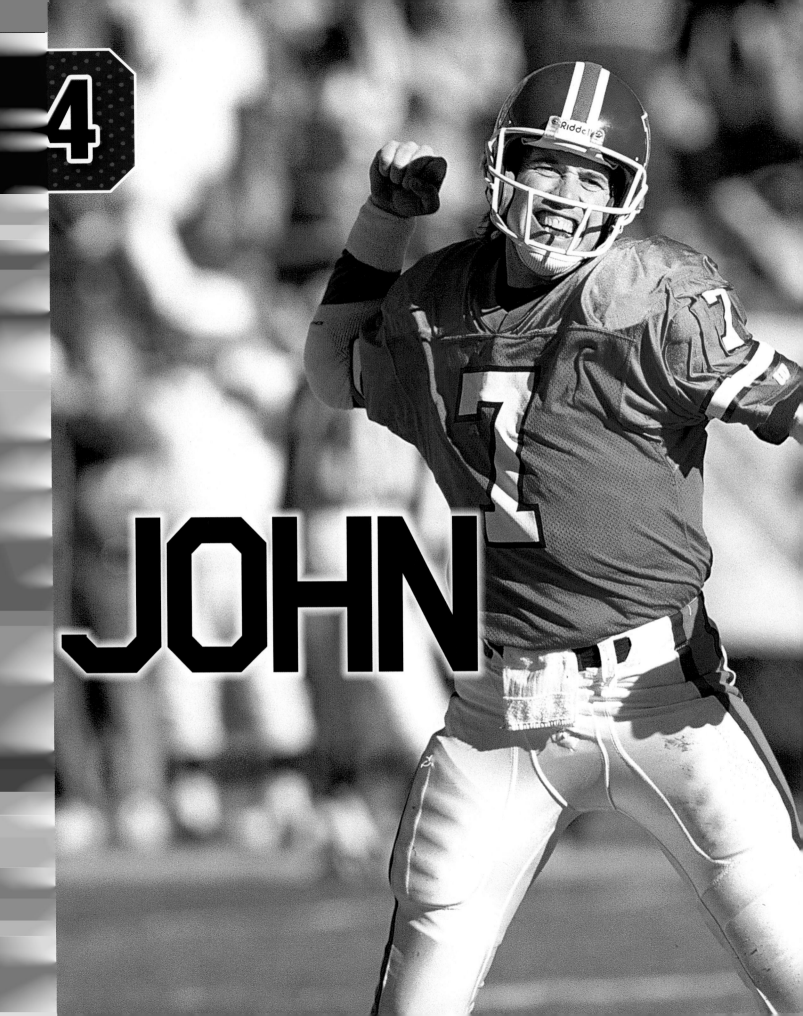

4

JOHN

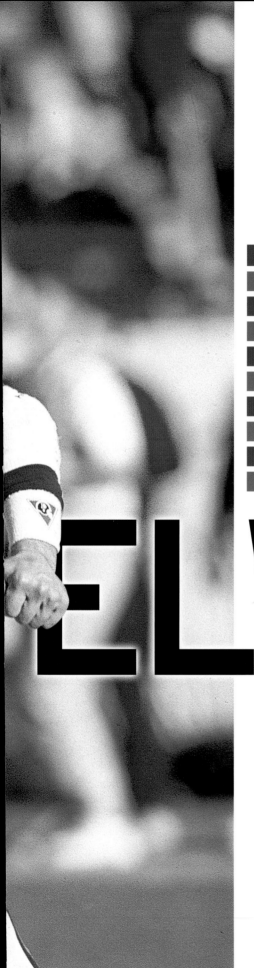

Armed and dangerous, Elway drove his Broncos to the top of the pro football world

Team, seasons:	
Denver Broncos, 1983-98	
Height: 6-3	
Weight: 215	
Born: 6-28-60	
College: Stanford	
Championship teams:	
1997, '98 seasons	
Career passing yards/TDs:	
51,475/300	

y the time John Elway joined the Denver Broncos, the franchise was light years beyond its days as the laughingstock of professional football. Only die-hard fans could remember—or cared to remember—when the Broncos wore vertically striped socks or failed to make a first down in an entire game or were unable to post a winning record in their first 13 seasons of AFL/NFL competition. Still, when 1983 rolled around, the Broncos weren't exactly reflecting

on a glorious past. Oh, they had made it to the Super Bowl in the magical-if-not-miraculous 1977 season and qualified for the play-offs three times. But no one viewed the Broncos as a juggernaut—and a 2-7 pratfall in the strike-shortened 1982 season stirred fear among the Denver faithful that a return to mediocrity or worse might be in the offing.

The team appeared to be at a critical juncture, in need of some-one to ride in on a white horse—a fitting piece of imagery, in view of the snorting stallion perched atop the scoreboard on the south stands of Mile High Stadium. And in rode rookie quarterback Elway, albeit by a circuitous route. Chosen No. 1 overall in the draft by the Baltimore Colts, Elway told the Colts thanks, but no thanks—he wouldn't play for the down-and-out AFC East team. His rights then were traded to Denver.

Elway never had led Stanford to a bowl game, and the school had a losing record in his four years there. But he possessed the quintessen-tial "gun" when it came to arm strength and had thrown for 77 touch-downs. He had the makeup to be something special at a position where the Broncos had been decidedly unspectacular over most of their previous 23 seasons.

"Special" hardly conveys what Elway turned out to be. He drove

NFL's showcase game in his seventh season.

Elway's late-game heroics, dazzling passing statistics and winning ways shot the quarter-

regular-season record in the Elway years.

Still, it took two postseason victories to thrust Elway and the Broncos into true greatness. With three crushing Super Bowl losses often obscuring Elway's wondrous accomplishments and Denver trying to live down the franchise's embarrassing 0-4 Super Bowl record, Elway and the Broncos swept past Green Bay and Atlanta in Super Bowls 32 and 33. At long last, the Broncos were at the pinnacle, and Elway had gotten his full due. And the guy on the white horse, choosing to save his very best for last, rode off into the sunset and retired from the game.

In his 16-year career, Elway led Denver on 47 game-winning or game-saving drives in the fourth quarter or in overtime.

the Broncos to the Super Bowl in his fourth season, 1986, winning a special place in NFL lore by taking Denver on a game-tying 98-yard drive in the fourth quarter of the AFC championship game at Cleveland. In his fifth year, he led the Broncos to another Super Bowl appearance, and he had Denver back in the

back and his team into prominence. In his 16-year career, Elway led Denver on 47 game-winning or game-saving drives in the fourth quarter or in overtime. He passed for 4,030 yards in one season and 51,475 yards in his career, and he threw 300 TD passes. And Denver fashioned a 161-93-1

'HE GOT ... THOSE RINGS.
HE DESERVES THEM.' *By Junior Seau*

lot of his game was improvising, but he knew the game and felt the game. When you have a guy with the ability of a John Elway, it's hard to practice for him, prepare for him.

It was always fun to try to fool him. He and Dan Marino were guys you could try to bluff a blitz, but they would know by your body language you were bluffing. It was always a chess game out there. John Elway was one of the best at it. He'd look at me sometimes and say, "I got it, stop." So back to cover 2 zone for me. He'd say it right in the middle of the play.

There was a game where he was coming down on a 2-minute drive, leading the way. It was in Mile High Stadium, and he was rolling out, and there was like 10 seconds left, and they were on maybe the 6-yard line. He was rolling out, and he went to throw the ball, and I was lucky enough to be in the vicinity and was able to grab the ball. I intercepted it, and the game was over. That didn't happen very often.

Another time, I took one of his slant passes and took it to the end zone. We were offside, and it got called back. He got the better of it because he scored on the next play.

If you're going to step in front of a John Elway pass, you better have body position because he could really throw the ball. Whether he was throwing a hitch pass, a 5-yard route or a 30-yard route on a comeback, it was going to be coming—fast. That second interception, the one that got called back, I didn't put my hands

out there trying to catch it, I'll say that. I closed my eyes, it hit my chest hard, and I took it off my pads. But for the most part, I caught it.

There hasn't been a quarterback who has had a stronger arm than Elway. His throws were not only precise, they were hard. You could see the way he'd put a ball between two defenders that he could wing it.

He was so good at improvising in terms of turning a bad play into a good play. He was a strong thrower, and he could run. He could run like a fullback, and he knew angles. And he had great vision—not just as a passer but also as a runner.

He was a one-man team for a long time. Nothing against anybody else, but he was carrying that offense for a while. Then Terrell Davis and Tom Nalen and Co. came in. They had the receiving corps. It worked out that he held on long enough that he got that ring—those rings. He deserves them.

THE DRIVE

January 11, 1987 was a day that will live in infamy in Cleveland. It was the day Broncos quarterback John Elway carved his name in NFL lore on his way to becoming a legend. It was the day Elway engineered a 15-play, 98-yard masterpiece in the mud to send the AFC championship game into overtime.

"For us, it was 98 yards to the Super Bowl, but, in the face of adversity, true champions are born," Denver wide receiver Mark Jackson said at the time.

"You'd be on the sideline, and (Elway) would have the ball, and you felt as hopeless as you possibly could," said Ozzie Newsome, the Browns' Hall of Fame tight end.

The Drive, Play by Play

Play No. 1: First-and-10 at the Denver 2 (5:32 remaining). Elway fakes a handoff to Gerald Willhite, then passes to Sammy Winder for 5 yards.

Play No. 2: Second-and-5, Denver 7. Winder, on a pitchout, runs for 3 yards.

DENVER CALLS TIMEOUT

Play No. 3: Third-and-2, Denver 10. Winder runs over left guard for a 2-yard gain and a first down.

Play No. 4: First-and-10, Denver 12. Winder runs over left tackle for 3 yards.

Play No. 5: Second-and-7, Denver 15. Forced out of the pocket, Elway scrambles for 11 yards and a first down.

Play No. 6: First-and-10, Denver 26. Elway hits Steve Sewell on a swing pass for a 22-yard gain and a first down.

Play No. 7: First-and-10, Denver 48. Elway hits Steve Watson over the middle for a 12-yard gain and a first down.

TWO-MINUTE WARNING

Play No. 8: First-and-10, Cleveland 40-yard line. Elway's pass intended for Vance Johnson is incomplete.

Play No. 9: Second-and-10, Cleveland 40. (1:52 remaining). Elway is sacked by Cleveland's Dave Puzzuoli for an 8-yard loss.

DENVER CALLS TIMEOUT

"When I went over to the sideline, (coach Dan Reeves) told me to try and go for only half of what we needed because we still had two plays to get the 18 yards," Elway said. "We called a 'Release 66' pass, with Orson Mobley as the primary receiver, about 10 yards over the middle. But as we lined up, I saw their strong safety (Ray Ellis) was playing very, very deep and that we had a good chance to go for the whole 18 yards. So, instead of looking for Mobley, I looked for Jackson."

Play No. 10: Third-and-18, Cleveland 48 (1:47 remaining). The play nearly is a disaster. Watson goes in motion, passing in front of Elway, who is in shotgun formation. The snap bounces off Watson's hip, but Elway isn't fazed. He grabs the ball and throws a strike to Jackson for a 20-yard gain and a first down.

Play No. 11: First-and-10, Cleveland 28 (1:19 remaining). Elway's pass intended for Watson is incomplete.

Play No. 12: Second-and-10, Cleveland 28 (1:10 remaining). Elway hits Sewell for a 14-yard completion and a first down.

Play No. 13: First-and-10, Cleveland 14 (:57 remaining). Elway's pass intended for Watson is incomplete.

Play No. 14: Second-and-10, Cleveland 14 (:42 remaining). Elway is flushed from the pocket and runs 9 yards to the Cleveland 5.

Play No. 15: Third-and-1, Cleveland 5 (:39 remaining). Elway drops back for the 12th time on the drive and hits a wide-open Jackson for the game-tying touchdown.

"I thought their cornerback (All-Pro Hanford Dixon) would bump Jackson at the line of scrimmage," Elway said, "but when he didn't, it was Mark against the safety, one-on-one. No problem."

Rich Karlis kicked the extra point to tie the score at 20-20 with 31 seconds remaining in regulation. Cleveland got the ball first in sudden-death overtime but gained only 8 yards and punted. On Denver's first possession in overtime, Elway took over at the 25 and marched the Broncos 60 yards in nine plays. The game ended when Karlis, a bare-footed kicker, whistled a 33-yarder just inside the left upright.

'JOHN CHANGED THE WAY YOU COACHED.
HE WAS JUST AN AMAZING PLAYER.'

By Marty Schottenheimer

ohn who? Sure, John Elway broke my heart, but I have great admiration for him. I think he ranks in that top category, that top echelon of the greatest players in the game.

Obviously, he had skills, but he had such a great competitive spirit and love for the game. That play in the Super Bowl against Green Bay, where he dove for that big first down, that's what I'm talking about. He had the physical ability to do that, and he also had the love and willingness to take a chance like that in a big situation.

He gave up everything when the game was on the line.

There are guys who might be a little faster—Michael Vick, Steve Young—but if you're talking about being athletically gifted and playing to a level of performance, no one was as good as John. Nobody matches his combination of skills and accomplishment.

The Drive? Periodically, I see something that triggers a memory of it. I don't spend time thinking about that game, but it was remarkable. The play that was the most remarkable, we had them in a third-and-18 or 20, a tough situation where you think you can get him. John was in the shotgun, and Steve Watson went in motion. Watson comes across, and the snap is just a little early, and it ricochets off Watson's hip. John had the presence and athletic ability to get the ball and still get the play. That one broke our backs. We go from having them backed up, to thinking for a second that it's over, to suddenly he makes this incredible play. That's the competitive aspect of him that I love.

We had schemes where we would try to flush him out to the left and get him to throw it against his body. That's all you could do, but even then, he could whirl around and throw it back to the other side of the field. In the 1987 AFC championship game at Denver, we put a spy on him. We put in D.D. Hoggard, a defensive back, at linebacker because we didn't have a linebacker who could catch John. D.D. was supposed to wait until John broke the pocket and then go after him. It worked OK for awhile, but John was so smart, he started sitting in the pocket until the last second before taking off. By that time, D.D. couldn't get to him before the throw.

John changed the way you coached.

Normally, when a quarterback starts running out of the pocket, you tell the defensive backs to give a little cushion if they're on the other side of the field, figuring they can catch up to the ball if the quarterback tries to throw it over the top. With John, his arm was so strong you couldn't give any cushion. You had to tell your guys to keep running all the way with the route even if he's running all over the field. He could throw it 70 yards back across the field.

He was just an amazing player.

'IF YOU CAN'T BEAT 'EM, JOIN 'EM.'

By Neil Smith

I have to say John really made my career. Hey, if you can't beat 'em, join 'em.

When I played against him, he was so competitive it brought my game to its highest level. He did the same thing for Derrick Thomas, too. Of course, no matter what we did, he was able to rise above us, especially when the Chiefs played in Denver. I came in the league in 1988, and we lost seven of our nine games at Mile High, including the first six in a row.

All those losses were frustrating. We were trying to get over the hump, and Elway was almost single-handedly keeping us pinned down in our own division. And the guy had that look, that grin. I'd always say, "I'm going to wipe that grin off his face!" to our guys, or his offensive line—I never said it to Elway because I didn't talk to quarterbacks—but it was always there. It was painfully obvious to me he was having fun every play. The harder you hit him, the quicker he got up. You had to respect the way he played the game, and he made you play at your best.

That didn't make me feel any better at the time because almost every one of those losses was a heartbreaker, and I was on the field for the end of all of 'em.

The worst one was probably the first game of the 1992 season, when we had Elway defensed as perfectly as you can for 58 minutes and led 19-6. In Denver! Naturally, we couldn't keep him down forever, and he took them down the field and threw a perfect touchdown pass to Mark Jackson in the corner. So it was 19-13, and everyone on our sideline is thinking, "Here we go again; Elway's going to get that ball one more time."

NFL Films was on our bench—if you haven't seen it on TV already, it's one of the highlights on John Elway's Greatest Comebacks. You hear Marty Schottenheimer trying to motivate us, making this great speech and about what a great opportunity it was for our team to make a statement and finally stop Elway with the game on the line.

Coaches can say whatever they want. We couldn't stop him. With less than a minute left, with our rush coming at him from both sides, Elway made his inevitable miraculous throws. And Denver beat us 20-19, with two touchdowns coming after the two-minute warning.

We didn't beat Elway on his turf until we got Joe Montana. That was in 1994, and it took Joe throwing a TD with eight seconds left. Even then, I came out with the defense for that last play thinking: "Elway will find a way. Superman to the rescue!"

I rate Elway as one of the top two quarterbacks ever, with Montana. If I had to make a choice … I am more proud I got to play on a team with John.

Our first game as teammates was the 1997 opener, against Kansas City, in Denver. John pulled me aside during warmups, gave me that grin and said, 'Welcome to the good side.'

When I came to the Broncos, I didn't hear personally from John, but I knew he personally helped bring me in because he restructured his contract to bring in players and win a Super Bowl. We won two. After the second, I made sure I was one of the first people to greet him as he came off the field for the last time, offering my congratulations and thanks.

Our first game as teammates was the 1997 opener, against Kansas City, in Denver. John pulled me aside during warmups, gave me that grin and said, "Welcome to the good side." We won. We won 12 games that season. We also played the Chiefs at Kansas City in the playoffs, and there wasn't any doubt we'd win that one; we had Elway. We understood this was his best chance to be a champion, and his destiny was ours.

Remember when we beat Green Bay in the Super Bowl, when Pat Bowlen held the trophy and said, "This one's for John?" Elway got all the acclaim and attention—but I got the game ball! After the Packers' incompletion on fourth down, while everybody was celebrating, I turned around and saw the ball just laying there on the field, so I picked it up. It's in my family room today. John, I owe ya.

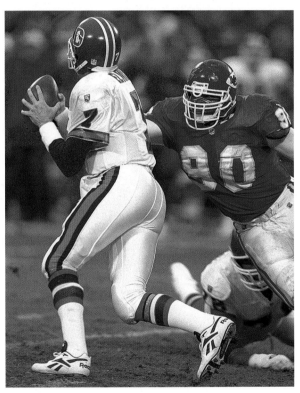

Before he was Elway's teammate, defensive end Smith played for rival Kansas City and tried to chase down the Broncos quarterback, usually without success.

5

SAMMY BAUGH

SA

No passing
fancy,
Slingin'
Sammy
helped
revolutionize
the game
with his
forward
thinking

MMY BAUGH

| Team, seasons: |
| Washington Redskins, 1937-52 |
| Height: 6-2 |
| Weight: 182 |
| Born: 3-17-14 |
| College: TCU |
| Championship teams: |
| 1937, '42 seasons |
| Career passing yards/TDs: |
| 21,886/187 |

he great divide of football came on a simple 5-yard pass.

In his first pro game and on the first play from scrimmage in Washington Redskins history, Slingin' Sammy Baugh, the great forward passer from Texas Christian University, hit Ernie Pinckert on a seemingly innocuous gain against the Giants in what ultimately become a landmark moment in the birth of the modern passing game.

Tall, rangy and pinpoint accurate, Baugh completed 11 of 16 passes for 116 yards in a 13-3 victory over the Giants. The five incomplete passes could be classified as drops. "No one had passing numbers like that in those days," said Riley Smith, who scored all of the Redskins' points that night. "No one thought about passing 16 times. But Sam was throwing that thing all over the place. It electrified the crowd."

It was September 16, 1937, a warm Thursday night in Washington's Griffith Stadium. And football never would be the same.

The three-downs-and-a-cloud-of-dust days were about to end. Baugh passed on first down and second down and even in short-yardage situations that begged for a run. His daring passes became the best NFL headlines since Red Grange a decade earlier. The Redskins captured NFL championships in 1937 and '42 and played in three other title games. Baugh claimed six passing titles in 16 seasons and almost single-handedly laid the groundwork for every major offensive scheme to come.

"Anytime you see a quarterback scramble, or throw on the run, or loft one perfectly in the corner of the end zone for his receiver, that's a reflection of Sammy Baugh," former Bears rival quarterback and good friend Sid Luckman said in a 1997 interview. "No one ever did those things before him, but a hell of a lot of people sure copied him—including me."

Baugh's skills and approach were 40 years ahead of their time. Think of Joe Montana's cool and Steve Young's efficiency. Baugh introduced a short-passing, ball-control, high-percentage offense that he called "short, safe and sure." If this strategy sounds familiar,

consider that Bill Walsh was 5 years old when Baugh introduced it to the NFL.

But to fully understand Baugh's enormous impact, you must understand his time and place. Pro football could not have been more raw. The rules to restrict passing "didn't make a damn ounce of sense," said Baugh.

To outline Baugh's significance in football and illustrate the remarkably adverse conditions by which he had to play, *Sporting News* went to The Slinger himself for some revisionist history:

'I can throw a little'

When Baugh entered the league in 1937, football was conservative and defensive-minded. A team rarely passed more than eight times a game, and passes usually occurred only on third-and-long. That's the way the college and pro game had been played for five decades.

When I was a boy, football was Jim Thorpe, Red Grange and the Four Horsemen of

Notre Dame running the ball. But I was one of those boys who just liked to throw the damn thing.

When I first came into the league, it was a boring game to me and about anybody who watched it. They didn't want you to throw the ball until you got to at least your 20-yard line. You didn't pass on first down, rarely on second and not on third unless you needed more than 7 yards. They wanted a running game. All the rules favored the running game.

The entire game was so conservative that most every team in the colleges and pros used the single wing. It was an offense geared to fool the defense because you had so many options for handling the ball—spinning, faking, reversing and, on occasion, passing. But the single wing was not a

spread-out, dropback-and-pass offense. There was no such thing as a quarterback in the single wing; the primary ballhandler was a tailback like me who lined up—in what is known today as a shotgun formation—5 yards behind the snapper. That tailback might be a runner, blocker, passer or quick-kicker.

The defense didn't have to be a bunch of geniuses to know you were going to run. It was a matter of whether you were going left, right or center.

What we did in the single wing in Washington was add the wrinkle of passing early in downs and controlling the clock. That's what we had done at TCU, and that's really all I knew how to do. The colleges were ahead of the pros in tinkering with their offenses. In the 1930s, teams began playing around with the Notre

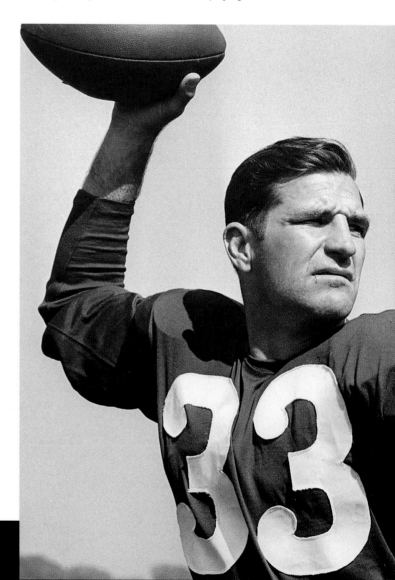

Dame Box, the double-wing spread—as we ran some in Washington—and loose versions of the T-formation, in which a back (named the quarterback because he was in front of the halfback and fullback) lined up directly behind center.

Ray Flaherty was our coach when I got to Washington, and he was a pretty typical coach for that time. Flaherty believed defense was the best way to win games, and he was pretty damn skeptical about me throwing. On my first day of practice, he comes over and says, "These receivers in the pro league expect their passers to be good. None of those wild heaves you see the college boys throw."

I'm shaking my head. "Yessir, yessir."

"They tell me you're quite a passer," Flaherty said.

"I reckon I can throw a little," I answer.

"Let's see it. Hit that receiver in the eye."

I cocked an eye toward Wayne Millner, who was running a little buttonhook pattern, and I turned to Flaherty and asked, "Which eye?"

Flaherty, who was a mean, hot-tempered sonofabitch, laughed like hell and after that never really questioned my decisions to throw the ball. We won games and, in the end, that's all that matters to a coach. But by 1940, only a few teams had truly gone away from the basic single wing, except for Notre Dame, Stanford and the Chicago Bears. And Stanford and Chicago were kicking people's ass using what they called the "modern T."

Bears coach George Halas said T stood for Total Offense Football but in truth the T had been a standard offense at the turn of the century, except for the passing aspect. Stanford coach Clark Shaughnessy had revived the T to include a man in motion and the quarterback having options, like passing, pitching or faking a handoff. And what that meant to the more aggressive passers like me and Sid Luckman of the Bears was widening the area of attack, spreading the defense and, best of all, throwing the damn ball in those areas opened by the spread.

But the T required a special skill in footwork, handling of the ball and the risk of having the ball snapped to the quarterback that much closer to the defense. It was an offense that scared 99 percent of the coaches. It was too risky, they thought.

But after the Bears beat the piss out of us, 73-0, in that '40 championship game ... well, you could literally see the game changing right in front of your eyes. A few weeks later, Shaughnessy's Stanford bunch finished 10-0 by beating Nebraska in the Rose Bowl. By the next season, almost everybody in football started messing with the T.

Since then, about every form of pro-style offense has been a cousin of the T. The triple option. The wishbone. The veer. You name it. So whenever you see what Johnny Unitas and Fran Tarkenton and Dan Marino and John Elway and all these great passers have been able to do, you can trace it back to 73-to-nothing.

The linebacker is born

No longer able to crowd the line of scrimmage with six- and seven-man fronts to stuff the run, teams had to more often move the defensive center off the line to help against the pass. That player became known as a linebacker.

What's really interesting about the pro game in the '40s is a lot of people talk about all the offensive innovations, with most teams switching to the T and Paul Brown developing pass protection in

'I was one of those boys who just liked to throw the damn thing.'

Cleveland. But I think the biggest changes at that time actually came on the defensive side of the ball. The rules also favored the defense. If an offensive lineman put his hands up on a boy's jersey to try and block him—*pow!*—holding, 15 yards.

The biggest change was the free-substitution rule, which was put into effect (later adopted in 1949-50) on a trial basis during the war. Back then, a lot of damn good offensive ballplayers were eliminated because they couldn't play defense well enough. There just wasn't any such thing as a specialist in those days. You had to be able to play both ways and play both damn well. If they only had to play offense, they might have become stars and I'm goddamn certain we'd have had as much offense as they have today. When we played and the fourth quarter came around, everybody, and I mean everybody on the field, was dog tired.

You knew teams were going to jam the line. So when we lined up on offense, I knew I was going to throw the ball right away. I wasn't going to run two plays and throw. But in the '40s, for the first time, the defensive man started using the freedom he was allowed to move into better position and cover a man. You started seeing more stunts, blitzes and disguises.

Because of boys playing both ways, you knew that the ends were meant to be blockers and defenders, not receivers. There were not going to be a lot of great receivers unless they were halfbacks who caught the ball. But when the passing game started up, teams still had to figure out how to play both sides of the ball—and how to protect that safety man in the

defensive backfield.

But so many of the defenses were so damn paranoid about the run that they wouldn't budge off the traditional 6-2-2-1 formation. That made it easy for the passer to toss little screens and flares, control the clock and move the ball and send those defensive ends scrambling to cover those short passing plays. They'd start creeping up, and then you'd burn that safety man's ass. That much about the game hasn't changed.

Things started changing on the defensive side of the ball in the early '40s when Greasy Neale of the Eagles created a 5-3-2-1 package that caused a lot of problems for an offense. That formation, spreading two men out to the corners to help the safety man, was the beginning of the 4-3 defense we know today.

Protecting the quarterback

A passer could be hit—HARD—as long as the play was alive, no matter where the ball was. That was changed in early 1938, just after Baugh's rookie season in which he had electrified the sport with his passes.

You'd throw the damn ball, the play would be 50 yards downfield and you'd be run-

Baugh, a former minor league player in the Cardinals organization, also is remembered as one of the best punters in NFL history. Baugh averaged a whopping 45.1 yards per punt over his long career.

ning for your life on the other end of the field. If you weren't paying attention, some sonofabitch would blindside your ass and be smiling about it. When we played in the '37 championship game, those goddamn Bears just about killed me.

Roughing the passer? Personal foul? My ass. Nobody had ever heard of those rules.

But I believe roughing the passer became a rule because of what happened in that championship game. I had already had my knee about twisted off, got my hand cut when somebody stomped on me and had my hip driven into the icy field after a play was dead. Dick Plasman threw a punch at me in front of our bench that started a big-ass brawl.

So one day shortly after the '37 season, George Preston Marshall, the Redskins' owner, called and said, "What if we

put in this rule that said you couldn't hit the quarterback after the pass was thrown?"

I said, "That'll put about 10 years on my life if you do." So Mr. Marshall and Mr. Halas got together, as they did when they wanted something changed, and agreed to make that rule. It was the first rule put in place for benefit of the passing game: a 15-yard penalty for hitting the passer too hard after the ball was thrown.

Penalty clauses

It took more than a dozen years for the NFL to fully rectify a handful of rules that hindered the passing game. Some of those crazy rules were beyond the wildest imagination. Most were changed in early 1938, just a few weeks after Baugh's impressive rookie season.

When Mr. Marshall and Mr. Halas got together after the '37 championship game, they realized the passing game attracted people. Fans liked the scoring. Football had been boring, and no one had ever thought of changing things.

The dumbest rule I ever saw was that you had to be at least 5 yards behind the line of scrimmage to pass or it was a penalty. They changed that one in 1933, my freshman year at TCU, but another was a 5-yard penalty if you threw two straight incompletions. That rule was why no one dared to pass earlier than third down, and you can make the argument that the game really didn't open up until they got rid of that rule in 1938 and offenses could pass earlier in the possession.

Think about this one: If you threw an incompletion from the end zone, you lost possession of the ball. You didn't hear much about that rule because you couldn't pay teams to pass out of the end zone. Why hell, that's why! So until they changed that stupid rule, also in '38, a lot of times when we were down inside the 10-yard line I would just quick-kick the ball away.

What happened in the 1945 NFL championship game in Cleveland beat all I've ever seen. It was 6 degrees that day, and it was so cold that players were bundled up in straw on the sidelines. The band came out at halftime to play, but their horns were frozen. All you could hear were the drums. It was a miserable day to play with those winds coming off Lake Erie.

On our first possession, from our own 5, I dropped the snap and had to run after the ball in the end zone. I picked up the ball and threw it up for grabs, trying to get rid of it, and was called for intentional grounding. That put the ball on the 2.

On the next snap, everyone was expecting me to quick-kick, so the defense stayed up close. I dropped back 10 to 15 steps into the end zone, underneath the goalpost, which was on the goal line in that day. Wayne Millner was as wide open as a barnyard and

just as I let the ball loose a gust of wind blew and ... the goddamn pass hit the crossbar and fell to the ground. The official called a safety because the pass did not get past the end zone line.

I couldn't believe it. We got beat 15-14, and I always felt like I cost us the damn game. We should have won, 14-13. If you wanted to hurt the passing game, you had stupid rules like that. It wasn't three weeks later that a forward pass was ruled an incompletion for hitting the goal post.

Throwing a watermelon

In 1933, the NFL adopted a slimmer, more standard ball, but it wasn't until 1941 that a modern, tapered ball was mandated and more carefully enforced. Before then, as the home team supplied game balls, if the

opponent happened to be a great forward passer like, say, Slingin' Sammy Baugh, the game ball might mysteriously be the width of a watermelon.

They said it never happened, but it did. You would warm up with a regulation ball from your own bag, but when the game started the home team would throw in some beat up old ball blown up to the size of a beach ball. Then when they were on offense, they'd throw in a ball that was slimmer and easier for their passer to handle.

Boys like Arnie Herber of the Packers and Ed Danowski of the Giants—real good passers in my day—went through the same damn thing I did. I was lucky; I had big hands and could usually adjust. But the boys with smaller hands? Hell, they couldn't throw that thing 20 yards. You never knew what

kind of ball you were gonna get when you played on the road.

The star attraction

Baugh almost immediately became the biggest star in pro football, the sport's version of Joe DiMaggio, Joe Louis or Jesse Owens. Baugh was the most photographed football player of a generation, starred in a rollicking Western serial called King of the Texas Rangers, raised $1.3 million for charities in his career and had his likeness on nearly two dozen products, by far the most of any football player of the time. "He had a charisma to attract fans," said Eagles great Bucko Kilroy. "I can remember in Philadelphia at Shibe Park, out on Lehigh, there would be 15,000 people wanting to see Sammy Baugh. Couldn't get in. He was an attraction."

The pro game didn't have any players with a national name when I came into the league, and the reason wasn't the players but the sport. Baseball, college football, boxing and even horse racing were far more popular. Pro football? Hell, I'd never really heard anything about it until I got to Washington.

Mr. Marshall was a showman, a real smart businessman, always thinking of the league and the team. He told me the game needed to be opened up and that I should keep passing. "Don't pay any attention to the coach," he said. He understood that passing the ball was exciting, that it was like hitting the home run in baseball.

6

DAN

That quick release and the ability to zip passes where none had gone before fueled a record spree that still separates Marino from most of the other great quarterbacks in NFL history

t didn't take long for Don Shula to realize he had robbed the bank. It was the Dolphins' first practice of 1983, and curly-haired Dan Marino—the sixth quarterback drafted that year—was zipping passes, laser like, through the muggy South Florida air.

A franchise known for its perfect 1972 season now had the perfect quarterback.

Quarterbacks have their trademarks. Roger Staubach flung it. Terry Bradshaw's body arced gracefully, as a former javelin thrower's should. And Marino? He didn't use his shoulders much and wasn't much of a dancer. It was all arm. Hand him a pint of beer and he'd look like a professional dart thrower.

It's simply referred to as The Release.

Marino dissected defenses as few ever have or will. His quick trigger allowed him to

Team, seasons:		
Miami Dolphins, 1983-99		
Height: 6-4		
Weight: 228		
Born: 9-15-61		
College: Pittsburgh		
Championship teams:		
None		
Career passing yards/TDs:		
61,361/420		

wait longer for receivers to get open and compensate for his lack of mobility, and his arm strength allowed him to make throws other quarterbacks could only dream about.

"Is there anyone else who had a quicker release?" said Ron Wolf, the former general manager of the Green Bay Packers. "Probably (Joe) Namath. In all my years, he is the only person who released it faster. But it's like Bum Phillips used to say about Earl Campbell, 'He may not be the

MARINO

best, but it doesn't take long to call the roll.' "

Marino is the most prolific passer in the history of the NFL, and you won't raise any eyebrows if you also say he is the best pure passer. Unfortunately for Marino, the sports world cares more about winning than his gaudy statistics: 61,361 yards, 420 touchdown passes and 4,967 completions, all NFL records. His legacy always will be tarnished by one career-deflating number: zero championships.

Marino never won a Super Bowl and only reached the championship game once, in

Namath, Steve Young and Bart Starr.

"Why is he No. 6?" growled Shula, obviously thinking his quarterback had been slighted. "The guy has all of the passing records."

Blackledge (Kansas City); Miami's Jim Kelly (Buffalo); Illinois' Tony Eason (New England); Cal-Davis' Ken O'Brien (New York Jets)—were drafted ahead of Marino in 1983, perhaps the richest draft ever for one position.

Marino was the 27th pick of the first round. That fall from grace wasn't just because of his poor senior season, though. There were rumors at the time—which turned out to be untrue—that he was involved with drugs.

"There were all sorts of rumors," Wolf said. "He should have never lasted that long."

History shows that the mediocre senior year actually propelled his pro football career to greater heights. Had he led Pitt to another 11-1 season, he might have been quarterbacking—and struggling—for the Colts instead of the Dolphins. Stuck in the wrong system, might he now be remembered as a rich man's Mike Pagel?

"The system is really important for a young quarterback, and Don (Shula) was a master at taking what a person could do and making the system work," said Floyd Reese, general manager for the Titans. "Whether it was Bob (Griese) handing off to (Larry) Csonka or (Jim) Kiick, or long-snapping to Dan, he would build a system to match his quarterback's strengths."

Marino is the most prolific passer in the history of the NFL, and you won't raise any eyebrows if you also say he is the best pure passer.

his sophomore season. His only appearance on the world's biggest stage ended in a 38-16 loss to San Francisco, a game that was more lopsided than the score indicates.

In 1995, Marino shattered most of Fran Tarkenton's major career passing records. But when each major record fell, the Dolphins lost. "That's the frustrating part," Marino said then. "The individual records are nice, but this is a team game."

Blame the Dolphins organization for his failure. It is hard to conceive that Marino could have done more for those teams. The Dolphins' inability to build a competent running game is unforgivable. They truly wasted the talents of this great player.

Marino's magical gifts, sans a ring or two, were enough to place him No. 6 on our list of greatest quarterbacks—squarely above notable Super Bowl winners Troy Aikman, Terry Bradshaw, Brett Favre,

ears ago, he was "Danny Marino." A product of a working-class neighborhood in Pittsburgh, he left Central Catholic High School as a baseball and football star. He chose football and the hometown Pittsburgh Panthers over baseball and the Kansas City Royals.

He led the Panthers to three consecutive 11-1 seasons, but his senior year began with a shock. He threw four interceptions against North Carolina, a harbinger for the rest of a forgettable year. His senior totals were 17 touchdowns and 23 interceptions. Because of those poor numbers, five other quarterbacks—Stanford's John Elway (Baltimore, later traded to Denver); Penn State's Todd

Shula said Marino was the second-rated quarterback (behind Elway) on the Dolphins' draft board. After that first practice, Shula was comfortable in the knowledge he had his man.

"We had all the guys on the field, and it was pretty evident he was going to be 'The Guy,' " Shula said. "David Woodley was an athlete playing quarterback. Marino was a quarterback playing quarterback."

The steal of the draft didn't start until the sixth game of his rookie season. In that game against Buffalo, Marino started poorly, throwing two interceptions. But he finished strong, passing for 322 yards. Miami lost in overtime, but Shula smiled as he left the field. Lottery winners do that.

That year, Marino set a record that still stands for rookie quarterbacks: lowest percentage of passes intercepted. During an exceptionally hot streak that year, Shula was asked when the NFL's new star was going to start throwing to the opponent.

"With this one, I wouldn't be so sure," Shula said at the time.

"What always impressed me the most about Dan is that if you look back over the last 25 or 30 years, you really can't find anyone who has started that strong and maintained it," Reese said. "Peyton Manning comes to mind. That's about it."

Marino's fabulous finish to his rookie season set the stage for 1984. Marino to Mark Clayton. Marino to Mark Duper. Marino to the record book. Records in pro football are meant to be broken. O.J. Simpson's 2,003-yard rushing record lasted for just 11 years.

Marino's 1984 record of 48 touchdown passes stood for two decades, until Manning fired 49 in a memorable 2004 season. For most of that 20 years, Marino's one-season TD mark seemed as unapproachable for NFL quarterbacks as Joe DiMaggio's 56-game hitting streak remains for baseball hitters. Marino began the 1984 season by torching Washington for five touchdown passes. He set many other records that year, including still-standing marks for most yards passing in a season (5,084) and most games with 400 or more yards passing (four). His records for most games with four or more touchdown passes (six) and most consecutive games with four or more TD throws (four) were tied and topped by Manning.

When Marino set the NFL

'To make him perfect,
you would have given him legs.' –Former Packers G.M. Ron Wolf

afire in 1984, his quick release wasn't just about getting the ball where he needed it to go in a hurry. It made the pass rush nearly impotent and almost wiped out its most effective weapon, the blitz. Use of the blitz had been increasing dramatically before Marino entered the league.

Gil Brandt, the former personnel guru for the Cowboys, remembers Marino torching his team in the 1984 season

finale on *Monday Night Football*, 28-21—a game that kept Dallas out of the playoffs.

Marino's arm frustrated defensive players who, time and again, saw him avoid a near sack with a flick of his wrist. Then the ball zipped 25 yards, a spiral as tight as two best friends.

"He didn't have outstanding mobility, but he didn't have cement feet either," Brandt said. "He just had a great understanding for the game. He just knew where the pressure was coming from."

"When you think of an immobile quarterback, you think of Drew Bledsoe," Wolf

said. "That's not Marino. He was able to walk around the rush; he had that gift, even though you wouldn't classify him as mobile."

hula's favorite Marino performance came not during the heady, Miami Vice days of 1984, but a year later when the undefeated Bears came to the Orange Bowl. That Dolphins team simply was protecting the legacy of its undefeated 1972 predecessor; Chicago was 12-0, and Miami had plenty of incentive to deny the

Bears a perfect regular season. It remains the highest-rated game ever on *Monday Night Football*.

"It was the best half of offensive football I've been around," Shula remembers, thinking back to Miami's 31 first-half points. "Most teams tried to pick up the 4-6 (Chicago's famed blitzing defense) by bringing people up to block. But our philosophy was we were going to spread the field. Their safeties couldn't cover Nat Moore in the slot."

And Marino's quick release got Moore the ball for two touchdowns. Final score: Miami 38, Chicago 24.

Marino's numbers: 14-of-27, 270 yards, three touchdowns.

A great release. A great arm. Great instincts. What was missing?

"To make him perfect, you would have given him legs," Wolf said. "Namath had legs, but his knees gave out. But you can say the same things about the great ones, if they could have run–(Johnny) Unitas, (Norm) Van Brocklin, (Y.A.) Tittle. But if Marino could have moved, there is no telling what he could have accomplished."

The release and sixth sense helped Marino avoid the rush and dodge injured reserve for a decade, but it was more bad luck than a bad hit that altered his career. Against the Browns in 1993, his 11th season, on a routine pass play, Marino took a funny step and tore his Achilles' tendon. From then on, the dart thrower moved less and less.

Marino thought he could play forever and that eventually a ring would come. Never one to cozy up to the media, he began to ponder out loud about his career ending without that elusive ring. Not that Marino gave up. His brash, almost cocky personality never would have allowed that. He was one tough, emotional, fiery competitor whose will to succeed pushed him through major injuries and kept his standard of performance impressively high even amid the constant disappointment of postseason flops.

As the years wore on, he took a tremendous beating. His 1993 injury didn't quench his thirst for a championship. "He came back strong," Shula said. "He could still move."

Still, the end tasted like sour milk.

Shula and Jimmy Johnson, hardly coaching slugs, failed to give Marino adequate running support. Perhaps Shula's was the greater sin because he had a much longer time to fix the problem. In creating an offense that spawned the NFL's most prolific passer, catering entirely to Marino might have been what kept Miami out of the Super Bowl in all but one of Marino's seasons. Johnson, who took over when Shula moved to the front office after the 1995 season, promised things would be different. After Johnson's first game as head coach, a win over New England, his postgame comments referred again and again to the running game. If that didn't work, "We still have No. 13 back there." It was quite a change in Miami.

But Marino's reduced role caused tension. Johnson never could build an effective running game, and while building a great defense–whose key players still are performing today–the Dolphins underachieved. The end for both men was a 62-7 playoff loss to Jacksonville in 1999.

Marino's Miami connection was revived in January 2004 with an ill-conceived, ill-executed plan that made him the Dolphins' president of operations. But it was just a way to assuage fans. He was going to be the face of the organization without any real power. It was a farce and Marino lasted three weeks before resigning. Nevertheless, he still owns Miami and always will, just as John Elway owns Denver. Marino's face still is everywhere–selling cars on TV, looming over commuters on billboards, selling jewelry and condos–and his bust rests comfortably in the Hall of Fame.

Marino's fans long ago reconciled the Super Bowl failures. They saw and still see a much bigger picture–a player so good for so long that he became a sports deity. He is Dan the Man. Miami never will see another one like him.

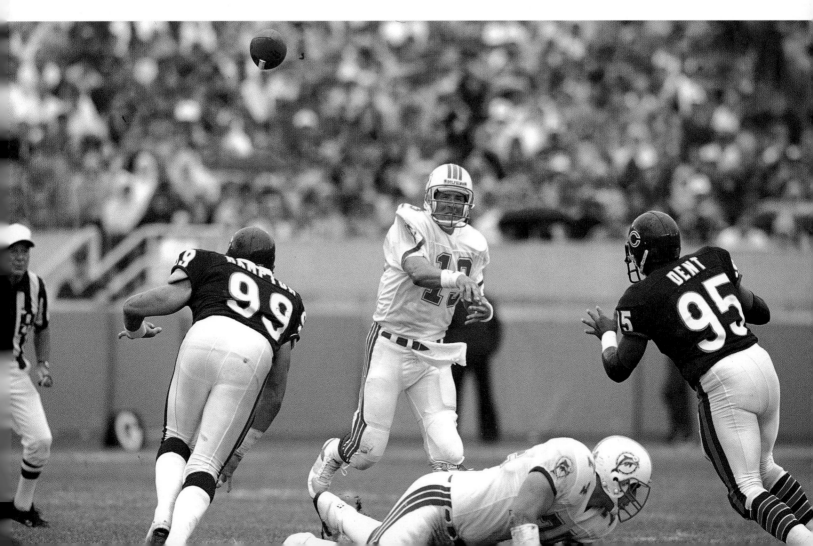

7

BRETT

BRETT FAVRE

72

PRO FOOTBALL'S GREATEST QUARTERBACKS

FAVRE

Fun-loving Packer has thrown caution to the wind and perfect spirals into the memories of Green Bay fans

Teams, seasons:
Atlanta Falcons, 1991; Green Bay Packers, 1992-present
Height: 6-2
Weight: 225
Born: 10-10-69
College: Southern Miss
Championship teams:
1996 season
Career passing yards/TDs:
49,734/376 (through 2004)

 t's his toughness and unbridled enthusiasm for the game. It's his infectious smile and passion for winning. It's his burning desire to compete and his willingness to laugh in the face of odds stacked against him. It's his charm and wit.

It's all those things that have made Brett Favre special.

Long before Favre fired his last touchdown pass, his name was etched among the all-time NFL leaders in every significant passing category. Long before he played his final game, his durability and poise had reached legendary status. But there is so much more to Favre than just numbers. His legacy won't be just the touchdowns he threw or the games he won but the passion he kindled in those on the field, in the stands and watching on TV. Favre's unquenchable spirit has been—and always will be—infectious.

He has made the game fun.

"People always want to know when he's retiring," longtime Packers trainer Pepper Burruss said before the 2004 season. "I often think about the perfect ending, and I think it will be just like the movie Forrest Gump when Forrest is always running down the road and then one day he all

of a sudden stops. When Brett quits having fun, he'll stop. He'll throw a touchdown pass, and then he'll walk off the field right through the tunnel, and that will be it."

As Favre's career wound to its inevitable conclusion, his place as one of the greatest quarterbacks in NFL history already was cemented. Numerous records were in his sights, including Dan Marino's seemingly insurmountable career touchdown mark of 420. But the one he already owned, the one that best defines his career and is unlikely to ever be challenged, is not a passing statistic. It's Favre's incredible string of consecutive starts, which had climbed to 205 regular-season games through the 2004 season, 224 including the playoffs.

During that amazing span, Favre had been injured and unable to finish a game only six

'My dad kicked me in the ass every time I wanted to be a wuss.' –Brett Favre

times. In only one other game was Favre forced to go to the bench because of an injury. The percentage of plays he had missed during 13 seasons as an NFL starter was miniscule. Since Favre took over the Packers' starting job in Week 4 of the 1992 season through 2004, injuries had forced him to miss fewer than 200 of the 13,123 total offensive plays from scrimmage the team had run.

And it's not like he hadn't been hurt.

He fought off a concussion in 2004. There was the broken thumb in 2003, the sprained lateral collateral ligament in his left knee in '02, the elbow tendinitis and mid-foot sprain in '00, the sprained thumb and sore shoulder in '99, turf toe in '98 and '97, a severely sprained ankle in '95, a bad hip bruise and abdominal pain in '94 and a separated shoulder in '92.

And those are just the bumps, bruises and breaks we know about.

In those 13 years with the Packers, he had been listed on the injury report 42 times; the other times, Favre just refused to show pain. It's one reason USA Today named him the "Toughest

Athlete in Sports" and Men's Journal chose him as the "Toughest Guy in America."

"I think when I get hit, it may not feel very good, but I'm trying my best not to let the opposing team know that," Favre said. "I may get up and laugh and slap the guy on the back or something. The guy goes, 'Oh, man, that guy's tough.' Inside, I'm going, 'Oh, God, how many more of those can I take?'

"It doesn't get any easier, I know that. But I think (what) it takes to play this game–not just to play one game but to play for a long period of time at a high level–it takes, more than anything, mental toughness. That doesn't mean being able to say, 'OK, this bruise doesn't hurt.' It's being able to overcome the good days, the bad days, the meetings, practice.

"There is so much that goes into being, I think, a great player. Not just for a season but for a long time. You just learn at some point how to deal with it."

hat makes Favre's streak so impressive is that he was not simply holding down a position in the lineup. At age 34, he led the NFL in touchdown passes for

the fourth time and posted a passer rating of 90.4, the sixth-highest in his career.

He wasn't as dominant in the late 1990s and 2000s as he was during the three-year span from 1995-97, when he threw 112 touchdown passes and won the league's MVP award each season, becoming the first player to win it three times in a row. Those were the salad days when Favre and the Packers ruled the NFC, playing in three consecutive NFC championship games, advancing to two Super Bowls and winning it all after

the '96 season.

It was the years leading up to the Super Bowl 31 title that were Favre's most difficult. In his first significant playing time as a Packer in '92, he replaced the injured Don Majkowski in the first quarter and led the Packers to a startling come-from-behind victory with a 35-yard touchdown pass with 13 seconds to go. The rest of the season went like a dream, and the Packers almost made the playoffs.

But 1993 was a nightmare as second-year coach Mike Holmgren attempted to har-

ness the wild side in his young quarterback. The two clashed frequently, and Favre threw a career-high 24 interceptions, including four in a regular-season finale against Detroit that cost the Packers a home playoff game.

If there was a sign Favre would be special, it came the next week when the Packers returned to Detroit for a wild-card playoff game and he connected with Sterling Sharpe for a game-winning 40-yard touchdown pass. It was the most improbable completion imaginable given Favre had

scrambled far to his left and threw all the way across the field—at least 55 yards—to Sharpe streaking down the right sideline.

It was then that people knew there was something special about No. 4.

"There are guys in history who seize the moment, and they're there," said Ron Wolf, general manager of the Packers from 1991-2001 and the man responsible for acquiring Favre in a trade with Atlanta. "It's like George Thomas at the Battle of Chickamauga. He's there.

'When I get hit, it may not feel very good, but I'm trying my best not to let the opposing

"What put him there? How did he get there? That's the reason the North won the Civil War. When all that stuff is around, certain guys stand tall. And this guy (Favre) happens to stand taller than all his peers."

avre's rise to prominence didn't come without growing pains. In the early days, Holmgren confined Favre to the outline of the West Coast offense and refused to let him revert to his schoolyard ways. Every day was a lesson in patience and discipline.

Holmgren demanded perfection, and Favre sought creativity. When Favre didn't comply, he usually wound up at the other end of a Holmgren tirade.

"I knew that I probably deserved a good chewing out, but I didn't particularly like it," Favre said. "So one way or another, maybe subconsciously, I would do something to make him even madder. He'd tell me, 'Whatever you do, don't scramble out of the pocket,' and I'd say, 'No problem.'

team know that.'
—Brett Favre

What's the first thing I would do? I'd scramble out of the pocket. If it worked, I'd be the first one to say, 'Now see.' And he'd just 'Mmmph.' When it wouldn't work, 'I want to see you,' and I knew what was coming."

In the end, they were perfect for each other, and they both got what they wanted.

When Favre looks back at those years, he realizes how important Holmgren was to his development and to this day speaks appreciatively about his former coach.

"He has meant a tremendous amount to my career," Favre said. "He stuck with me through the hard times. He called plays to my liking. They suited me. He allowed me to become the MVP. Yeah, sure I made great plays and did some wonderful things, but someone had to call them, someone had to put me in that situation, someone had to believe in me to call those plays. There's no question Brett Favre wouldn't be who he is without him."

Favre's flamboyant style is an extension of his carefree personality. Teammates describe him as a big, fun-loving kid without the ego that usually goes with multimillion dollar paychecks and MVP trophies.

"I think when Brett goes through his first two options and then has to improvise, that is when a play really starts. He just keeps making plays and breaking your heart," said safety John Lynch, who battled Favre at least twice a year when he played for the Buccaneers.

After five seasons under Holmgren protege Mike Sherman, Favre still was seeking that one more Super Bowl title as the 2004 season came to a close. Since 1997, he had not come close to reaching the big game, even though the Packers had finished .500 or better in 13 consecutive seasons, the second-longest active streak at the time.

Favre finished 2004 ranked third on the all-time list in passing yards (49,734) and attempts (7,004), second in completions (4,306) and second in touchdowns (376). His career rate of 29 touchdown passes per season had him on pace to pass Marino sometime during the 2006 season, an ambitious—if not unrealistic—goal.

But what is real is the impact Favre has had on the NFL and the indelible memories he has produced for millions of Packers fans spread across the 50 states and beyond. Few will forget the December 22, 2003, Monday night game in Oakland when, a day after learning of his father Irvin's death, Favre threw for 399 yards and four touchdowns.

It was a glimpse of the emotion Favre brings to everything he does. It was Irvin, a high school football coach and teacher, who taught Brett to be tough. "My dad kicked me in the ass every time I wanted to be a wuss," Favre said. That Monday night in Oakland was a reminder that behind the numbers is a special person.

"I don't think the thumb, ankle or whatever injury he has suffered could compare with that kind of pain," Burruss said. "Nothing amazed me more than the way he dealt with his father's death, the way he stood up and spoke to the team and how he performed. It was one of the top moments in sports I've ever seen and goes into the legacy of Brett Favre."

8

TERRY

The golden-armed 'gunslinger' passed every NFL test and led the powerful Steelers to four Super Bowl victories in a memorable six-year span

unch Ilkin was there that day in 1983 at Shea Stadium. Like his other teammates with the Steelers, Ilkin did not realize he was witnessing the final performance of the first quarterback to win four Super Bowl trophies. He did not realize that what he was experiencing on a cold December afternoon would be a lifetime memory. Nobody did. Not even the man who was going out with one final grand performance, Terry Bradshaw.

The Steelers had lost three in a row leading up to their Week 15 game against the Jets, and they needed a victory to clinch a playoff berth. Bradshaw did not play in the first 14 games because an injury to his right elbow had neutralized the golden arm that had made him a No. 1 overall draft choice in 1970 and helped produce four championships in a six-year span of the 1970s.

But on this day, needing a victory to qualify for the post-season and provide a lift to the team's sagging psyche, Chuck Noll decided to start his injured quarterback against the Jets. To ease the burden on Bradshaw's elbow, Noll put together a game plan that would emphasize the running game and control the clock. Bradshaw had other ideas.

"We come out throwing on the first series, and Brad goes zip-zip-zip right down the field," said Ilkin, a right tackle who played with the team from 1980-92. "Next series, we get the ball, and Brad goes right

down the field again—zip-zip-zip—and throws another touchdown. Just like that, we're up 14-0.

"We're over on the bench, and I said to him, 'Hey, Brad, I thought we were supposed to

run the ball.' He looks at me and says, 'Tunch, ol' boy, I'm a gunslinger, not a mailman.' "

Ilkin and the Steelers never saw Terry Bradshaw behind center again.

The Steelers beat the Jets that day, 34-7, and made the playoffs. But Bradshaw was finished. The two series against the Jets were too much for his injured elbow. When he threw the second—and what proved to be his final—touchdown pass to Calvin Sweeney, Bradshaw came off the field clutching his arm.

The Steelers lost their regular-season finale and then to the Raiders in their playoff opener. Bradshaw had surgery on his elbow after the season, and his arm never was the same. He retired before the 1984 season, a quiet and unexpected end to a career that helped redefine a

Teams, seasons:		
Pittsburgh Steelers, 1970-83		
Height: 6-3		
Weight: 215		
Born: 9-2-48		
College: Louisiana Tech		
Championship teams:		
1974, '75, '78, '79 seasons		
Career passing yards/TDs:		
27,989/212		

BRADSHAW

franchise.

"I knew I couldn't play anymore," Bradshaw said. "I was finished. Maybe underneath all that was the hidden disappointment I couldn't finish the way I wanted."

To the contrary, Bradshaw gave everybody—teammates, coaches, fans, even himself—one last glimpse of the extraordinary abilities that made him one of the greatest quarterbacks in NFL history. It was vintage Bradshaw—disdaining the game plan, throwing the ball downfield, taking out his opponent.

"I don't think Bradshaw would have been a very successful quarterback under a regimented system," said John Stallworth, the Steelers' all-time leader in receptions (537), receiving yards (8,723) and receiving touchdowns (63). "You talk about a West Coast system where the receiver has to run a certain route and the quarterback has to go a certain way with the ball; Bradshaw would not have been very successful in a system like that. I don't know that I would have been. Chuck adjusted to the way Terry Bradshaw liked to play.

"(Bradshaw) looked to throw the football. He liked to hear you say, 'Brad, I'm going deep on this one' or 'Brad, let's go deep.' He got excited to hear that."

As a result, Lynn Swann and Stallworth not only produced big numbers, they produced big plays. And usually at big moments.

Swann's tumbling 53-yard catch against Dallas in Super Bowl 10, acrobatically securing the ball with Cowboys cornerback Mark Washington helplessly trapped beneath him, is one of the most replayed moments in Super Bowl history.

Stallworth's 73-yard touchdown catch from Bradshaw in Super Bowl 14 put the finishing touch on a victory over the Rams and gave the Steelers their fourth Super Bowl triumph. Bradshaw and Stallworth had run the same play—62 Slot, Hook & Go—

earlier in the game and it produced another big play.

Those plays are snapshots in Pittsburgh's collective memory, moments that defined the team's greatness and crystallized the abilities of players who now are enshrined in Canton.

"His knowledge of me was that I was going to do what I could to catch the football,

whether it was to jump up high for it or dive for it or go through someone," said Stallworth. "I would give supreme effort to catch the ball. I think that gave Terry a lot of confidence in me.

"If he had confidence in you, he was going to throw up the

> 'If he had confidence in you, he was going to throw up the ball, even if you were covered. That felt good.' –John Stallworth

ball, even if you were covered. That felt good. And he had the kind of arm to make that happen. If it was a high-velocity throw, he had the capability to do that. Given a choice whether I was going up to get it or Lynn was going up to get it or a defensive back was going to knock it away, seven out of eight times we were

going to get the ball if he threw it up there."

Perhaps because he attended Louisiana Tech and had the mannerisms of a country boy, Bradshaw was labeled as a dummy early in his career, something he resented. Before Super Bowl 13, former Cowboys linebacker Thomas "Hollywood" Henderson said Bradshaw couldn't spell "cat" if you spotted him the "c" and the "a."

To be sure, there were times Bradshaw went to the line of scrimmage and called out plays that didn't exist in the Steelers' playbook. If Mike Webster, the thick-armed center, didn't correct Bradshaw in the huddle, he simply would turn around from his crouched position at the line of scrimmage and tell Bradshaw to call something else.

None of that, though, seemed to deter Bradshaw.

He had the arm to throw soap bubbles through a telephone pole. And his receivers seemed to have butterfly nets for hands.

"He had good days and bad days," Stallworth said. "There were days when he made things very easy for me and Lynn. And there were days where what looked like throwaways we were able to make catches.

"I remember (former Colts quarterback) Bert Jones saying once after a game, 'I wish I had receivers like you guys.' On the other hand, we had just beaten the Cowboys in the Super Bowl, and I was talking to Drew Pearson and Tony Hill, and they said they wished they had a quarterback like Bradshaw because he gives you guys a chance to make plays."

He was a gunslinger, right till the end.

Always laughing— on the outside

Terry Bradshaw's life never has been lacking for theatrics or football heroics. He was a No. 1 overall draft choice and the first quarterback to win four Super Bowl rings. He rocked the steps of Canton when he was inducted into the Hall of Fame.

In between, he sulked and feuded with his coach, tried to ignore suggestions he couldn't spell "cat" if you spotted him the "c" and the "a" and, for 19 years, turned his back on the town that loved him more than any of the other former Steelers greats.

It was only after he retired as one of the greatest quarterbacks in NFL history that Bradshaw's life came into sharper focus. He discovered he suffered from depression and lacked the ability to study and focus, something for which he now takes medication.

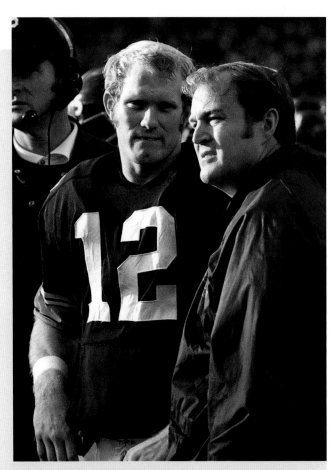

Bradshaw with Noll, the former Steelers coach who figured out his free-wheeling quarterback and designed his offense accordingly.

On the outside, Bradshaw was as happy-go-lucky as the free-wheeling style with which he played. On the inside, though, he was Hall of Fame center Mike Webster—scrapping and churning and fighting, mainly just to like himself. And, perhaps more debilitating, to make those around him like him even more.

"I think Chuck had me figured out," Bradshaw said, referring to his Hall of Fame coach, Chuck Noll. "He says I have a childlike attitude. He knew it long before I did. I'm sure that's why our offense was as simple as it was. I just had this God-given talent."

It took Bradshaw years to find peace in his relationship with Noll, whom he criticized for being an uncaring taskmaster. And he never really got over the hurt of being portrayed as stupid when the Steelers drafted him out of Louisiana Tech in 1970.

Despite his success with the Steelers, Bradshaw felt he had a frosty relationship with people in Pittsburgh. That's one of the reasons he didn't attend the 1988 funeral of team owner Art Rooney Sr., a man for whom Bradshaw claimed to have great affection. Bradshaw now admits that was a huge mistake.

"The thought of coming to Pittsburgh for Art's funeral, it sent cold chills down my back then; the

thought I had to go face those people," Bradshaw said. "I was bitter, mad that I left and felt unappreciated. I hate the fact I did that. I can't believe I did it, but I did."

Bradshaw, of course, is a Pittsburgh icon. No other former Steeler, not even Jack Lambert, is more revered. Bradshaw's belief otherwise brings into focus the inner struggle he endured all those years.

Bradshaw understands now. He has kissed and made up with Noll, with the city, with himself.

Not only is he a television star and author, he is a rare former jock who can make you laugh. Bradshaw always has been laughing on the outside.

It's on the inside where he fights his biggest battle. It is part of the reason he has been divorced three times.

"I am happy," Bradshaw said. "I'm as happy as I've ever been.

"I wish my personal life, my marriages, could have been different so I could've had that one real constant thing in life. But one of the things that's constant in life is changing, and, unfortunately, I've never liked changing wives.

"I laugh at it, which is kind of a healing thing. If you don't laugh ... you know people are talking about it anyway, (so you) might as well laugh at it. It's sad really. ..."

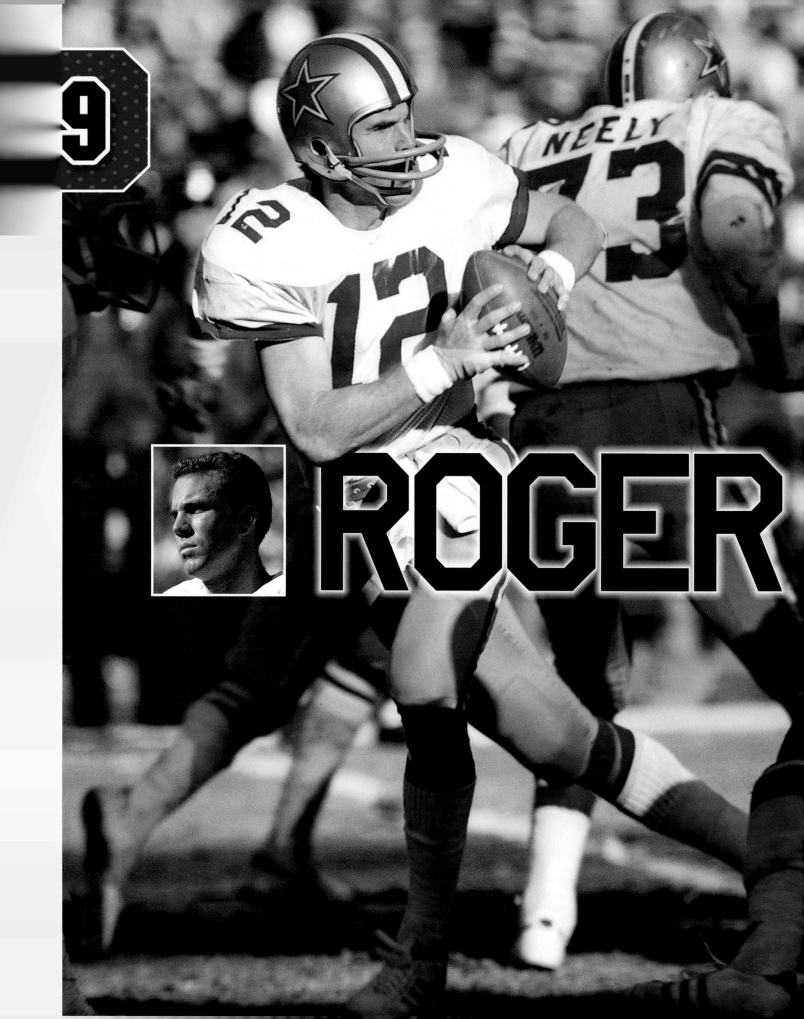

9

ROGER

There's much more to Staubach than what he did on Sundays in the 1970s. He's the All-American boy, the Heisman Trophy winner who went to Vietnam before he went to the NFL, the Hall of Famer.

In three years in college and 11 years in the NFL, Roger Staubach played for one losing team, his senior season at Navy, and he was injured for a big chunk of that year. With the Cowboys, he played in four Super Bowls, winning two of them, and six NFC championship games, winning four. He retired with what was at the time the highest quarterback rating in history. But he wishes he had done more.

"I feel guilty I didn't win more Super Bowls," he said.

Staubach's charm is that he can say that and mean it. He's humble without acting as if he doesn't know he was one heck of a football player. There's much more to Staubach than what he did on Sundays in the 1970s. He's the All-American boy, the Heisman Trophy winner who went to Vietnam before he went to the NFL, the Hall of Famer.

STAUBACH

The success has continued. Staubach began working in real estate in the offseason while with the Cowboys. Today, The Staubach Company, working exclusively in office, industrial and retail space, has more than 1,100 employees in 50 offices in the United States, Canada, Mexico and Brazil.

The years have been kind to Staubach. He looks as lithe and wiry as he was when he was nicknamed "Captain Comeback" for his late-game heroics as the leader of America's Team. He still has a

Team, seasons:		
Dallas Cowboys, 1969-79		
Height: 6-3		
Weight: 197		
Born: 2-5-42		
College: Navy		
Championship teams:		
1971, '77 seasons		
Career passing yards/TDs:		
22,700/153		

strong arm, which he showed while throwing out the first pitch before a San Diego Padres game in 2004.

For a guy who played with such bravado, he has an understated personality. You would think a guy who played with so much attitude would be gregarious. He's not. He's thoughtful and soft-spoken. He's full of opinions, not full of himself, and shares them, albeit quietly. He would make a lousy politician; he doesn't care whether those around him share his views. He's a devout Catholic who stresses

his company is ecumenical.

His interest in leadership didn't retire when he quit playing football; he yearns to become better at it. "You can't compartmentalize it," he said. "Really great leaders live their personal lives as well as they do their professional lives, whether it's their business or their football life. That isn't always the case."

At the company headquarters in Dallas, one wall of Staubach's modest office is covered with pictures of his children and grandchildren. On another wall are autographed pictures of

Staubach with two presidents, both named George Bush. During a 90-minute interview, he fielded questions about life, leadership and coining the phrase Hail Mary pass.

You grew up a good Catholic boy in the Midwest but you didn't go to Notre Dame. Tell me that story.

My coach in high school switched me to quarterback, and I didn't want to do that. My senior year in high school was my first year as quarterback, and we didn't throw a lot. I ran, scrambled. And then I just developed as a quarterback. I really started liking it. I didn't like it at first. I didn't want to be a quarterback; that wasn't my choice.

The coach switched me there. The reason, he said, is the other players listened to me. It changed my life. I really enjoyed being a quarterback. Looking back, I say, "Man, how could I have not wanted to be

Much of the perseverance and fortitude Staubach displayed in the NFL was learned from his college days at the U.S. Naval Academy.

backs, but to go to the next level, you have to have the ability to get the ball between defensive backs, who every one of them is good. That ability is what they're trying to judge of college guys today.

Having the mental capacity to be a leader and run the

I was a supply officer in Vietnam. I was on shore duty there and had over 100 sailors working for me. So I learned the responsibility of having people work for you. We were responsible for the shipping and receiving, supporting all the Marines.

are human beings working for you—you're responsible for their actions; you're an example to them. The academy taught me the importance of that.

As an athlete, the thing that I most represented to the players is that I was expecting a lot out of them and I was going to give a lot back, work out just as hard as they would.

Which was better, beating Army or beating the Redskins?

There in front of 4,100 midshipmen, beating Army was a big deal. If I had my choice, I'd go with beating Army, but the Redskins would be right up there. And the Steelers would be right there, too.

Sports really teach you a lot. It's like the high-occupancy vehicle lane. You have goals and ambitions, and you're determined to move down the road. But you have to take someone with you. You can't do things by yourself. Once you start thinking it's all about you, sports teach that's not the case. Those athletes that start thinking it's all about them—instead of being a great asset to the team—they become a liability.

Football really is a wonderful team sport. But you as a quarterback have a tremendous amount of responsibility that is not only physical but mental. You've got to be able to handle that and want that responsibility. And I did want that responsibility.

'Really great leaders live their personal lives as well as they do their professional lives.' –Roger Staubach

a quarterback?" That's what coaches are for, right?

The guy probably made a good decision.

In my case, it was. I grew up in Cincinnati. By the time I went to the Naval Academy, I had spent one year in Roswell, New Mexico (in junior college), which was a great year for me. There were about 20 of us from the Naval Academy. They had some West Point and Air Force guys there, too. I had a coach named Bob Shaw. He had a wide-open offense, and I really learned more of a passing, pro-style offense. At Navy, we had a very good offense. Wayne Hardin was a great coach at Navy.

When you go to the next level, it really is about having arm strength. There are a lot of really good college quarter-

football team, make things happen and make plays, get other players' confidence, are ingredients that are sometimes hard to measure until a guy is a quarterback in the NFL.

How did the experience in the Navy and Naval Academy prepare you for the NFL and life after that?

I was very focused and very competitive and did everything I could to prepare myself every year I played. I think the Navy gave me that determination and perseverance. Some of it is just in your gut; it's something you have. Things don't come easy in life. You've got to really stay after it.

In terms of leadership, how did the Navy prepare you?

I had a lot of responsibility. In the service, I was in charge of people who worked for me.

I grew up fast, but I wasn't in danger of being shot at.

I was in a support role for a year, then I went to Pensacola Naval Air Station and had responsibility for logistics out of Sherman Field, which was on the base there, (and) had probably about 50 people working for you there. When you're young— and these

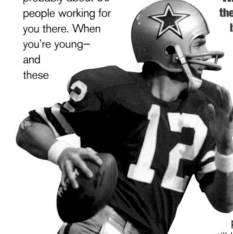

What's the parallel between the sports world and the business world?

What keeps me going now is the responsibility of trying to lead a company. I'm learning every day how to be a better leader, how to do things differently, how to be a better company.

We're concerned about doing the things the right way. To continue to see the company grow and get better, I still have a passion to do that. I

One that got away

Roger Staubach's memories of Super Bowl 13, which the Cowboys lost to the Steelers, 35-31:

I think about winning that Super Bowl. I think more of the interception I threw to Mel Blount before the half. I don't blame Jackie. (Hall of Fame tight end Jackie Smith dropped a pass in the end zone late in the game.) Jackie was just one play. Jackie's just a great guy.

We played a great team. That game, we had some breaks that were our fault. We also had the lousiest call in the history of the game of football by the referee, Fred Swearingen, on Benny Barnes. (Swearingen flagged Barnes for tripping Lynn Swann.) It was the play of the game. The Steelers were going nowhere in the third quarter, and on that play, Bradshaw (Terry) threw it up for grabs.

I had one of the best games I've ever played, except for before the half, I actually threw the ball to the right, to Drew (Pearson) on a play-action. Mel Blount saw the motion and ran to the middle. I didn't see him. Billy Joe (DuPree) was covered by Dirt Winston out there. Billy Joe was my No. 1 receiver. I looked at him and immediately threw to Drew. Blount made a hell of a play. He should've been where Billy Joe was, but they switched when they saw the formation. They tricked us. I just looked out there and saw someone on Billy Joe and thought it was Blount. It was Winston.

What happened is, he intercepts it, and Billy Joe clocks him. A great hit. And they gave him a 15-yard penalty. It is a joke that they called a penalty. The last play of the half, they throw the ball to Rocky Bleier for a touchdown. Instead of us kicking a field goal, we had a 10-point swing. That was the only bad play I had the whole game.

Jackie got screwed on that deal (being blamed by many Cowboys fans for losing the game). Jackie Smith did not deserve that. So you know, I do think about that game.

don't actually do deals or receive commission; I'm enjoying trying to build a business.

It could've been the Our Father pass, the Glory Be pass. Tell me that story.

It was 14-10 in a playoff game; we played decent the whole game. Drew (Pearson) hadn't caught a pass the whole game. The last drive, we were at the 15- or 20-yard line, and he caught a couple of passes. One of them was like fourth-and-17. He got knocked out of bounds, and a guy on the sideline kicked him, one of the security guards.

It gave us a first down, but he was tired. I threw a ball out to Preston Pearson, just to let Drew catch his breath. Thankfully, Preston dropped it.

I don't know what would have happened. There were only 30 seconds left, and we didn't have any timeouts. We still would have gotten another play off, probably.

Drew came back to the huddle and said, "Hey, what can you do?" I said, "See if you can just go deep; I'll look off (Vikings safety) Paul Krause." When I pumped, Krause did take two steps. Nate Wright was playing Drew. The ball

was a little underthrown, and he caught it. Of course, they accuse him of pushing off. Even Nate Wright said he kind of slipped on the play.

But anyway, he went in the end zone, and we won the game, 17-14. After the game, they said, "What were you thinking about?" I said, "I closed my eyes and said a Hail Mary." I got knocked down on the throw. The next day, it was in the press: "Hail Mary wins game."

Take me inside the huddle in one of your comebacks.

Some of it is preparation. You've worked on two-minute drills in practice. So it's making sure the mechanics are there; we've got one timeout left, we've got no timeouts left.

We're calling two plays in the huddle. After the first play, half the guys forget, so you have to get up there and say, "Hey!" You're kind of yelling at them, especially when you're calling two plays.

In that Redskins game (in the final regular-season game of 1977, Dallas won in the last minute, 35-34), we were down there, and we had played the Redskins earlier that year. We called this 12-pass to the tight end, who runs a little turnout, and the fullback runs in the flat. We ran it against the Redskins in Washington, and they blitzed and trapped me. Now we're playing them in Dallas, and we're driving down there, and the score was 34-28.

It was the same exact play, and I knew they might blitz. So I tell Tony Hill, who's the split end out there, "Really make a good move out there because I'm going to go to you if they blitz." He would've never done that; he was just out of the play. I figured I might need him.

That's exactly what happened. As soon as I saw the blitz, Tony made the move, and I threw the ball in the corner, and he caught it. He would not have made that move because we were only on like the 4-yard line. That's what it's like out there. You're talking to players about going to them.

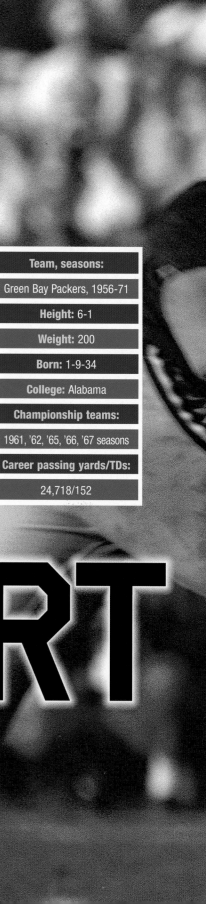

He was a star in name only, a silent winning machine who powered an NFL dynasty

Team, seasons:
Green Bay Packers, 1956-71
Height: 6-1
Weight: 200
Born: 1-9-34
College: Alabama
Championship teams:
1961, '62, '65, '66, '67 seasons
Career passing yards/TDs:
24,718/152

There would have been no Green Bay Packers as we know them without Vince Lombardi. His impact was incalculable in scope. It also is safe to say there would have been no Vince Lombardi as we knew him without a 6-1, 200-pound, blond-haired, blue-eyed quarterback named Bart Starr.

When you look at the names of the 11 players whose time with the Pack spanned all those championship years—Starr, Willie Davis, Boyd Dowler, Forrest Gregg, Henry Jordan, Jerry Kramer, Max McGee, Ray Nitschke, Bob Skoronski, Fuzzy Thurston and Willie Wood—you see a team of all-stars. In fact, Starr played with nine Hall of Famers and 25 Pro Bowl players during the 1960-67 glory years. And it is largely because of that star-studded cast that Starr often is overlooked.

Yet not one of those other 25 players was indispensable to the success of the team. As important as Paul Hornung and Jim Taylor were (both were league MVPs), for example, the Packers won their last two championships essentially without them. The celebrated Kramer missed major chunks of time with serious injuries. Most of the other Pro Bowl players were not pivotal throughout the entire Packers reign. One was.

The Packers could not and did not win without Starr.

No one knew that better than Lombardi. "Without a good quarterback," he said with typical bluntness, "you just don't operate." So critical to the team's success was Starr that

BART

STARR

by '62, the fiery mentor had changed his focus from teaching to creating as calm an atmosphere as possible for Starr. "By the nature of his position, your quarterback is your No. 1 man, and we are the champions, and I know that Bart feels that he has the whole burden of our offense on his shoulders, and I will have to try to relax him."

Despite a changing cast, Starr quarterbacked the team throughout Lombardi's tenure. In fact, other than linemen Skoronski and Gregg, only Starr started all 10 playoff games during the championship era. And Starr did not simply hand off and pass. He didn't just audible from time to time, changing the play brought in from the sidelines, as has pretty much been the case since the 1970s. Starr called the plays.

There is no higher trust a coach can place in a quarterback than to allow him to call the plays. This would be particularly true for the detail-obsessed perfectionist Lombardi, who had been the offensive coordinator for the venerable New York Giants of the late '50s. By the time Starr took over in Green Bay, the sun already was setting on the era of quarterback play-calling. There were coaches around the league—Paul Brown and Tom Landry among them—who had taken over the task, shuttling plays in from the sidelines.

Lombardi trusted Starr to make the calls. Moreover, it was probably his turning over the offense to the quarterback that sealed their bond. Starr, as polar opposite as he was from Lombardi temperamentally, became the coach's alter ego. "If this is a game through which you find self-expression—and if it isn't, you don't belong in it— then that quarterback is the primary extension of yourself, and he is your greatest challenge," Lombardi wrote in his book *Run to Daylight*.

Lombardi had total confidence in his leader. He praised Starr's stability and judgment. "Your quarterback has to be stable, though, and Bart is that. Starr is so stable that out of the 65 or 70 plays we run in a game, I don't send in more than 10. Then he has the right, not in the huddle but on the line, to negate anything I send in."

Starr's control was so complete that he was, in effect, the offensive coordinator as well as the chief executive of the offense. As meticulous as Lombardi's preparation was, according to Lombardi biographer David Maraniss, it was a standing joke among the players that once the game started,

cussed the previous three days, and that meant he had a great memory, dedication and desire." Perhaps the highest honor Lombardi bestowed on his quarterback came, ironically, when Lombardi left Green Bay after the 1968 season to coach the Washington Redskins. He asked Starr for his game notes. "He wanted all my game notes," Starr told Maraniss, "all my team game plans for the teams we'd played over the years. I had my own detailed folders, filed by teams in a cabinet, and I gave them to him, and he copied them all and sent them back. It was the nicest tribute he ever paid me."

here is no single way to determine who is the greatest quarterback in football history. The task is muddied by the changing nature of the game. Statistical brilliance is rarely associated with Starr, yet he must be in the conversation. For example, he threw 2,000 fewer passes than Unitas and was outgained by more than 16,000 yards.

Yet, it is in the statistics that much of the case for Starr's greatness can be made. Nearly 30 years ago, football analyst Bud Goode determined that "yards per passing attempt" was the premier statistical correlate with winning. Since 1958, only Bill Parcells' 1996 Patriots have played in an NFL championship game despite allowing more yards per passing attempt than they gained. Over the last two decades, the team that won that simple statistic won 80 percent of the time. Just below yards per attempt in importance is interception percentage.

Starr lapped the field in these two categories throughout the '60s. His career inter-

Lombardi was the most useless man on the field. Defensive coordinator Phil Bengtson directed the defense, and Starr called the offense. Lombardi did not even bother to wear a headset.

Starr's indispensability never was in doubt. When the Packers took over for the final time in the '67 Ice Bowl against the Dallas Cowboys, trailing 17-14, a shivering, frost-bitten Nitschke stood on the sideline with hope. "We're losing," he said, "but we have the ball. And we have Starr." Thurston said every time Starr stepped into

the huddle, the 10 other players believed the team was going to score. "That's just the way he was," Thurston said, "the feeling he inspired in everybody."

uch has been made of Starr's intellect, his capacity to perform surgery on opposing defenses. His knowledge was nearly total. And to play for Lombardi, it had to be. "His IQ must be above average," wrote the coach in describing a quarterback's role,

"because he must not only be able to absorb the coach's game plan each week, but he must also have a thorough knowledge of what everyone does on every play, and he must know the opponent, the qualities and characteristics of each individual on the other team."

Not nearly enough has been made of Starr's football acumen. Early on, he mastered everything. "At our quarterback meetings," said Lombardi, "even though he was not first string, he could repeat almost verbatim everything we had disception percentage is the lowest of any passer in the decade, and his yards per attempt is near the top. His 7.85 yards per attempt is better than that of Roger Staubach (7.67), Sonny Jurgensen (7.56), Joe Montana (7.52) and Dan Marino (7.37). Furthermore, Starr stepped up as his career progressed. In the early '60s, the Packers were regarded as a running team, featuring Taylor and Hornung. By the middle of the decade, that reputation was more myth than a reality. In a 14-team league, Green Bay ranked 11th in rushing in 1965 and 13th the next season. Yet, the team won NFL titles both years; Starr was named league MVP in '66. In that year, he had 14 touchdown passes and just three interceptions and averaged nine yards per attempt.

The flamboyant Hornung often was cited as a clutch player, but the best big-game performer in Green Bay was Starr. In each of his 10 playoff games, Starr exceeded his regular-season yards per attempt and interception percentage numbers. In the postseason, Starr was 9-1, completed 61 percent of his attempts and threw 15 touchdowns with only three interceptions. His passer rating was 104.8, the best ever in playoff history.

"Bart Starr utilized everything God gave him," said Nitschke. "He rose to the challenge. His best games were in the big games."

espite a sterling resume—five NFL titles, four All-Pro selections, two-time Super Bowl MVP, one-time NFL MVP, leading the league in passing three times—Starr never was a universally acclaimed, main-

stage performer. Even in '66, his league MVP season, Starr's individual brilliance was obscured amid the dominance of a 12-2 Green Bay team, one in which 11 teammates were named All-Pro or selected to the Pro Bowl squad. Starr was consistently dwarfed by the magnitude of Lombardi's personality and the attention-grabbing behavior of Hornung. As a quarterback, he played his entire career in the shadow of Johnny U.

Starr, however, handles it well. He tells of a letter he received from some of his friends attending a medical seminar in Japan. It came in an envelope addressed simply, "To the Greatest Quarterback

'Bart Starr utilized everything God gave him. He rose to the challenge. His best games were in the big games.'

–Ray Nitschke

in the World." That was it. It bore no name, no city, no state. Amazingly, the envelope arrived at Starr's Green Bay address. When he got home that evening his wife, Cherry, greeted him with, "Hi, honey. The most interesting thing happened today. You received a letter that was obviously intended for Johnny Unitas."

Curiously, this understatement, this lack of recognition, has as much as anything endeared Starr to the Packer faithful. He was Every Man, a self-made superstar. He was an inspiration to every youngster with less-than-extraordinary athletic gifts who nonetheless yearns to be one of the greats.

"The true measure of

success," Starr told Kramer, "is what you've contributed to your community and your nation. I've tried to live a life pleasing to my family and my God."

Starr, in contrast to so many others, has lived a purpose-driven life. While many chased after fame, comfort, fun and ease, Starr has forever remained focused. It is perhaps why he became such a remarkable leader but also a reason he is not easily understood. Nonetheless, that mission statement of life, of itself, is not the stuff of great self-revelation. Indeed, few do know Starr because intense self-revelation is not part of his makeup.

"Bart came as close to perfection as any man I ever met, perfection as a quarterback and as a human being," Kramer said. "Bart never said he was perfect, but he did say he tried to be."

Starr has often been described as shy. Self-contained is perhaps a more accurate term. "My emotions often ruled me," confessed Kramer. "Bart ruled his." Emotional control is fundamental to understanding who Bart Starr is. It has cost him much, yet given him more. It has cost him celebrity while giving him poise. It has meant perhaps fewer close personal relationships, yet greater respect from those with whom he has come in contact. It has meant less jocularity, yet greater purpose and vision. It has made him less of a peer, yet more of a leader.

This story is an excerpt from Bart Starr: When Leadership Mattered by David Claerbaut (Taylor Trade Publishing), which is in bookstores now. It can also be purchased by calling 1-800-462-6420 or online at www.taylortradepublishing.com.

1

Teams, seasons:
Minnesota Vikings, 1961-66, 1972-78; New York Giants, 1967-71
Height: 6-0.
Weight: 190
Born: 2-3-40
College: Georgia
Championship teams:
None
Career passing yards/TDs:
47,003/342

FRAN TARKENTON

here are scramblers. And then there is Fran Tarkenton. Although he eventually developed into one of the most prolific passers in NFL history, that's not what makes him unique. It's his legs—those skinny, unimpressive limbs that could transform him into one of the most elusive, evasive jitterbugs ever to put on a pro uniform.

"Frustrating, really frustrating," is how linebacker Sam Huff described playing against Tarkenton, particularly in his early years with the expansion Vikings, who didn't protect him well or provide him with a lot of other playmakers. If Minnesota were to have any offensive success, it was up to Tarkenton, who learned to survive in the NFL despite being a slight 6-0 and 190 pounds. He mastered the art of dashing around behind the line, faking and dodging and cutting back and buying precious seconds before passing or running.

Perhaps the only Viking who didn't like Tarkenton's style in those early years was his coach, Norm Van Brocklin, a former traditional dropback passer who wanted his quarterback to stay in the pocket, not scramble recklessly. But Tarkenton was no fool. If he stayed in the pocket, he had no chance. Tarkenton made that discovery in the opening game of his rookie season, when he upset the Bears, turning his ad-lib forays into four touchdown passes and one touchdown run. That was the start of a career that lasted 18 seasons; it was a miracle that his body held up that long.

But his individual successes—he retired with NFL career records for passing yards, completions and touchdowns—were marred by one enormous disappointment. He led the Vikings to three Super Bowl appearances, but they came away losers every time. He was inducted into the Hall of Fame in 1986.

It's his legs—those skinny, unimpressive limbs that could transform him into one of the most elusive, evasive jitterbugs ever to put on a pro uniform.

12

'He was strong and steady and smart, and he could kill you with his ability to throw the football.' –Ron Wolf

TROY AIKMAN

ou are the Golden Boy, the can't-miss prospect, the next Great One. Your reward? You're drafted by the worst team in the NFL, saddled with a terrible offensive line that results in a horrific physical beating in a dreadful rookie season and questions that maybe you are overrated. Yeah, sure. Twelve years later, you retire prematurely, sent to the broadcast booth after too many concussions. Before you go, though, you win three Super Bowls and establish yourself as one of the true stars of a generation.

That is Troy Aikman's legacy. The great prospect who became the opposite of the bust, the rare elite talent who lived up to every expectation, who became a franchise quarterback, the triggerman of a Cowboys offense that evolved into one of the most efficient and respected of its time. More than anything, Aikman established himself as one of the most accurate passers in league history. His career completion percentage of .615 is impressive but doesn't truly indicate his talent. He directed a downfield-passing

offense, which, unlike the West Coast scheme, is not designed to produce high completion ratios. Yet Aikman flourished because of his quick delivery, flawless

mechanics and good decision making.

"I rank him among the best who have ever played," said Ron Wolf, former Packers general manager. "He was strong and steady and smart, and he could kill you with his ability to throw the football. He was all about winning, too. It didn't seem to matter to him if he ran up big numbers or not—as long as the Cowboys won."

Aikman retired holding or tying 47 team passing records. He always will be linked with two other offensive stars of those Cowboys teams, running back Emmitt Smith and wide receiver Michael Irvin. Aikman was the least flashy of the bunch but always the most reliable.

Team, seasons:		
Dallas Cowboys, 1989-2000		
Height: 6-4		
Weight: 220		
Born: 11-21-66		
Colleges: Oklahoma, UCLA		
Championship teams:		
1992, '93, '95 seasons		
Career passing yards/TDs:		
32,942/165		

TROY

AIKMAN

13

STEVE

andlestick Park. October 30, 1988. The 49ers were playing the Vikings in a rematch of the previous season's playoff, and legendary quarterback Joe Montana was sidelined with a back injury. Steve Young, acquired from Tampa Bay the year before for second- and fourth-round draft picks, took Montana's place. Young threw a 73-yard touchdown pass to John Taylor early in the game, but it was his late-game scramble that endeared him to 49ers faithful.

The 49ers trailed, 21-17, late in the fourth quarter. The following is play-by-play announcer Lon Simmons' call on the 49ers Radio Network. Analyst Wayne Walker chimes in at the end:

Simmons: "Young, back to throw, in trouble. He's going to be sacked. No, gets away. … He runs. … Gets away again! … Goes to the 40! … Gets away again! … To the 35, cuts back at the 30! … To the 20 … the 15 … the 10! He dives! Touchdown 49ers!

"Young is exhausted! He stumbled as he got to the 2. He could barely move. He dived into the end zone, and the 49ers have taken the lead with 1:58. A 49-yard touchdown run by Steve Young."

Walker: "You won't see many better runs in your life than that."

The play earned the 49ers a 24-21 victory and a bit of revenge. It also embodied Young's never-say-die attitude—he eluded at least four tacklers before stumbling into the end zone—and showcased a special dimension of his game.

"It looked like a guy in the

desert looking for that last glass of water," said 49ers offensive lineman Bruce Collie.

Sportscasters around the country replayed the run over and over, putting Young on the NFL map. He won NFC Offensive Player of the Week honors, but not a starting job. Montana returned two weeks later and led the 49ers to two more Super Bowl victories before Young took over in 1991.

Young, who played his first two professional seasons in the USFL, finished his NFL career as a two-time league MVP, and he earned seven Pro Bowl selections. He also threw for 33,124 yards and 232 touchdowns and ran for 4,239 yards and 43 TDs. His career-defining moment came in Super Bowl 29 when he fired a record six touchdown passes in a 49-26 victory over San Diego.

Teams, seasons:
Los Angeles Express (USFL), 1984-85; Tampa Bay Buccaneers, 1985-86; San Francisco 49ers, 1987-99
Height: 6-2
Weight: 215
Born: 10-11-61
College: BYU
Championship teams:
1988, '89, '94 seasons
Career passing yards/TDs:
33,124/232 (NFL)

YOUNG

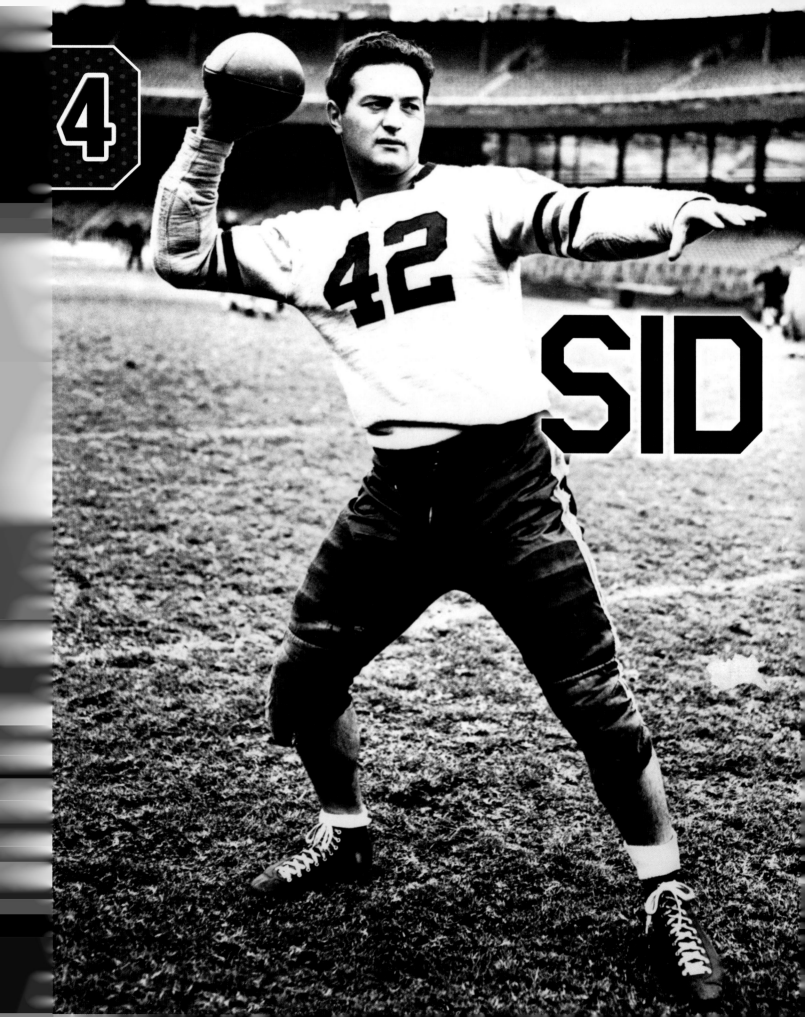

'In Sid, we created a new type
of football player, the T quarterback.' – George Halas

LUCKMAN

here is only one way to spell Sid Luckman—with a "T"–for the offensive formation he made famously effective for coach George Halas. As the legend goes, Luckman was exposed to an updated version of this once-tried-but-scrapped offense but struggled as a rookie with the complexity of plays. He fumbled and bumbled until he was moved briefly to halfback.

Returned to quarterback a year later, the quick and crafty Luckman handled the new formation with a record-setting touch

during the Bears' 73-0 championship game victory over the Redskins in 1940. It was the first of four championships for the Bears, their trendy offense and their quarterback who worked it to a T.

Even in 1940, the NFL was a den of copycats, and teams throughout the league immediately shifted to the T-formation. Many tried the new scheme, but few tasted the success of Luckman, who was the chief apostle spreading the gospel of back-to-the-line, freeze-the-

defense deception by the quarterback that characterized the T offense, similar to the way Joe Montana was the Paul of today's West Coast scripture.

"In Sid, we created a new type of football player, the T quarterback," Halas said. "Newspapers switched their attention from star runners to star quarterbacks. It marked a new era for the game."

By 1943, the success of the Brooklyn-born quarterback was legendary, and the Bears were welcomed to New York's Polo Grounds on November 14 for Sid Luckman Day. The Chicago quarterback starred in his old home with seven touchdown passes during a 56-7 triumph over the

Giants on his way to MVP honors. Luckman, who was elected to the Hall of Fame in 1965, also capped the 1943 season with five touchdown passes in the Bears' 41-21 championship game win over the Redskins.

Team, seasons:
Chicago Bears, 1939-50
Height: 6-0
Weight: 195
Born: 11-21-16 **Died:** 7-5-98
College: Columbia
Championship teams:
1940, '41, '43, '46 seasons
Career passing yards/TDs:
14,686/137

Luckman (left) celebrates with teammates George McAfee (center) and Ray McLean after the Bears' victory over the New York Giants in the 1946 NFL championship game.

15 PEYTON MANNING

Like father like son: NFL success for Colts star quarterback was an all in the family production

hen Peyton Manning was growing up in New Orleans, he didn't need to go far to find a role model. He sat with him at the kitchen table every morning for breakfast—his dad, Archie, who remains the most popular player in the city after a 15-year career with the Saints.

Peyton modeled much of his game after his dad, the way he prepares, the way he conditions, the way he deals with teammates and the public. There is just one major difference. "I can't run a lick," he said.

Archie survived on mobility. Peyton survives with his almost-perfect throwing technique. A pure drop-back passer, he has methodically developed his game, becoming more precise in his reads, more accurate with his throws, more sure of his role as leader.

The result has been stunning. Over his first seven seasons, Peyton was more productive than any quarterback in NFL history, throwing for 29,442 yards and 216 touchdowns. Manning is obsessive in every aspect of his approach, even to having a film room at his house so he can put in extra study time. His quest for perfection reached a new pinnacle during the 2004 season when he threw 49 touchdown passes—breaking Dan Marino's NFL record for TD passes in a season—while completing 68 percent of his passes and posting a league-record passer rating of 121.1.

Teams, seasons:		
Indianapolis Colts, 1998-present		
Height: 6-5		
Weight: 230		
Born: 3-24-76		
College: Tennessee		
Championship teams: None		
Career passing yards/TDs:		
29,442/216 (through 2004)		

During one amazing five-week stretch, Manning was as perfect as any quarterback ever, throwing for 24 touchdowns. The touchdown feast might have created a frenzy of attention usually confined to record pursuits in baseball. But those last two numbers— 68 and 121.1—are equally as impressive to football purists who never thought any quarterback could be both this accurate, particularly one who throws downfield so frequently, and this close to perfection, particularly against today's sophisticated defenses. His record season culminated with a second league MVP award; he shared the '03 award with Tennessee's Steve McNair.

"I remember when I first got into the league, I thought how it would be nice to have a year when you were the best," he said. "That means your team is probably winning. ... I am very appreciative of the opportunity and of my teammates and coaches for putting me in this position. I know how hard it is to win games and to have some success, and I appreciate the chance I am getting."

For Manning, it is all about hard work and preparation and focus. If you can master those things, everything else—the statistics, the victories, the accolades—comes along for the ride. Certainly, few quarterbacks have enjoyed a more rewarding regular season than the one Manning experienced in 2004.

It is difficult to completely comprehend it: the numbers were that dazzling. But the

consistency of his career also is impressive. He is the only player to throw for 4,000 yards in six consecutive seasons and the first to throw for 3,000 in his first seven. He also finished 2004 with 112 consecutive regular-season starts, never having missed one since he

became a Colt in 1998. And just think: He said he wants to play another 10 years or so.

"I have tried to get better every year, and I feel I should get better every year," he said. "I am a year older, I am in the same system, I am more comfortable, we have better timing. All those things should show in better results."

Yet, despite all of Manning's records and accolades, his Colts teams have not won a conference title, keeping them out of the Super Bowl. His playoff record stands at 3-5. His 2003 and '04 postseason runs ended with bitter defeats at New England. Statistics are one thing and rings are anoth-

er, and Manning understands the ultimate success of his career will be measured accordingly. He understands how really fickle his world is, where a quarterback's career somehow must be validated by a championship, and that even Marino and Dan Fouts and Fran Tarkenton, as good as they were, could never distance themselves from that asterisk.

It's a subject that annoys him. Don't people understand that if you and your team do everything possible to put yourself in position to win and it is not good enough, there is nothing demeaning about that kind of failure? Sometimes the

other guy is just better. He fully believes this, yet he still beats himself up over the losses; he can remember every play, good and bad, of every one of the past playoff games, and when he recalls his mistakes, he punishes himself: How could I have made that throw, how could I have called that audible? These playoffs will become his next laboratory, and he'll be driven by the intellectual challenge of training himself to translate what he sees during film study into instant on-field recognition so he can put his team in the perfect play every time based not on a whim, but on solid, empirical evidence, all within a

'I can't do anything about how people think. … We have not won a Super Bowl. … It's something I have to deal with, but it also is something that pushes me. No one wants a championship more than I do, for sure.'

Manning-to-Harrison success story has been choreographed through the same set of eyes

Figure Peyton Manning threw 18 of his first 82 career touchdown passes to Marvin Harrison using his favorite play.

It happened in the second quarter against the Falcons in December 2003. The call was for Manning to throw to Harrison on a post route after a play fake. The Colts anticipated Falcons safety Cory Hall covering Harrison on his outside shoulder, but Hall played on the inside of the receiver. Harrison recognized it and, knowing Manning would, too, altered his route. Manning threw to Harrison's outside shoulder instead of in front of him, and the Colts had a 17-yard touchdown in the corner of the end zone.

This is how Manning and Harrison operate, seeing 100 yards and 11 defenders through the same pair of eyes. If there were devices inside their helmets that enabled their neurons to transmit signals to each other, no one would be surprised. The trust they share on the field defies the laws of relationships. "They not only know what they're going to do, but they feel each other," said linebacker Junior Seau, a 12-time Pro Bowl pick.

Figure Manning threw 1,100 passes to Harrison in regular-season games in their first seven seasons together. Of those, 702 were complete. Figure he threw another 65 passes in eight playoff games, with 39 of those being complete.

Manning-to-Harrison is at the top of the list of most productive quarterback-to-receiver duos ever. During the 2004 season, Manning and Harrison passed former Bills Jim Kelly and Andre Reed for most completions (663) by a duo and entered the 2005 season just 128 yards shy of Kelly's and Reed's yardage mark (9,538) by a duo. They finished the 2004 season four touchdown passes behind the NFL record of 85 set by Steve Young and Jerry Rice.

Given the frequency of injuries and roster turnover in today's NFL, it is possible Manning and Harrison are creating records that will stand for eternity, the football equivalent of Joe DiMaggio's 56-game hitting streak. One viable threat to Manning and Harrison, Minnesota's Daunte Culpepper passing to Randy Moss, was broken up after the 2004 season when Moss was traded to Oakland. "Having those records would mean a lot—that two guys can do what we've done in such a short time," Manning said, referring to his first seven years with Harrison.

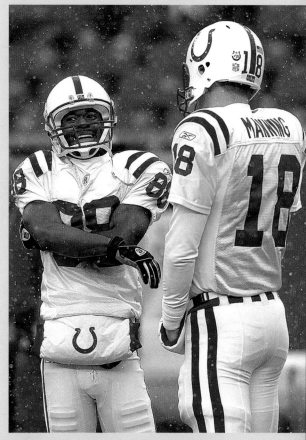

Manning and favorite receiver Harrison have been inseparable, joined at the hip statistically as well as physically during Colts games and practices.

Figure Manning has thrown more than 12,000 passes to Harrison in regular- and postseason practices. Another 10,000 in training camp and preseason practices. And another 8,500 in offseason workouts.

Harrison was the 19th pick in the 1996 draft; Manning was the first selection in '98. There is no lack of ability here. There also is no lack of humility. How else could you explain the way they come to work every day—even after 11 Pro Bowls between them—wanting to sweat as if they were undrafted free agents from Division III schools?

Sitting on a golf cart after one training camp practice, Manning estimated he throws 33 passes in a typical practice to Harrison. There are 10 he throws "versus air," another 10 in the one-on-one segment of practice, another five in seven-on-seven and another eight or so in the team period.

Colts coach Tony Dungy, who, as a player, assistant coach and head coach has been part of

self-imposed environment where nothing is ever good enough, no statistic, no victory, no season. It is hard to conceive the NFL has ever had a smarter quarterback, yet he is so obsessed that even his father worries. "Peyton," Archie tells him, "you need to relax more."

But Peyton can't be concerned; he wants only to focus on these next obstacles. "Reality is reality," he said about the validation that comes with a ring. "This is my seventh year, and we have done a whole bunch of things, but not what we ultimately want to do. I can't do anything about how people think, and to tell you the truth, I don't spend much time worrying about it. We have not won a Super Bowl. ... It's something I have to deal with, but it also is something that pushes me. No one wants a championship more than I do, for sure."

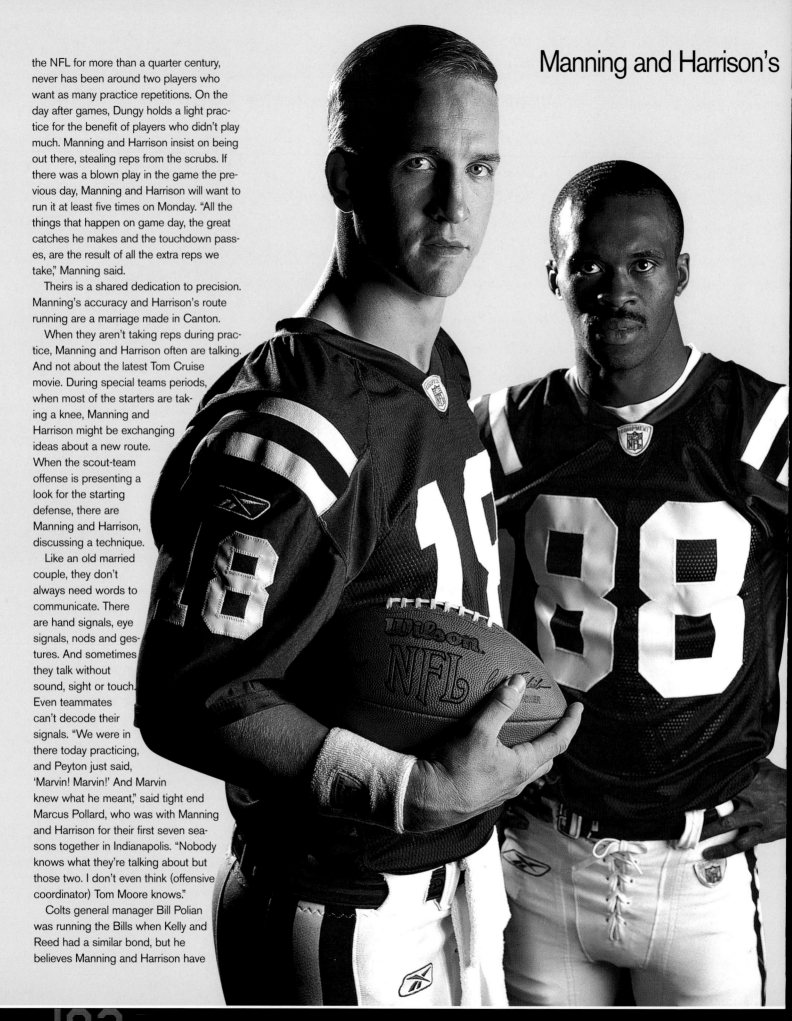

the NFL for more than a quarter century, never has been around two players who want as many practice repetitions. On the day after games, Dungy holds a light practice for the benefit of players who didn't play much. Manning and Harrison insist on being out there, stealing reps from the scrubs. If there was a blown play in the game the previous day, Manning and Harrison will want to run it at least five times on Monday. "All the things that happen on game day, the great catches he makes and the touchdown passes, are the result of all the extra reps we take," Manning said.

Theirs is a shared dedication to precision. Manning's accuracy and Harrison's route running are a marriage made in Canton.

When they aren't taking reps during practice, Manning and Harrison often are talking. And not about the latest Tom Cruise movie. During special teams periods, when most of the starters are taking a knee, Manning and Harrison might be exchanging ideas about a new route. When the scout-team offense is presenting a look for the starting defense, there are Manning and Harrison, discussing a technique.

Like an old married couple, they don't always need words to communicate. There are hand signals, eye signals, nods and gestures. And sometimes they talk without sound, sight or touch. Even teammates can't decode their signals. "We were in there today practicing, and Peyton just said, 'Marvin! Marvin!' And Marvin knew what he meant," said tight end Marcus Pollard, who was with Manning and Harrison for their first seven seasons together in Indianapolis. "Nobody knows what they're talking about but those two. I don't even think (offensive coordinator) Tom Moore knows."

Colts general manager Bill Polian was running the Bills when Kelly and Reed had a similar bond, but he believes Manning and Harrison have

relationship mostly is about pushing each other.

taken their connection to a higher ground. "They have a communication level that's probably unique in pro football," he said.

They are so comfortable with each other and the offense the Colts have used since Manning's rookie year that Harrison occasionally will change Manning's play at the line of scrimmage. Three years ago against the Ravens, he lined up in the slot and saw a linebacker outside of him and a safety about 10 yards off, waiting to bracket him. Harrison recognized that it was an effective defense for the play that had been called, a 7- or 8-yard hitch. So Harrison came in motion toward Manning and, as he passed him, said, "I'm going to pump it." Harrison took off toward the end zone, and it was the right call. Only an overthrow by Manning prevented a long touchdown. Even though they missed on that one, the two had 11 touchdowns of 50-plus yards going into the '05 season.

You wouldn't call them kindred spirits, but you would call them friends. Manning likes country music; Harrison likes hip hop and R&B. They eat out together a couple times every season. Harrison often stops by Manning's house for postgame parties. Manning has stayed at Harrison's house in Philadelphia. Harrison has worked at Manning's football camp in New Orleans. Their relationship mostly is about pushing each other. "If I were to slack for some reason, 'P' still would be the energy," Harrison said. "He's always upbeat. If I run a route and don't get open, I might think, 'Shoot, I let him down. I have to turn it up.' And it would be the same way the other way around."

As is the case with most quarterbacks and receivers, some occasional tension can creep into their relationship. During a 1999 game against the Giants, a critical third-down pass to Harrison was ruled incomplete. It looked like a catch to Manning, who wanted to challenge the play. When he asked Harrison if he had caught it, Harrison did not respond and kept walking to the sideline, probably because Manning's throw was off. On the sideline, they exchanged

some nasty words. But on the next series, Manning found Harrison on a slant for a key reception. "They both strive for perfection," Pollard said. "When things don't go perfect, somebody is going to hear it."

There is too much history between them for a disagreement to fester. Harrison didn't really arrive as an NFL receiver until Manning arrived. Harrison averaged 13.1 yards per touchdown catch before Manning and has averaged 24.7 yards per TD catch since. When Manning came to Indianapolis, all apple-cheeked and yes-sir, no-sir, Harrison was one of the veterans he leaned on.

Manning's first pass as a pro—in a preseason game against the Seahawks—was a quick slant to Harrison after Manning picked up a zone blitz. Harrison made the catch in stride, burst past cornerback Shawn Springs and scored a 48-yard touchdown.

Figure Manning has thrown more than 110 passes Harrison's way in preseason games, completing about 70 percent.

They went to the Pro Bowl together for the first time after the 1999 season and have been there together five times. The one time Harrison made it without Manning, after the 2001 season, Harrison bought him a Rolex. "I felt real guilty," Manning said. "He's thanking me for helping him, but look what he does for me."

Their familiarity with each other has enabled Harrison and Manning to save each other repeatedly. Three years ago against the Cowboys, Manning was flushed out of the pocket to his left. Harrison saw it, stopped the route that was supposed to take him across the field in the other direction and ran in the same direction Manning was running. Manning was able to complete a pass to Harrison for a first down.

Manning also helps Harrison, who is slightly built at 170 pounds, avoid big hits. "He bails me out by working with me, and I can save him a headache by throwing it away from the defender," Manning said.

Avoiding knockout blows is no small part of their success. Asked to explain the productivity of Manning and Harrison, Titans coach Jeff Fisher, with great reverence, said simply, "They both stay healthy."

Manning never has missed an NFL game. Harrison missed the last four games in 1998 with a separated shoulder and one

game in 2003 with a pulled hamstring. "Marvin's always there," Manning said. "He's always been there. He never comes out. He never said, 'I need a breather.' He never takes a practice off."

Manning's iron man performance at his position is even more remarkable but less celebrated because his streak of 112 consecutive starts is 93 behind the streak of Green Bay's incomparable Brett Favre.

Figure Manning has thrown about 7,300 passes to Harrison in pregame warmups.

While other players use the time before a game to socialize with opponents, nap or listen to music, Manning and Harrison are working. As a warmup to the team warmup, they go through the entire route tree and run additional special plays. Their pregame ritual is done without words or signals. "It puts you in a good frame of mind, especially when you go on the road, on different fields with different throwing levels and different angles," Manning said.

As much as Manning and Harrison work together on the field, you would suspect they watch game tape together. But Harrison doesn't watch tape much outside of team meetings. It has not limited him, in part because he, like Manning, can visualize a play based on words. "Some guys have to write it down or see it on the board," Manning said. "But if you can visualize it as a quarterback, it's a great advantage. For a receiver to be able to do it is amazing."

Also amazing is their shared ability to recall prior plays. During a game against the Dolphins in 2002, the Colts found themselves in the red zone facing a combination coverage in which the Dolphins "kind of built a wall" on the 10. Manning thought back to when the Colts faced the same situation against the Bills three years earlier in the season opener. "Buffalo, '99, at home, same thing," he told Harrison. No other words were necessary. Seconds later, the pair resurrected the play, which was not in the game plan, for a 16-yard touchdown.

Figure between offseason workouts, training camp, preseason, regular-season games, postseason games and in-season practices, Peyton Manning has thrown about 40,000 passes to Marvin Harrison, give or take a hundred or two. Is it any wonder they are ringing history's doorbell?

 hen Michael Jordan began wearing baggy shorts in the early 1990s, he started a fashion revolution. When Steelers quarterback Terry Bradshaw sported a full beard in Super Bowl 10, it didn't quite have the same effect. Bradshaw's gritty play, however, inspired at least one player, second-year quarterback Dan Fouts, to adopt the lumberjack look.

And he hasn't shaved his beard since—"though I have trimmed it," Fouts said.

Perhaps the beard was good luck: That next season, Fouts completed better than 50 percent of his passes for the first time in his career. But Fouts' luck really panned out with the arrival of coach Don Coryell in 1978. Coryell came to the Chargers with a plan: Build an offense around the strengths of his young quarterback. And "Air Coryell" was born.

Air Coryell was based on precise throws, perfect routes and patience in the pocket. Fouts didn't have the strongest arm or fastest 40 time, but none of that mattered.

Team, seasons:		
San Diego Chargers, 1973-87		
Height: 6-3		
Weight: 204		
Born: 6-10-51		
College: Oregon		
Championship teams:		
None		
Career passing yards/TDs:		
43,040/254		

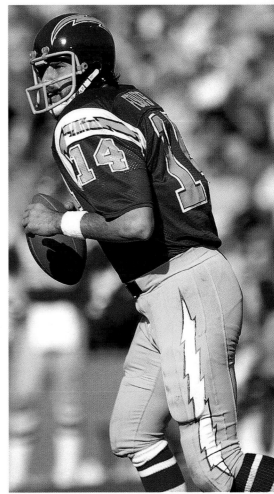

'He was not an athlete.
Ask him to run,
and you were in trouble.
But boy, he could throw.'

−John Jefferson

DAN FOUTS

"We gave him trouble about those skinny legs," former Chargers receiver John Jefferson said. "He was not an athlete. Ask him to run, and you were in trouble. But boy, he could throw."

It was a perfect match between player and system: In Fouts' first five years in the NFL, he averaged 120 yards passing per game. In his next five after Coryell arrived, Fouts more than doubled his average to 270. In 1986, he became only the third player to pass for more than 40,000 yards in a career.

With the help of a superstar cast of receivers—Jefferson, Kellen Winslow, Charlie Joiner and Wes Chandler—Fouts led the league in pass attempts twice, completions twice and passing yards four times. He led the formerly hapless Chargers to four AFC West titles—but never to the Super Bowl.

The inability to garner a Super Bowl ring makes him no less a legend. Today, Fouts' bearded bust sits shoulder-to-shoulder with several hundred other NFL greats in Canton.

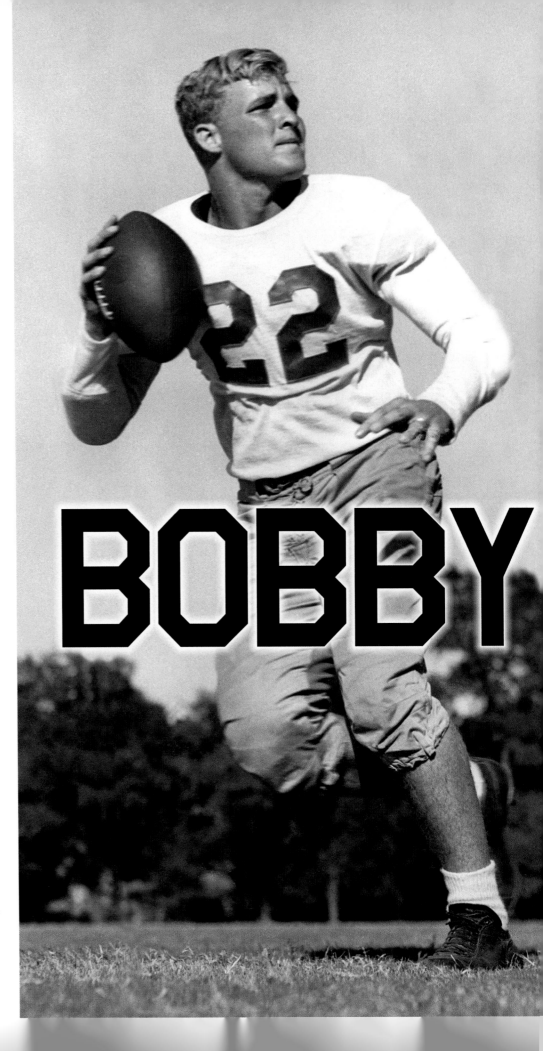

BOBBY

Who knows how many games Bobby Layne played with a hangover. It certainly was more than a handful. Living the good life was as important to him as throwing a touchdown pass, and somehow he managed to figure out a way to do both. He certainly was unconventional, both in personal conduct and passing technique. But neither prevented him from producing one of the most amazing and colorful careers in NFL history.

Layne's approach could be tolerated only by a few coaches, and he was fortunate that Buddy Parker was coaching the Lions. Parker realized the gem he inherited when Layne joined Detroit in 1950 after single seasons with the Bears and New York Bulldogs. Layne's impact was almost immediate. The Lions won division titles in 1952, 1953

Teams, seasons:
Chicago Bears, 1948; New York Bulldogs, 1949; Detroit Lions, 1950-58; Pittsburgh Steelers, 1958-62
Height: 6-1
Weight: 201
Born: 6-19-26 **Died:** 6-1-86
College: Texas
Championship teams:
1952, '53, '57 seasons
Career passing yards/TDs:
26,768/196

He was an incredible leader, so gutsy and impervious to pressure that he elevated teammates with his bravado.

LAYNE

and 1954 and beat the mighty Browns in 1952 and 1953 for the league championship.

No one ever enjoyed his livelihood more than Layne. He was an incredible leader, so gutsy and impervious to pressure that he elevated teammates with his bravado. They loved him, and why not? His larger-than-life personality and good-times approach were mesmerizing. He smoked and drank and partied and loved women and eating, and it didn't matter because he always was ready to play at a level that

earned him Hall of Fame election in 1967.

Nothing showcased Layne's special abilities more than the dramatic 80-yard drive he engineered in the 1953 title game. The Lions got the ball at their own 20 with 4:10 left and Layne scratched and willed them into the end zone, sealing the victory with a 33-yard pass to receiver Jim Doran. Even after being traded to the Steelers in 1958 and reuniting with Parker, Layne had enough left to direct Pittsburgh to three winning records, including a 9-5 mark in 1962, his final season.

8

NORM VAN

His gift was a right arm fashioned by the gods, a weapon that he used to carve up defenses for 12 colorful NFL years.

I f you are looking for an ornery, obstinate, difficult, determined and incredibly tough quarterback, end your search with Norm Van Brocklin. He was outspoken and almost ridiculously competitive, so sure of his abilities that he took passing risks that made his coaches cringe. But to the Dutchman, no receiver was ever uncovered, no pass impossible to complete.

His gift was a right arm fashioned by the gods, a weapon that he used to carve up defenses for 12 colorful NFL years. Never one to shy away from a battle or controversy, Van Brocklin considered himself the best and carried himself accordingly. That swagger endeared him to teammates, who fed off his confidence, but angered opponents, who took great delight in beating him—something that didn't happen very often. Van Brocklin was a multi-talented athlete who also led the league twice in punting average.

Teams, seasons:		
Los Angeles Rams, 1949-57; Philadelphia Eagles, 1958-60		
Height: 6-1		
Weight: 190		
Born: 3-15-26 **Died:** 5-2-83		
College: Oregon		
Championship teams:		
1951, '60 seasons		
Career passing yards/TDs:		
23,611/173		

He left the University of Oregon a year early in 1949 to join the Los Angeles Rams, who already had a star quarterback, Hollywood celebrity Bob Waterfield, who was married to movie star Jane Russell. These were opposites, the gruff Dutchman and the polished Waterfield. The Rams won four division titles and one league championship during Van Brocklin's nine years. But he had to share playing time with Waterfield for the first four, and neither handled the situation well. Still, Van Brocklin won passing titles in 1950 and 1952.

In 1951, he demonstrated his explosiveness by throwing for five touchdowns and a still-standing record 554 yards in a game against the New York Yanks.

Van Brocklin finished his career on top, thanks to a 1958 trade to the Eagles. In three years, he helped transform Philadelphia from last place to NFL champion. After beating the Packers, 17-13, in the 1960 championship game, he retired; 11 years later, he was voted into the Hall of Fame.

BROCKLIN

9

TOM

His statistics and athleticism are not super, but the results he gets certainly are

Jim Schwartz, the Titans' defensive coordinator, spoke at a sports banquet before the 2004 season. The host asked him a question: What NFL quarterback would you select, other than Steve McNair, to start one game? When he picked Tom Brady, guests in the audience stirred. "The guy looked at me and said, 'Tom Brady?' and I laughed," said Schwartz. "I mean, he's won Super Bowls, he's a clutch performer, and people still don't see him as a marquee player. What hasn't he done?"

What Brady hasn't done is move out of the shadow of *It*. When those who passed on him in the 2000 draft and those who can't beat him now try to explain how this kid—the one they remember out of Michigan with the weak frame, average arm, terrible feet and limited mobility—can possibly possess three Super Bowl rings, the fallback position always is, blame *It*, that mysterious, seemingly indefinable something that some quarterbacks have and many

don't, and when you have *It*, you win and when you don't, you are Ryan Leaf. They simply didn't realize Brady had *It*.

Now, they are wiser. Brady's cup of *It* runneth over. Charlie Weis, the Patriots' former offensive coordinator, gives *It* a name: moxie. "And Tom is the epitome of having that special moxie," he said. Scouts speak about *It* in reverent tones as if *It* has form and breathes and invisibly stalks the playing field. "*It* is leadership, poise, judgment, competitiveness, an edge," said John Dorsey, the Packers' director of college scouting. "You know *It* is there, but can you find *It*? When you do, you eventually will get the trophy. But the search drives us crazy."

Brady still is driving them bonkers. They so much want to look at him

BRADY

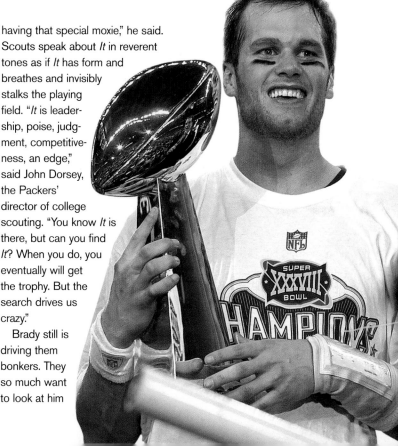

differently. They see the Unitas-like accomplishments, how the Patriots have won three Super Bowls in his first four seasons as a starter, how he never lost any of seven overtime games heading into the '05 season, how the Pats have lost just once with him in 19 games decided by six points or fewer, how he has pieced together 16 winning drives in the fourth quarter or overtime. Yet, even with this resume, which carves out space among the all-time greats, their vision still is clouded by the shadow cast by his close pal *It*. With Peyton Manning and Brett Favre and Donovan McNabb and Steve McNair and Michael Vick, you can see all the natural talent and a decent amount of *It* mixed in, too; they've always seemed more suited than Brady to be elite NFL quarterbacks. Maybe with him, the success is too much, too soon. When you are a draft afterthought, when your coaches at Michigan worked so diligently to replace you as a senior with young Drew Henson and his All-American gifts, and now to be considered an equal of Manning, who has been part of our quarterback mindset forever, well, the NFL always has been slow to change perceptions.

Listen to the inner debate of Bills general manager Tom Donahoe. "If you rated Brady's skills, he is not the top-rated quarterback in the league," he said. "To put him skill-wise with Favre or Manning, you just can't do it." OK, but ... "All he

does is win Super Bowls. You can argue all day long who is the best athlete, but you still have to win. And no one has won more than him recently." So where does that leave Donahoe? "How old is Tom, 28? He's 27? Wow, that is even worse for the rest of us. If the Patriots keep going and the rest of us don't find a way to stop them, he will put together a record as good as anyone who has ever played." Like so many in the league, Donahoe walks right to the edge with Brady, but hesitates to take the next step.

For sure, Brady can be buried by numbers. Manning and Favre are all over the record book. Manning might even challenge Dan Marino's career statistics one day, a notion once considered unfathomable. Within the Patriots' offense, Brady never will accumulate gaudy totals. He never has led the league in passer rating, yards or completions. He never has been named to the All-Pro team. In

the 2003 and '04 seasons, despite winning 28-of-32 regular-season games and all six playoff games, he wasn't a contender in the MVP balloting, finishing behind co-winners McNair and Manning in 2003 and Manning in '04. Yet, neither has beaten Brady in a meaningful game. It's unfair, and it's wrong.

But that will change. Brady certainly is not depending on *It* to fuel the rest of his career. What you see emerging now is the culmination of a transformation—a quarterback who recognizes he can be even more special by complementing *It* with significantly improved skills. What you see emerging from the shadow of *It* is the best quarterback in football.

hen Randy Mueller was general manager of the Saints, he scouted Brady. "Skinny kid, average arm, average athlete,

average physical skills," said Mueller, who went on to become an ESPN analyst. "Not much there. None of us saw *It*."

But Mueller looked at Brady again during the 2004 season, evaluating him as if he were scouting for the draft. He was mesmerized by the change. "He has improved his skills light years, even from the first Super Bowl win," he said. "That doesn't happen. But it has with him. He could have sat back after the first ring, but it was like he went back to the drawing board and said, 'I am going to keep doing what I am doing, but even better.' He has improved his arm strength, his fundamentals. Before now, he's gotten most of his credit for the way he manages the game. But that isn't appropriate anymore. Now, he is a playmaker."

Indeed, Brady quietly assumed more pre-snap responsibility than any quarterback Weis and Bill Belichick had coached. Brady is not nearly as flashy at the line as Manning, who spends much of the clock orchestrating the next play. But on virtually every down, Brady has the freedom to change the call. "He is the next closest thing to a coach," said Weis. "It has gotten to the point where by the end of the week, he knows the game plan like a coach knows the plan."

Brady's masterful grasp of the offense is particularly significant considering the Patriots run a game-plan scheme. They are not a proponent of a particular style—West Coast, vertical, power rushing—but instead vary their approach weekly depending on the defense. To make this philosophy flourish, it is essential the quarterback has the mind and desire—here is *It* showing up again—combined with the requisite physical ability to execute the demands.

"I use three elements to measure success by quarterbacks in this league," Schwartz said. "One is intangibles—leadership, knowledge of game, work ethic, competitiveness. Two, does he make the right decisions? Every coverage has strengths and weaknesses. Does he recognize the coverage, does he move the ball around, how does he handle the blitz? Three, can he throw an accurate pass after he makes the decision, and put it where I can catch it? That is different from throwing it through a wall or breaking someone's hand with your velocity. It's touch. If you can't get past these three things, you can't play quarterback in the NFL. You are screwed. And Tom Brady is three-for-three."

Brady has moved from heavily *It*-dependent to the player we see now, confident in his reads, able to quickly scan the field, locate the open receiver and then throw a wonderfully catchable pass. He jokingly said his favorite receiver is "whoever's open," but that remark is reflective of the Patriots' spread-the-field approach, which depends on Brady to find the uncovered option. "Brady is a brilliant football guy," said Donahoe. "And what they are doing on offense fits their players and quarterback perfectly, all the five-wide

receiver stuff and spreading out, putting it on his shoulders."

Brian Baldinger, an analyst for FOX Sports and *Sporting News*, is fascinated by the continued evolution and maturity of Brady's game. "He is seamless in his decision-making," he said. "I'm watching him against Arizona. He starts to pass, the defensive back closes, he pulls back, moves just enough in the pocket to buy some time and then finds the

open guy and puts it right on his hands. It's all so fluid that you forget how hard it is to do that consistently. But he does it all the time."

Here's where he has improved the most:

• Brady is a career 61.6 percent passer, but Belichick still sees noticeable progress in his quarterback's mechanics and accuracy. "A lot of that is combined with good decision-making," said Belichick, "where if you throw the ball to a more open space, there is a little bit more margin for error than if you throw into a really tight space."

• Brady showed marginal footwork coming out of college, slow and not fundamentally consistent, so bad that it turned off Mike Holmgren, who believes

strongly that quarterbacks with poor foot mechanics can't win in the NFL. Now, Brady has learned to keep those feet planted, always under control. Baldinger sees in him the nimbleness of a Derek Jeter, "the way he turns, the perfect footwork. It's frustrating to play against a guy like him. He's so sound."

• He was physically weak as a rookie. But even after three Super Bowl wins and two Super Bowl MVPs, Brady

works as hard as any Patriot, continuing the change from a formless 220-pound kid to a robust 225-pound man. At 6-4 and with a more developed body, he is closer to that physical prototype sought by NFL teams. An offshoot of this heavy lifting is additional arm power. It never will be at the Favre or Vick level, but he now is a confident downfield passer with sufficient zip and range to expand how much of the field opponents must defend.

"From 2001 to now, it is night and day," Weis said of Brady's development. "The one thing he had walking in the door was mental ability. He had moxie, and he had character and he had that competitive fire. He had all the qualities that allow you to develop into (a top quarterback), but there are a lot of people that have thrown abilities away and have never reached their potential. Who knows what his potential is as a football player?"

is weight room work has other, less noticeable residuals, particularly within the fabric of this carefully constructed, closely managed team. The most diligent participant in the Patriots' offseason program receives a premium parking spot just a few steps from the players' entrance at the training facility. The reserved space is a carrot dangled for all players, who for two of the last four seasons have had to walk past Brady's pickup truck in that spot.

"We saw him in there, pushing himself, and that gives all of us confidence in him," said safety Rodney Harrison. "He wants to be perfect. He wants to win championships. It is not about individual things, and people here respect that."

Brady easily is the most famous player on a roster of role players and marginal stars. Yet somehow he still is one of the guys. "The thing that I'm happy about with playing for the Patriots is that you feel like you're one of the guys," Brady confirmed. "That's all I want to be." Mueller watched a training camp practice in the summer of 2004 when Belichick, upset at the lackluster performance of his offense, called out the players and sent them on a punishment lap, as if they were still in middle school. Brady was the first to take off, running hard. The rest followed him.

He knows how to interact with teammates, when to be their friend and when to get in their face and push them beyond their limitations. No Patriots player works out as hard or studies more diligently. His impact can be felt through the entire franchise, just as he promised owner Bob Kraft during their first stairway

'He is the next closest thing to a coach. It has gotten to the point where by the end of the week, he knows the game plan like a coach knows the plan.' –Charlie Weis

NOT JUST AN AVERAGE JOE

hose who know Joe, see Joe in Tom. Those who know Tom, see Joe in Tom. Tom Brady won't accept that he is the reincarnation of his boyhood idol, Joe Montana, and Joe himself refuses to see Tom as Joe or even understand why anyone would expect Tom to be Joe.

"I think that is something that is crazy," Brady said. "He was the best quarterback in the history of the NFL. I think a lot of times it is flattering, but at the same time I think it is pretty unrealistic, too."

On February 3, 2002, at 24 years and 184 days, Brady became the youngest starting quarterback to win a Super Bowl, topping the previous mark of 25 years and 227 days held jointly by two guys named Joe: Namath and Montana. Twenty years before his first Super Bowl, Brady was a 4-year-old 49ers fan in San Mateo, Calif., watching Montana claim his first ring.

"We always had tickets, and one of Tom's earliest games was the one where Dwight Clark made The Catch," said Tom Brady Sr. "For the next 10 or 12 years, Tommy went to a whole bunch of 49ers games, and the games that he didn't go to we saw on TV. Joe Montana was the icon. To this day, he's the best quarterback I've ever seen. In many respects, the attributes that Joe had were attributes that I see Tommy developing."

Is it possible that Brady is experiencing an elevated level of success because of the amount of Montana he saw while growing up in the Bay Area? "For any NFL quarterback, I can't imagine they couldn't learn something or pick something up just from watching those guys and by the way they carry themselves or their mechanics," said Patriots coach Bill Belichick.

Consider the skills Brady brings to the field. Not speed. Not incredible arm strength. Grace, poise, intelligence, leadership and passing accuracy make a winning combination for Brady. Just like Joe.

"If there is reason to compare Brady to anybody, it would be Joe," said former 49ers coach Bill Walsh. "Their styles are very similar, their appearance is very similar and their results are very similar."

Brady is accumulating wins and rings at a pace to match—and perhaps even exceed—Montana. Heading into the 2005 season, Brady had won 77.4 percent of his starts, the best mark in the Super Bowl era, just ahead of Roger Staubach and well ahead of Montana's 71 percent, the third-best mark for a quarterback. Add in Brady's 9-0 playoff record, and his winning percentage is an off-the-charts .792.

"Something may look like somebody else, but in most cases I don't think any of the (quarterbacks) really grow up and model themselves by saying, 'Well, I'm going to do this exactly like he did it,'" Montana said. "You enjoy watching somebody—like when I was growing up, I enjoyed watching Namath and Bradshaw and Unitas—but I never really went out and tried to throw like them or did anything where I said, 'I'm Joe Namath today.' You get to where you are by being yourself. That's what Tom has done."

The two quarterbacks with seven Super Bowl rings and five Super Bowl MVP trophies between them also share the same chiropractor, who brought them together for a lunch at Montana's home before the 2003 season. "It was more about the things that take place outside of the game as much as the things going on inside the game," Montana said.

The style and manner by which Brady deals with pressure and finds ways to make good things happen is the overwhelming reason for all the Montana talk. Some Brady-Montana comparisons are based on statistics, but the resemblance is less physical and more intangible. In a uniform, Montana and Brady have that something special only the most elite performers possess. It's not something that can be coached or taught, because it's a charm or personal magnetism that compels teammates to listen and follow and watch and believe.

Brady, 8, as a Joe Montana fan.

path-crossing, hours after New England selected Brady in the sixth round of the 2000 draft. Brady is as acute with his leadership skills as he is with his passing touch.

Still, Brady is different. He is a celebrity yet remains relatively unpretentious and boyishly charming. He loves his parents, is close to his sisters, is adored by his teammates, respected by his coaches.

"He has a presence, almost regal-like," said tight end Christian Fauria. "It's the same presence of a JFK, someone like that. When they come into the room, you aren't awestruck by him, but you feel it. I mean, this guy has met the Pope, the President, he's dating a movie star. May I carry your bag, sir?"

Brady wants to hear none of this superstar stuff. Even after three Super Bowl victories, he flinches at being compared to Joe Montana. Brady sees himself as a work unfinished, still so much to patch. "There are so many things I would like to improve on," he said. "My recognition of what the defense is doing and making better decisions with the ball, especially late in the game. I want to take better advantage of late-game situations and putting up points and turning those three-point wins into 10-point wins where it is not critical at the end."

His coaches are pushing him hard to refine even the smallest of details. Take a pass into the flat. Belichick wants the ball in a specific spot. Not in the facemask, not too low or too high, but one foot in front of the receiver's number. When Brady isn't perfect, his coach tells him, loudly. It's his way of letting teammates know the quarterback, even this one, isn't immune to reprimand, either.

Still, how much can you correct a guy with this much *It*—and this much skill?

20

SONNY JURGENSEN

 o town has ever loved a quarterback more than Washington D.C. loved Sonny Jurgensen. The fans loved his approach to life, where a cigar, a good drink and a big meal figured prominently, and they loved what he could accomplish amid the disarray that was the Redskins during much of his time in Washington. He was their symbol of hope, one of the few stars on a team that danced annually with mediocrity.

He was a heroic figure, a classic dropback passer with a short, quick, quirky release that made him difficult to sack and even more difficult to defend. He made the hard throw seem easy; he had so much faith in his skill that if an opponent gave him the slightest throwing lane, he was sure he could squeeze in the completion. For most of his 11 seasons with the Redskins—he spent his first seven NFL years with the Eagles—he took a tremendous pounding while playing for terribly bad teams.

Vince Lombardi gave him one winning record in 1969, and George Allen gave him four more, but by then Jurgensen was sharing

Jurgensen with Vince Lombardi in 1969.

Teams, seasons:		
Philadelphia Eagles, 1957-63; Washington Redskins, 1964-74		
Height: 5-11		
Weight: 202		
Born: 8-23-34		
College: Duke		
Championship teams:		
1960 season		
Career passing yards/TDs:		
32,224/255		

playing time with Billy Kilmer. And when the Redskins lost to Miami in Super Bowl 7, Jurgensen sat out with an Achilles' tendon tear.

"He was one of the most determined people you could ever want," Kilmer said. "He had supreme confidence in himself, and he didn't fear anyone. And man, could he throw the football."

That he could. Jurgensen won three passing titles and five times surpassed 3,000 yards in a season. He was inducted into the Hall of Fame in 1983.

21

JIM

KELLY

 he first thing you noticed about Jim Kelly was his brashness. He would call it confidence, but it was more than that. It was one of those stick-your-chin-out kind of things, where the tough guy on the block says, "OK, anyone want to take me on?" He played quarterback like that, a rough-edged, physical, confrontational guy who really longed to be a linebacker, even though playing quarterback made him very, very rich and very, very famous.

It was this pugnaciousness that helped Kelly make the transition from the USFL to the NFL and helped establish the Bills and their prolific, high-speed offense as one of the most dangerous in the league. He was afraid of no one or no team, and that fearlessness became the hallmark of the Bills as well.

It was not a pleasant experience playing against Kelly and his mates, particularly when the quarterback would seek out defenders to run over on scrambles. He was one of those throwback kind of guys who would have been just as comfortable playing with leather helmet and no facemask.

Only when it came to Super Bowls did his style fail. Four times he led the Bills to the brink of an NFL championship, and four times they lost—a crushing blow for him and the franchise. But because they were so tough, they recovered from the devastating missed field goal in Super Bowl 25 against the Giants and went on to play in three more title games.

Through it all, Kelly never backed off, never conceded that his Bills weren't good enough or that he wasn't a quarterback worthy of a championship ring. He just ran out of games. Kelly was inducted into the Hall of Fame in 2002.

He played quarterback like a rough-edged, physical, confrontational guy who really longed to be a linebacker.

22 Y.A. TITTLE

Teams, seasons:

Baltimore Colts (AAFC/NFL), 1948-50; San Francisco 49ers, 1951-60; New York Giants, 1961-64

Height: 6-0

Weight: 192

Born: 10-24-26

College: LSU

Championship teams:

None

Career passing yards/TDs:

28,339/212 (NFL)

 n his knees, grimacing to find a breath in the after-shock of a cartilage-tearing hit to the sternum, with rivulets of blood trickling down his helmetless, balding head, the enduring image most people have of Y.A. Tittle is not pleasant. Tittle's most memorable moment is captured in an award-winning 1964 photo-graph that remains a powerful portrait of a violent sport as well as a champion in the twi-light of his athletic glory.

"It's one day in my life that ended my career," Tittle said. "Lots of people recognize me now through that picture, but that doesn't bother me at all to talk about it because I don't feel the pain anymore."

"I was gasping for my breath," Tittle said about dam-age inflicted in an early-season game by the Steelers' John Baker and not, as some believe, by the resulting inter-ception returned for a touch-down by Chuck Hinton. So much from that play is nega-tive for Tittle, and yet he is the ultimate benefactor because

"more than anything in the world, that picture has kept me in the public eye for 40 years."

Tittle's Hall of Fame career is more than a single snap-shot: 33,070 passing yards over 17 professional seasons

with the Colts, 49ers and Giants, 242 touchdowns, three consecutive division championships with the Giants, two league MVP sea-sons, two years with 30-plus touchdown passes, one famous photo and no regrets.

LEN DAWSON

Teams, seasons:
Pittsburgh Steelers, 1957-59; Cleveland Browns, 1960-61; Dallas Texans, 1962; Kansas City Chiefs, 1963-75

Height: 6-0

Weight: 190

Born: 6-20-35

College: Purdue

Championship teams:
1962, '66, '69 seasons

Career passing yards/TDs:
28,711/239

ften overlooked—because of the highly physical and downright brutal conditions that are at the essence of pro football—is the dominant influence of poise and intelligence. Brainpower is a significant factor in winning games and championships.

After five bench-riding seasons with Pittsburgh and Cleveland, Len Dawson finally was allowed to show how a brain can prevail over brawn in 1962 when he joined the AFL Dallas Texans and another great mind, coach Hank Stram. In eight of the

next 14 seasons, including six straight from 1964 through 1969, Dawson charted his path to the Hall of Fame with the best completion percentage in the league.

Dawson knew the limitations of his dimensions and his arm. He recognized his best assets were standing next to him in the huddle, and his role was to maximize their talents with his less measurable and intangible qualities. "I was a thinking type of quarterback," Dawson said, "not necessarily a

muscle guy who can throw the ball through a wall."

Dawson was the league MVP in 1962 while guiding the Texans/Chiefs franchise to the first of three AFL championships. In Super Bowl 4, Dawson's accuracy was on display; he completed 12 of 17 passes and earned MVP honors in the Chiefs' 23-7 victory. Statistically, his greatest day didn't produce any overwhelming math, but typically his precision and poise added up to a winner.

LEN DAWSON

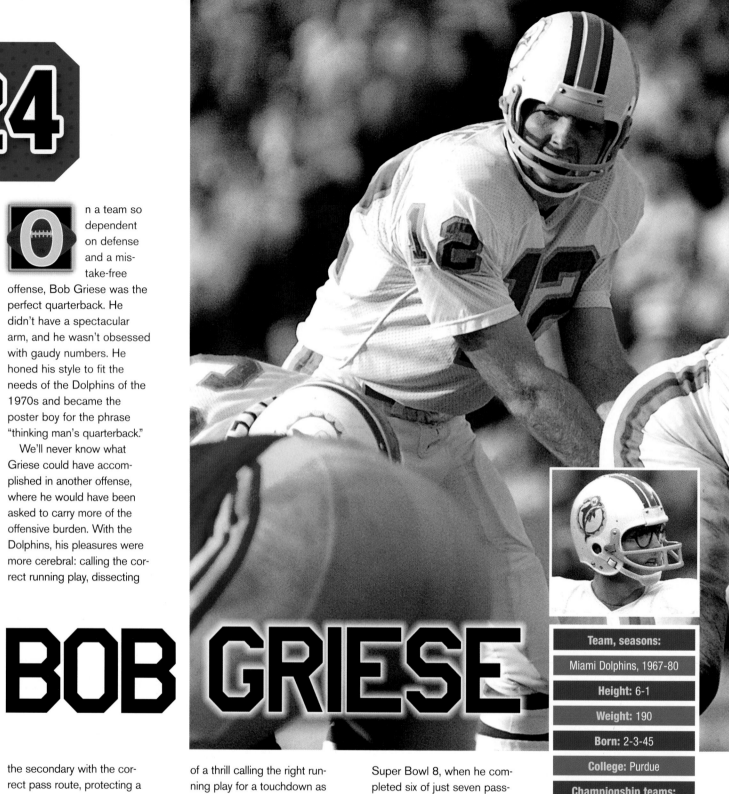

On a team so dependent on defense and a mistake-free offense, Bob Griese was the perfect quarterback. He didn't have a spectacular arm, and he wasn't obsessed with gaudy numbers. He honed his style to fit the needs of the Dolphins of the 1970s and became the poster boy for the phrase "thinking man's quarterback."

We'll never know what Griese could have accomplished in another offense, where he would have been asked to carry more of the offensive burden. With the Dolphins, his pleasures were more cerebral: calling the correct running play, dissecting

BOB GRIESE

Team, seasons:
Miami Dolphins, 1967-80
Height: 6-1
Weight: 190
Born: 2-3-45
College: Purdue
Championship teams:
1972, '73 seasons
Career passing yards/TDs:
25,092/192

the secondary with the correct pass route, protecting a lead with a long and methodical drive and making sure the ball was distributed with consistency among such playmakers as Larry Csonka, Jim Kiick, Paul Warfield and Mercury Morris.

"(Griese) is probably the most unselfish guy I've ever been around," coach Don Shula said. "He got as much

of a thrill calling the right running play for a touchdown as he did throwing a bomb. That's just his makeup."

Griese was a grump—curt and focused and incredibly intense. He didn't have the flamboyance of Joe Namath or some of his other peers. The playing field was his laboratory; the challenge was to keep his team on track. Never was his role more evident than in

Super Bowl 8, when he completed six of just seven passes; yet the Dolphins won their second consecutive title, 24-7, over the Vikings and completed a two-year run that included a 17-0 record in 1972—the last undefeated season in the NFL.

In 1980, Griese became the 14th quarterback to pass for 25,000 yards. Ironically, he sustained a shoulder injury

during the game in which he reached that milestone, forcing his retirement after the season. He was inducted into the Hall of Fame in 1990.

Broadway Joe. One of the great nicknames of all time. Say it out loud, and the image is unmistakable. Joe Namath in a full-length fur coat, blonde on each arm, heading into a New York nightclub for his version of in-season training. If you are searching for a player who helped turn the NFL into the money monster it has become, you don't need to go much beyond Namath, who developed into one of the first glamorous megastars of the modern era.

He had some game, too. His numbers don't reflect that in all categories—he was careless with his passes and took far too many low-percentage chances—but he was a naturally gifted athlete who, before a series of serious knee injuries, had special mobility. He starred under pressure; he relished the big moments when expectations were the highest. Few have that quality; it's also a major reason statistics are so meaningless sometimes. Certainly, the Baltimore Colts respect Namath and the way he guaranteed his Jets and the upstart AFL would win Super Bowl 3—and delivered, crafting one of the most brash and wonderful moments in sports history.

That supreme confidence led to Namath making millions of dollars in an era when even quarterbacks didn't pull down megasalaries. He signed with the Jets out of Alabama for a record $400,000, and succeeding contracts reflected his importance to the game. In 1967, he became the first quarterback to pass for more than 4,000 yards in a season, and he was the AFL's most valuable player in 1968. Who knows what else he could have achieved if his knees hadn't betrayed him? Still, he squeezed out 13 seasons and was inducted into the Hall of Fame in 1985.

The flamboyant Namath was always in the spotlight, whether throwing touchdown passes or making movies with the likes of Ann-Margret.

JOE NAMATH

Teams, seasons:	
New York Jets, 1965-76; Los Angeles Rams, 1977	
Height: 6-2	
Weight: 200	
Born: 5-31-43	
College: Alabama	
Championship teams:	
1968 season	
Career passing yards/TDs:	
27,663/173	

WARREN MOON

Teams, seasons:

Edmonton Eskimos (CFL) 1978-83; Houston Oilers, 1984-1993; Minnesota Vikings, 1994-96; Seattle Seahawks, 1997-98; Kansas City Chiefs, 1999-2000

Height: 6-3

Weight: 210

Born: 11-18-56

College: Washington

Championship teams:

None

Career passing yards/TDs:

49,325/291 (NFL)

Maybe it's useless to speculate but still, with Warren Moon, it's hard to resist. What would have happened if he had played his full career in the NFL? If he hadn't come along at a time when black quarterbacks were saddled with an unfair stigma: not good enough to start in the NFL? How much would he have achieved, spending six more years in the NFL instead of developing his talents in the Canadian Football League?

Of course, NFL coaches and general managers were wrong. Moon was good enough from Day 1 to compete in this league. Instead, he was undrafted and had to win five Grey Cups with the Edmonton Eskimos before getting a chance in the NFL. Here's how good Moon was: Despite spending six of his prime seasons in Canada, he retired among the top five NFL passers in four major career categories. He led the league in passing yards twice, in completions three times, in touchdowns once.

As the quarterback of the Houston Oilers' run-and-shoot offense, which disdained the running game and put the burden of winning on its quarterback, Moon was brilliant and durable. In 1991, he threw 655 passes. Later, with the Vikings, he attempted 601 and 606 in back-to-back seasons. That makes his career completion percentage of .584 all the more remarkable. That's a lot of passes for a lot of years.

Yet, despite 17 seasons of trying and all of his impressive statistics, Moon couldn't win an NFL championship. The most heartbreaking of his chances came in 1992. In an AFC wild-card game, the Oilers blew a 32-point lead, wasting a sensational first-half performance by Moon, to lose to the Bills in overtime, 41-38. After playing for the Vikings, he finished his career in Seattle and Kansas City.

GEORGE BLANDA  27

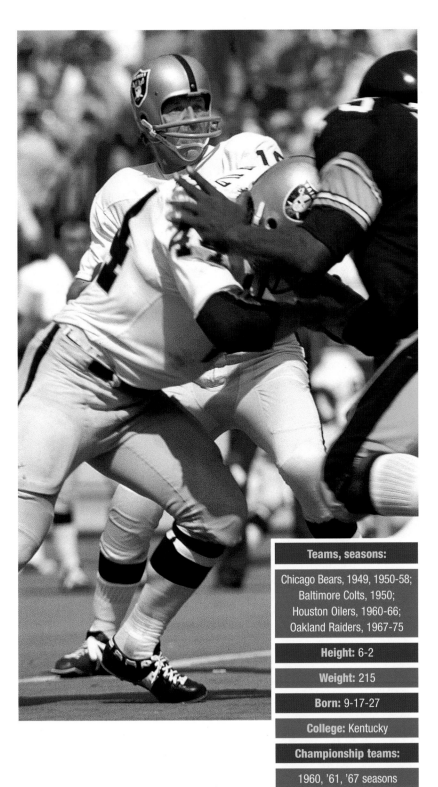

 George Blanda never got old; he just got better. During 26 incredible pro seasons, he threw 236 touchdown passes and posted 2,002 points as a kicker and quarterback. But the real legacy of George Blanda is the magic he created as an American folk hero who continued to deliver clutch performances in his fourth football decade, until the amazing age of 48.

Blanda was a scoring machine for 10 years as a Chicago Bears kicker, an icy competitor when he finally got his first call as a long-term starting quarterback and led Houston to championships in the AFL's first two seasons. Blanda fired 36 touchdown passes in 1961, a record-tying seven in one game. But nothing could match the dramatic impact Blanda brought to the Oakland

Raiders from 1967 until his 1975 retirement as the oldest player in football history.

In a magical 1970 season, at age 43, the Old Man came off the bench in five consecutive games to deliver a dramatic kick or touchdown pass that produced a win or tie. The heroics continued in subsequent seasons as the blazing blue eyes, protruding jaw and craggy face of No. 16 became a highlight film staple.

The former Kentucky star was a popular, sometimes-testy leader who played in a then-record 340 games, including one Super Bowl and 11 AFL/NFL championship games, in a career that produced 335 field goals, 943 extra points and 1,911 pass completions for 26,920 yards. Blanda was inducted into the Hall of Fame in 1981.

Teams, seasons:
Chicago Bears, 1949, 1950-58; Baltimore Colts, 1950; Houston Oilers, 1960-66; Oakland Raiders, 1967-75

Height: 6-2

Weight: 215

Born: 9-17-27

College: Kentucky

Championship teams:
1960, '61, '67 seasons

Career passing yards/TDs:
26,920/236

GEORGE BLANDA

From the Kentucky blue-grass of Morehead State to donning Giants blue, Phil Simms always wore his heart on his sleeve. He didn't have the most powerful arm or the most athletic body, but he knew how to win games as the leader of Bill Parcells' best New York teams.

Simms' defining moment was his near-perfect MVP performance in Super Bowl 21. The 1986 Giants were known for defense, but without Simms completing 22 of 25 passes for 268 yards and three touchdowns, they wouldn't have beaten John Elway's Broncos.

Even though Simms didn't have gaudy statistics—only one 4,000-yard season in 14 years—his small-town sensibility allowed him to thrive under the critical microscope of big-city media.

Team, seasons:		
New York Giants, 1979-93		
Height: 6-3		
Weight: 216		
Born: 11-3-54		
College: Morehead State		
Championship teams:		
1986, '90 seasons		
Career passing yards/TDs:		
33,462/199		

PHIL SIMMS

PHIL SIMMS

BOB WATERFIELD 29

Bob Waterfield was that rare NFL star who was known equally for whom he married and what he accomplished on the field. He was the high school sweetheart-turned-husband of actress Jane Russell, best known for her sizzling screen debut in *The Outlaw*.

Waterfield became a matinee idol in his own right by leading the Cleveland Rams to the NFL championship as a rookie while earning league MVP honors. That success continued after the franchise's move to Los Angeles, where the team advanced to three consecutive title games, culminating with another championship in 1951.

Waterfield pictured with actress/wife Jane Russell.

In a powerhouse offensive cast with fellow Hall of Famers Norm Van Brocklin, Elroy "Crazylegs" Hirsch and Tom Fears, Waterfield often found his name at the top of the marquee. He was a virtual superman–a talented quarterback-placekicker-punter-safety who gave new meaning to the concept of versatility–known for his big-play ability and poise under pressure.

Teams, seasons:
Cleveland/Los Angeles Rams, 1945-52
Height: 6-1
Weight: 200
Born: 7-26-20
Died: 3-25-83
College: UCLA
Championship teams:
1945, '51 seasons
Career passing yards/TDs:
11,849/97

30

Teams, seasons:

Brooklyn Dodgers, 1937-41; Boston Yanks, 1945; New York Yankees (AAFC), 1946

Height: 5-10

Weight: 178

Born: 5-17-12

College: Duke

Championship teams:

None

Career passing yards/TDs:

3,935/22

ACE PARKER

s a triple-threat halfback, punter, kicker, return man and ballhawking defender, Clarence "Ace" Parker helped turn a 7-year-old Brooklyn Dodgers franchise into a contender. He was neither fast nor athletically superior to the players he competed against. But he had the knack for making a perfect cut or throw and the playmaking instincts many star-quality players lacked.

Ironically, football was his destiny, not his choice. Parker preferred baseball, but a two-year average of .179 for the Philadelphia A's redirected his attention to football. The masterpiece season of his war-interrupted career was 1940, when he passed for 817 yards and 10 touchdowns, scored five TDs and led the Dodgers to an 8-3 record en route to league MVP honors.

Parker, who was inducted into the Pro Football Hall of Fame in 1972, led the AAFC's New York Yankees to a division title in 1946, his final professional season. The Yankees lost in the championship game to powerful Cleveland.

KEN STABLER

31

en Stabler's name forever will be linked to the "Holy Roller" play against San Diego, in which his forward fumble led to a game-winning touchdown and an NFL rulebook change. But Stabler's passing proficiency and success are equal parts of his legacy.

"The Snake" led Oakland to five consecutive AFC title games in the '70s and one Super Bowl victory, compensating for his mediocre arm with his ability to read coverages and hit the open receiver.

Former Raiders coach John Madden, in the book *Raiders Forever*, credits Stabler's cool demeanor as another key to his success, citing a double-overtime playoff win over Baltimore in 1977:

"It was during the sixth period, and we had the ball in scoring range when I called timeout. Ken came over and had his helmet tilted on the back of his head, and I was carrying on and blubbering, and he says to me, 'You know what, John?' and I'm thinking he's going to suggest a play, and I said, 'What, Kenny?' He said, 'These fans are sure getting their money's worth,' and then goes back out on the field and throws a touchdown pass to (Dave) Casper. He never let the excitement affect him. He probably tuned me out."

KEN STABLER

32

JOE THEISMANN

Teams, seasons:		
Toronto Argonauts (CFL), 1971-74; Washington Redskins, 1974-85		
Height: 6-0		
Weight: 192		
Born: 9-9-49		
College: Notre Dame		
Championship teams:		
1982 season		
Career passing yards/TDs:		
25,206/160		

JOE THEISMANN

When Joe Theismann arrived in Washington, he was the odd-man out in a three-man quarterback rotation with Redskins legends Billy Kilmer and Sonny Jurgensen. Despite that rocky beginning, Theismann's characteristic determination won out and helped him become a star.

Theismann, runner-up for the 1971 Heisman Trophy, was drafted by the Dolphins but became embroiled in a contract dispute and opted to play three seasons for the Toronto Argonauts of the CFL. After Washington traded for his rights in '74, Theismann waited his turn and even volunteered to return punts.

Soon, however, Theismann seized the quarterback reins and began carving out a prolific career. He led the Redskins to victory over the Dolphins in Super Bowl 17. The next season, 1983, he directed the powerful Redskins to a 14-2 record and then-NFL record 541 points, won league MVP honors and played in another Super Bowl, where his team was upset by the Raiders.

Although his career was cut short when Giants linebacker Lawrence Taylor broke his leg in 1985, Theismann still holds Redskins records for career passing yards (25,206), completions (2,044), attempts (3,602) and most consecutive passes without an interception (162).

A decade before Donovan McNabb brought his dual-threat talents to Philadelphia, Randall Cunningham dazzled Eagles fans as a perpetual playmaker—both in and out of the pocket. Whether it was with his strong arm or his active legs, Cunningham always was confident going downfield.

He reached elite status in 1988, and his rise culminated with 407 yards passing in the "Fog Bowl" playoff game at Chicago's Soldier Field. In 1990, he put together one of the best all-around seasons ever—30 touchdown passes and 942 yards rushing.

When his Eagles career ended in 1995, Cunningham left the league for a year and started his second career—in the granite industry. But with a change of heart and renewed interest in the game, he returned when the Vikings gambled that he had a strong third career left in him.

He rewarded Minnesota with a magical season in '98, posting a lofty 106.0 quarterback rating while leading the team to a 15-1 record, an NFL-record 556 points and a berth in the NFC championship game.

Teams, seasons:

Philadelphia Eagles, 1985-95;
Minnesota Vikings, 1997-99;
Dallas Cowboys, 2000;
Baltimore Ravens, 2001

Height: 6-4

Weight: 212

Born: 3-27-63

College: UNLV

Championship teams:

None

Career passing yards/TDs:

29,979/207

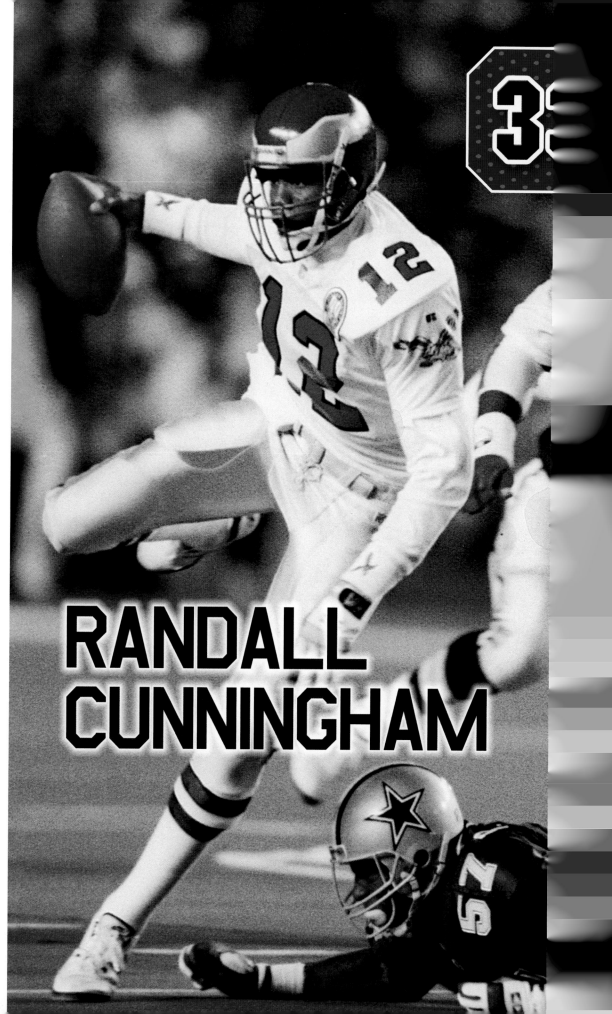

RANDALL CUNNINGHAM

34

DARYLE LAMONICA

Nicknamed "The Mad Bomber," Daryle Lamonica had a knack for big plays and deep throws that helped him make a name for himself with the Bills and Raiders. Lamonica was drafted by the NFL's Packers in the 12th round but signed with the AFL's Bills as a 24th-round pick. Instead of chafing over the prospect of being Jack Kemp's backup, Lamonica complemented Kemp, regularly coming up with clutch plays to help the Bills win AFL titles in 1964 and '65.

Just when Lamonica was set to become a starter, he was traded to Oakland. He says it was a touchdown pass he threw under pressure in a 1964 victory over the Raiders that convinced Al Davis to acquire him: "(Defensive tackle Ben) Davidson really unloaded on me. I was told later that when Al Davis saw me take the hit and get up on one knee to see if the pass was completed, he wanted to get me as a quarterback."

In his first season with the Raiders, Lamonica fueled the team's passing game, throwing for 3,228 yards and 30 touchdowns to lead Oakland to Super Bowl 2. He matched those statistics in each of the next two seasons.

A five-time Pro Bowl selection, Lamonica also is remembered for his role in the infamous Heidi game in 1968. Viewers missed seeing the Raiders' comeback victory over the Jets, fueled by Lamonica's four touchdown passes, because NBC switched to its scheduled program, the movie *Heidi*.

Teams, seasons:		
Buffalo Bills, 1963-66; Oakland Raiders, 1967-74		
Height: 6-3		
Weight: 215		
Born: 7-17-41		
College: Notre Dame		
Championship teams:		
1964, '65 seasons		
Career passing yards/TDs:		
19,154/164		

Boomer Esiason, a second-round pick from Maryland in 1984, gave the NFL a different look. Esiason's strong left arm and flowing blond hair could have been a good fit for Hollywood, but he settled in to the less glitzy lifestyle of Cincinnati.

Esiason earned his first Pro Bowl bid while leading the NFL's most productive offense in 1986. In '88, he led the NFL with a 97.4 passer rating and guided the Bengals to Super Bowl 23, where they were beaten by the 49ers on Joe Montana's last-minute TD pass to John Taylor.

Traded to the Jets in 1993, Esiason earned a fourth Pro Bowl selection and in three New York seasons climbed to fourth on the franchise's career passing yardage list (he still ranks fifth). After playing a year in Arizona, he returned to Cincinnati, where he ended his career with 2,969 completions on 5,205 pass attempts (57 percent) for 37,920 yards and 247 touchdowns.

Now a TV/radio analyst, Esiason also is known for his fundraising work in the fight to cure cystic fibrosis.

BOOMER ESIASON

Teams, seasons:
Cincinnati Bengals, 1984-92, 1997; New York Jets, 1993-95; Arizona Cardinals, 1996
Height: 6-5
Weight: 224
Born: 4-17-61
College: Maryland
Championship teams:
None
Career passing yards/TDs:
37,920/247

BOOMER ESIASON

36 KEN ANDERSON

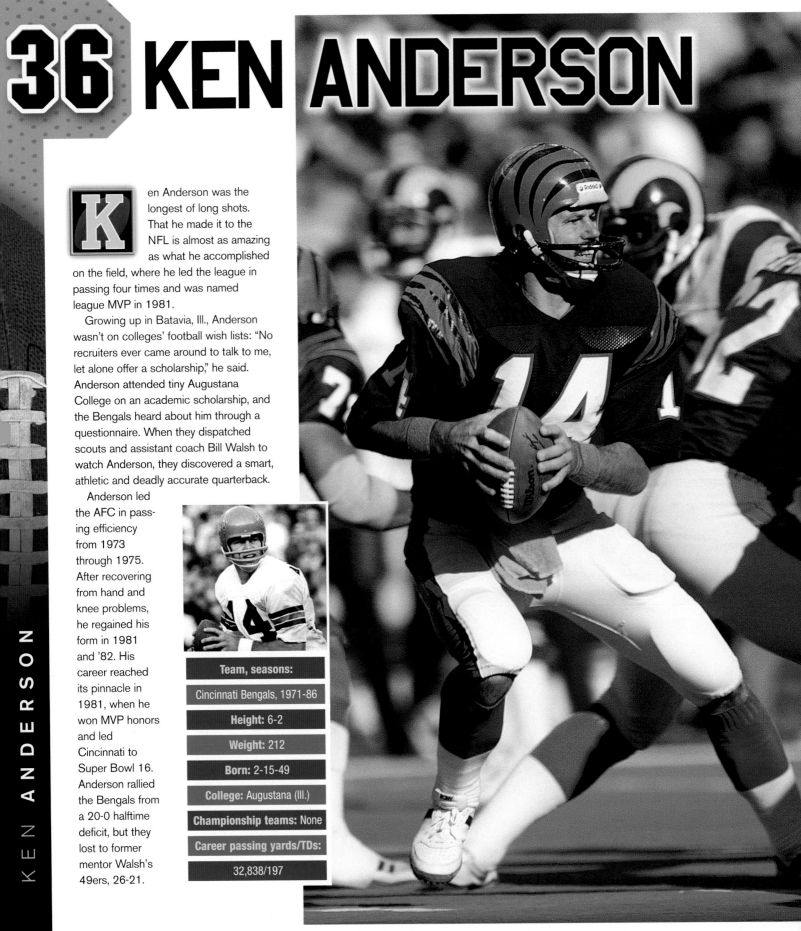

 en Anderson was the longest of long shots. That he made it to the NFL is almost as amazing as what he accomplished on the field, where he led the league in passing four times and was named league MVP in 1981.

Growing up in Batavia, Ill., Anderson wasn't on colleges' football wish lists: "No recruiters ever came around to talk to me, let alone offer a scholarship," he said. Anderson attended tiny Augustana College on an academic scholarship, and the Bengals heard about him through a questionnaire. When they dispatched scouts and assistant coach Bill Walsh to watch Anderson, they discovered a smart, athletic and deadly accurate quarterback.

Anderson led the AFC in passing efficiency from 1973 through 1975. After recovering from hand and knee problems, he regained his form in 1981 and '82. His career reached its pinnacle in 1981, when he won MVP honors and led Cincinnati to Super Bowl 16. Anderson rallied the Bengals from a 20-0 halftime deficit, but they lost to former mentor Walsh's 49ers, 26-21.

Team, seasons:		
Cincinnati Bengals, 1971-86		
Height: 6-2		
Weight: 212		
Born: 2-15-49		
College: Augustana (Ill.)		
Championship teams: None		
Career passing yards/TDs:		
32,838/197		

ARNIE HERBER

 t was almost predestined that Arnie Herber would be a Packer. He was born in Green Bay and was a football star at the city's West High School. He sold programs at Packers games as a teenager and later worked as a handyman in the Packers' clubhouse.

One day, coach Curly Lambeau–who left few stones unturned in his search for talent–gave the 20-year-old kid a tryout. Impressed by what he saw, Lambeau signed Herber to a contract calling for $75 a game. In the Packers' long, storied history, the club has made few better investments.

Herber helped the Packers win four NFL championships in the 1930s and earned three passing titles in his 13 professional seasons. Herber, who played eight years without a helmet, is considered by many to be pro football's first great downfield passer–a distinction often bestowed on Sammy Baugh.

Herber was part of the NFL's first great passing combination–he was the first quarterback for Hall of Fame receiver Don Hutson. Herber also was an accomplished runner, defensive back and punter.

Teams, seasons:		
Green Bay Packers, 1930-40; New York Giants, 1944-45		
Height: 5-11		
Weight: 203		
Born: 4-2-10		
Died: 10-14-69		
College: Wisconsin, Regis		
Championship teams:		
1930, '31, '36, '39 seasons		
Career passing yards/TDs:		
8,041/81		

38 JOHN HADL

Teams, seasons:

San Diego Chargers, 1962-72;
Los Angeles Rams, 1973-74;
Green Bay Packers, 1974-75;
Houston Oilers, 1976-77

Height: 6-1

Weight: 214

Born: 2-15-40

College: Kansas

Championship teams:

1963 season

Career passing yards/TDs:

33,503/244

or more than half of his 16 NFL seasons, John Hadl guided San Diego coach Sid Gillman's prolific aerial assault of the 1960s and early '70s. Hadl, an All-American at Kansas, was a key component in the offense that helped take professional football "vertical" and the quarterback who helped turn Lance Alworth into a Hall of Fame wide receiver.

Alworth was Hadl's go-to receiver for nine outstanding seasons, and it was that combination that sparked San Diego's 1963 AFL championship and the Chargers' run to two more title games. Hadl's best statistical season was 1968, when he led the AFL in passing attempts (440), completions (208), yardage (3,473) and touchdowns (27)—categories he also led three years later after the AFL/NFL merger.

After a brief stopover in Los Angeles, Hadl was traded midway through the 1974 season to Green Bay, where coach Dan Devine, who had followed Hadl since high school, was shopping for an experienced quarterback. Following his playing days, Hadl went into coaching. One of his stops was Denver, where he coached John Elway in his rookie season.

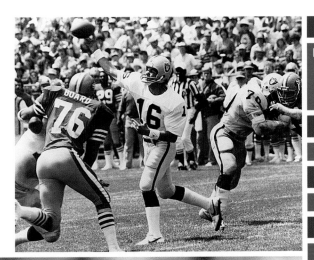

Teams, seasons:
New England Patriots, 1971-75; San Francisco 49ers, 1976-77; Oakland/Los Angeles Raiders, 1979-86
Height: 6-3
Weight: 220
Born: 12-5-47
College: Stanford
Championship teams:
1980, '83 seasons
Career passing yards/TDs:
25,882/164

As a child, Jim Plunkett overcame the obstacles of having a mother who was totally blind and a father who was legally blind to become a standout five-sport athlete in high school. Then, after having a benign tumor (first feared to be cancerous) removed from his neck before his freshman year at Stanford, Plunkett went on to become the Cardinal's only Heisman Trophy winner.

Plunkett, the first pick in the 1971 draft, bounced around for a decade before landing in Oakland. He didn't play a down in 1978 and threw just 15 passes the following year while backing up Ken Stabler.

Plunkett's NFL career really took off in 1980. In the fifth game that year, Oakland's starting quarterback, Dan Pastorini, suffered a broken leg and Plunkett stepped in and led the Raiders to victory in 13 of their next 15 games. He capped his memorable season with three touchdown passes in a 27-10 victory over the Eagles in Super Bowl 15.

"They said Jim didn't have it anymore," Raiders wide receiver Cliff

JIM PLUNKETT

Branch said. "But all he needed was good people around him."

Plunkett didn't stop there. In 1983, he passed for 2,935 yards and 20 touchdowns and led the Raiders to another Super Bowl. He connected with Branch on a 12-yard TD strike in the Raiders' 38-9 win over Washington.

JIM PLUNKETT

40

T he telltale sign of a great player is that opposing coaches devise game plans around him. When Patriots coach Bill Belichick and his staff put together their defensive plan to contain the Eagles before Super Bowl 39, Donovan McNabb was the focus.

Game-planning McNabb, a five-time Pro Bowl selection, is one of the most challenging tasks a defensive staff will encounter because of his ability to beat opponents with his arm or legs. McNabb, one of the finest scrambling quarterbacks in football, took his

DONOVAN McNABB

game to a new level in 2004 when he completed 64 percent of his passes, a significant improvement over his career mark of 57 percent. The arrival of Terrell Owens, one of the NFL's most gifted receivers, aided in that accuracy bump, but much of it can be attributed to McNabb's maturation as a quarterback.

"Now, he reminds me of Steve Young," said Panthers safety Mike Minter. "I remember my rookie year playing against San Francisco on a Monday night. I don't think a pass ever touched the ground. That's how Donovan is getting. He understands the West Coast offense to a T. He has it down pat."

Staying in the same offense for his entire career has benefited McNabb, who took the Eagles to four consecutive NFC championship games and the one Super Bowl from

Team, seasons:		
Philadelphia Eagles, 1999-present		
Height: 6-2		
Weight: 240		
Born: 11-25-76		
College: Syracuse		
Championships teams:		
None		
Career passing yards/TDs:		
16,926/118 (through 2004)		

2001-04. McNabb wins consistently because he rarely makes mistakes—his 2.20 career interception percentage was the lowest among active quarterbacks with 1,500 attempts through the

2004 season—and because he is a great leader.

McNabb, who boasted a career winning percentage of .709 through 2004, has turned boos to cheers in the toughest of sports towns.

JOHN BRODIE 41

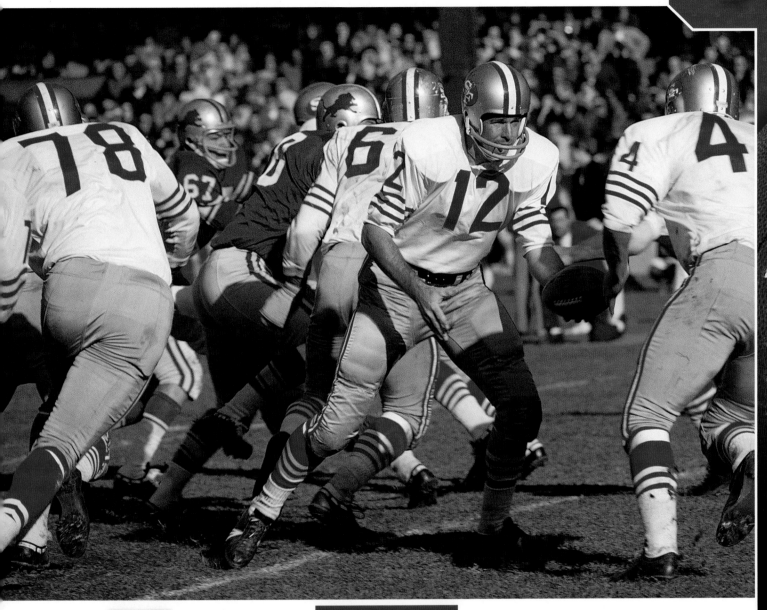

 he 49ers have been fortunate to have a rich history of passers for half a century, but none of their quarterbacks have worn the cardinal and gold longer than John Brodie's 17 years. Brodie began his NFL career as the backup to Hall of Famer Y.A. Tittle; a half century later, his passing numbers, 31,548 yards and 214 touchdowns, still rank second in team history behind Hall of Famer Joe Montana.

Like another 49ers Hall of Famer,

Team, seasons:		
San Francisco 49ers, 1957-73		
Height: 6-1		
Weight: 198		
Born: 8-14-35		
College: Stanford		
Championship teams:		
None		
Career passing yards/TDs:		
31,548/214		

Steve Young, Brodie had his best years in his 30s. In 1965, he enjoyed his finest individual season with a league-leading 3,112 yards and 30 touchdown passes.

He won a league MVP award in 1970 when he passed for an NFL-high 2,941 yards and 24 TDs while guiding the 49ers to the first of back-to-back NFC championship game appearances. Eight of his 10 career 2,000-yard passing seasons came consecutively from 1964 through 1971.

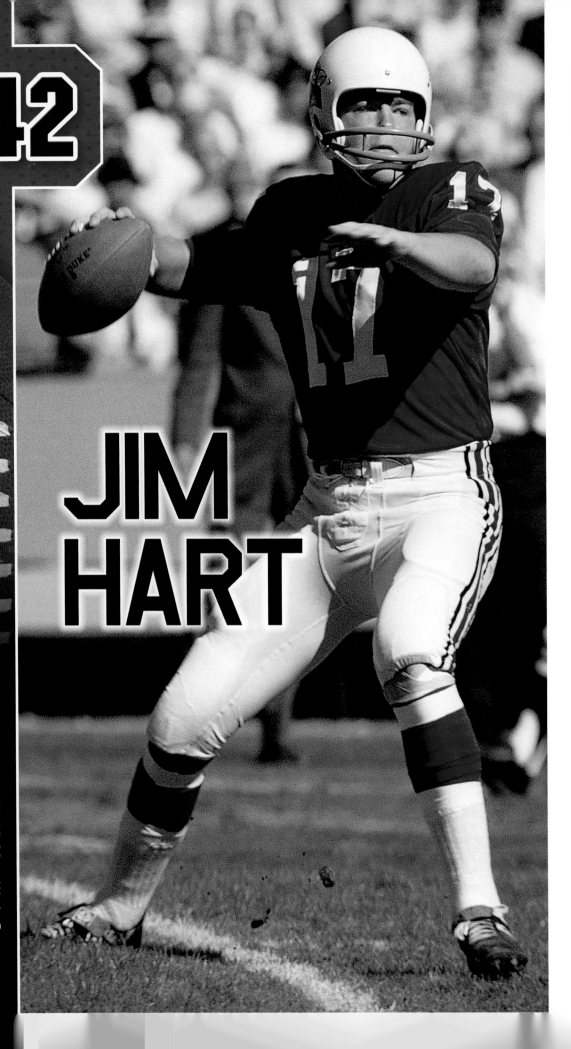

42

JIM HART

Although he wasn't selected in the NFL draft following his senior season at Southern Illinois University, Jim Hart went on to become the longest-tenured player in Cardinals franchise history, leading the club in 18 of its 28 years in St. Louis. In 1967, when incumbent Charley Johnson was drafted into military service, Hart stepped up and eventually guided the club to back-to-back playoff appearances in 1974 and '75.

Hart owns (with receiver Ahmad Rashad) the NFL record for the longest non-scoring pass in league history–98 yards–and he was selected NFC Player of the Year in 1974 after directing the "Air Coryell" Cards to the NFC East title and the team's first postseason appearance in 27 years.

Hart, who was named to four Pro Bowls, still ranks among the top 20 all-time in passing yardage (34,665). Hart, a three-time team MVP, was awarded the NFLPA's Byron "Whizzer" White Humanitarian Award in '76.

Teams, seasons:
St. Louis Cardinals, 1966-83; Washington Redskins, 1984
Height: 6-1
Weight: 215
Born: 4-29-44
College: Southern Illinois
Championship teams:
None
Career passing yards/TDs:
34,665/209

CHARLIE CONERLY

Team, seasons:
New York Giants, 1948-61
Height: 6-0
Weight: 184
Born: 9-19-21
Died: 2-13-96
College: Mississippi
Championship teams:
1956 season
Career passing yards/TDs:
19,488/173

Wherever he played, Charlie Conerly blazed a trail. He played two seasons at tailback for Ole Miss before serving three years in the Marines during World War II. After returning to school, he played quarterback in the new T-formation offense. The man later dubbed "Chuckin' Charlie" set a school record for touchdown passes in a season and finished fourth in the Heisman voting as a senior in 1947.

Conerly was drafted by the Redskins while in the Marines but was traded to the Giants in 1948. The deal paid off quickly as Conerly passed for 2,175 yards and 22 touchdowns. As a quiet but effective leader, he guided the Giants to four title games, including a 47-7 NFL championship win over the Bears in '56. He is one of 11 Giants players to have his number retired.

He set numerous team records that stood more than 30 years and eventually were broken by Phil Simms.

CHARLIE CONERLY

44 PADDY DRISCOLL

lthough he garnered notice during his playing days at Northwestern and his brief pro baseball stint with the Cubs, John "Paddy" Driscoll truly began making his mark on the Chicago sports scene in 1920, when the Chicago Cardinals hired him for $300 per game, a big-money deal at the time.

The Driscoll investment paid off nicely: Not only did he double as player/coach in his first three seasons and lead the Cardinals to a championship in 1925, he was a drawing card for fans and helped elevate football's status at a time it was searching for its niche. Driscoll finished his Hall of Fame career with the rival Chicago Bears after being traded in 1926.

A gifted quarterback and tailback, Driscoll also was football's first great kicker. He drop-kicked two 50-yard field goals in his career and possessed remarkable accuracy as a punter—a feat that earned him his share of scorn during a 1925 game. With 36,000 fans gathered for Red Grange's pro debut, Driscoll repeatedly punted away from Grange. Driscoll's reasoning was simple: "I decided if one of us was going to look bad, it wasn't going to be me. Punting to Grange is like grooving a pitch to Babe Ruth."

Team, seasons:	
Chicago Cardinals, 1920-25; Chicago Bears, 1926-29	
Height: 5-11	
Weight: 160	
Born: 1-11-1895	
Died: 6-28-68	
College: Northwestern	
Championship teams:	
1925 season	
Career rushing/passing TDs:	
25/16	

45

t the NFL Scouting Combine in 1999, then-Saints coach Mike Ditka sat down to interview a prospect from Central Florida University, looked him in the eye and said, "I'm going to make you a tight end."

One can only imagine the circuitous route Daunte Culpepper's career might have taken if Ditka had wrapped his paws around him. Instead, Culpepper was drafted by the Vikings to play quarterback. And now it looks like his road is headed toward Canton.

Culpepper is strong of arm. In a 2000 game against Buffalo, he rolled to his right and threw back across his body, hitting Randy Moss in the back of the end zone. The play covered 39 yards, but the pass traveled at least 60. Culpepper also is mobile. He can move around in the pocket and avoid the rush until he finds an open receiver—or take off running if he can't. He is deceptively fast. Once, at the end of practice, he beat Moss in a sprint.

But what really makes him different is his size. You don't see many 6-4, 264-pound quarterbacks. And that XL frame can deliver punishment as well as absorb it. On an 8-yard scoring run that capped a 20-16 comeback win over the Bucs in 2001, Culpepper crashed into linebackers Derrick Brooks and Shelton Quarles. Only one player got up right away. The quarterback.

Had it not been for record-setting Colts quarterback Peyton Manning, Culpepper might have been the NFL's MVP in 2004. He completed 379-of-548 passes for 4,717 yards and 39 touchdowns, with only 11 interceptions. And he became the first quarterback in league history to throw five touchdown passes in three different games in one season. Culpepper completed 69.2 percent of his passes—falling just short of Ken Anderson's single-season record of 70.6—and his 110.9 passer rating was the fourth highest of all time.

As a tight end, Culpepper probably could have been pretty good. As a quarterback, he has been extraordinary.

Team, seasons:		
Minnesota Vikings, 1999-present		
Height: 6-4		
Weight: 264		
Born: 1-28-77		
College: Central Florida		
Championship teams:		
None		
Career passing yards/TDs:		
18,598/129 (through 2004)		

DAUNTE CULPEPPER

PRO FOOTBALL'S GREATEST QUARTERBACKS

46

DUTCH CLARK

arl "Dutch" Clark was a jack-of-all-trades and a master of most. Kordell Stewart once was hyped as the ultimate "slash" threat, but he had nothing on Clark, a charter member of the Hall of Fame.

Clark was a tremendous threat running, an adept defensive back and an accurate drop-kicker. He also was no slouch as a quarterback, leading the Lions' famed "Infantry Attack" and completing 45.6 percent of his passes en route to three NFL scoring titles.

Clark's teams had their share of talent, but there was no doubt he was the leader. "If Clark stepped on the field with (Red) Grange, (Jim) Thorpe and (George) Gipp," former college coaching great Clark Shaughnessy once said, "he would be the general."

DUTCH CLARK

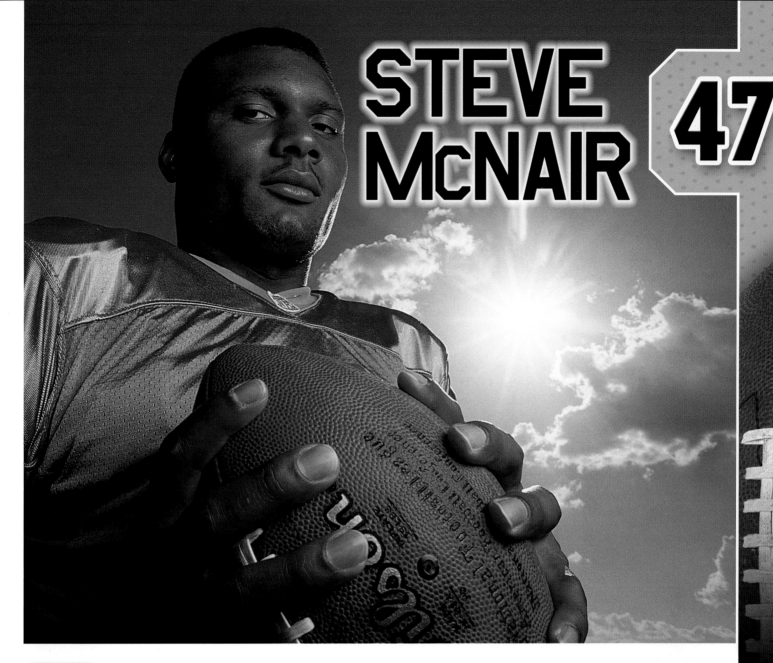

STEVE McNAIR 47

teve McNair is a warrior's warrior. During the season, he seldom wakes up without a body part—or parts—throbbing. He fights through the pain, digs deep and leaves everything he has on the field, inspiring both his teammates and the Titans faithful.

The injuries that have cost him considerable practice time over the years have not subdued his desire for game participation. From 1997 through 2003, he missed only nine of a possible 112 regular-season starts—and five of those

resulted from back surgery. He could have played in several others if they had been important games. Case in point: He never missed a postseason start.

In 2003, McNair shared MVP honors with Peyton Manning while leading the Titans to the playoffs for the fourth time. In '04, however, he battled through his toughest season, sidelined for half the games by a bruised sternum while the Titans fell to 5-11, the franchise's worst record since 1994.

Injuries have diminished the glossiness of his statistics and chances for a long

career, but numbers are not the marks of McNair anyway. As other quarterbacks pile up stats, McNair piles up hits while passing, running and leading—all in pursuit of victory. Few have played this position with the relentless fight of this Titan.

Team, seasons:		
Houston Oilers/ Tennessee Titans, 1995-present		
Height: 6-2		
Weight: 235		
Born: 2-14-73		
College: Alcorn State		
Championship teams:		
None		
Career passing yards/TDs:		
23,980/140 (through 2004)		

STEVE McNAIR

48

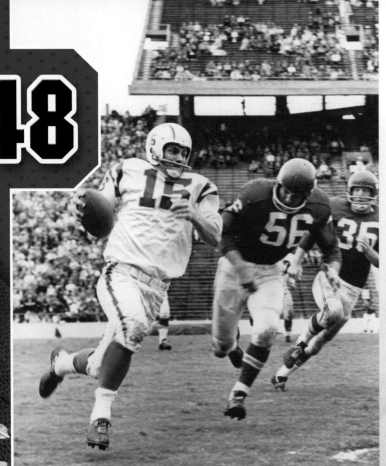

JACK KEMP

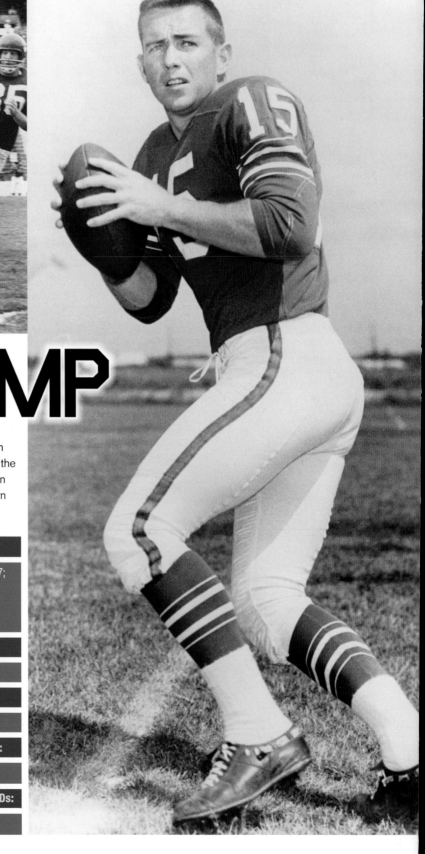

 hen the Bills claimed Jack Kemp on waivers from the Chargers at midseason in 1962, it changed the fate of his career and the city of Buffalo. The man who had grown up and played in sunny Southern California all his life quickly became the pride of wintry western New York.

Kemp showed great athleticism for the position, but his trademark was on-field leadership. He led the Bills to back-to-back AFL championships in 1964 and '65, winning MVP honors the latter season. He was a steady star in the fledgling league's decade of existence and was the first AFL quarterback to pass for more than 3,000 yards.

After pro football, Kemp represented the Buffalo region in the U.S. House of Representatives from 1971-89 before serving as Housing Secretary for President George H.W. Bush from 1989-93. Kemp was Republican presidential nominee Bob Dole's vice presidential running mate in '96.

Teams, seasons:
Pittsburgh Steelers, 1957; Los Angeles/San Diego Chargers, 1960-62; Buffalo Bills, 1962-69
Height: 6-1
Weight: 201
Born: 7-13-35
College: Occidental
Championship teams:
1964, '65 seasons
Career passing yards/TDs:
21,218/114

BENNY FRIEDMAN

 During an era when completing 35 percent of passes qualified as good, Benny Friedman once connected on an extraordinary 52.5 percent of his throws. When Friedman, a two-time All-American at Michigan, turned pro, he was greeted with fanfare that was exceeded only by the media attention given Red Grange a few years earlier. Friedman made such a dramatic impact on pro football—he was all-pro in his first four seasons—that Giants owner Tim Mara purchased the Detroit franchise in 1928 so he could get Friedman.

Friedman could run, kick and, most important, pass the ball better than any player who preceded him and most who followed. In 1928, he led the NFL in rushing touchdowns and touchdown passes; no other player has accomplished that. His 20 touchdown passes in 1929 stood as an NFL record for years.

Friedman, who retired after the 1934 season with Brooklyn, was elected to the Hall of Fame in 2005.

Teams, seasons:
Cleveland Bulldogs, 1927; Detroit Wolverines, 1928; New York Giants, 1929-31; Brooklyn Dodgers, 1932-34
Height: 5-10
Weight: 183
Born: 3-18-05 **Died:** 11-23-82
College: Michigan
Championship teams:
None
Career Passing yards/TDs:
929 (1932-34)/66

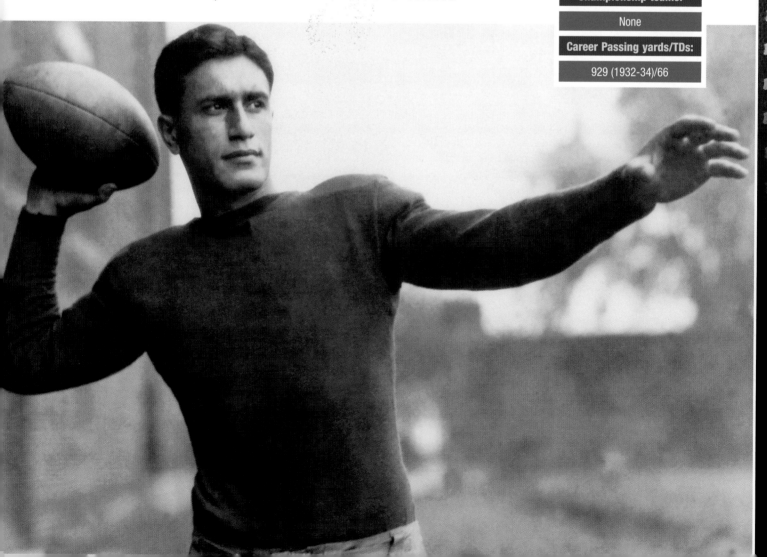

BENNY FRIEDMAN

ARCHIE MANNING

et's do it," said Peyton Manning to his brother Eli. Eli nodded. They approached each other grimly. "OK," said Peyton. "Turn around." Eli obeyed. They stood back to back.

"So who's taller?" Peyton asked. Eli stood on his toes. "Now, don't you do that," said Peyton.

Eli stopped. They settled down. It was 6-5 Peyton by half an inch. No question.

"See, I knew I still have you," said the older brother, triumph in his voice.

Some things in the pecking order of brothers never change, even if you are Peyton Manning, maybe the best player in the NFL, and Eli Manning, the No. 1 choice in the 2004 NFL draft. Eli might be the better basketball player and might be able to fling a Nerf Vortex football 15 yards farther ("I destroyed him," said Eli proudly). But he still is younger and smaller.

Eli also is the last of the fabulous Manning boys, the final star in the

Teams, seasons:
New Orleans Saints, 1971-82; Houston Oilers, 1982-83; Minnesota Vikings, 1983-84
Height: 6-3
Weight: 212
Born: 5-19-49
College: Mississippi
Championship teams: None
Career passing yards/TDs:
23,911/125

ARCHIE MANNING

...THE PATRIARCH OF THE NFL'S FIRST FAMILY

most remarkable family in the history of pro football. We've never seen anything like this: father Archie, second pick in the 1971 draft by the Saints before embarking on a highly lauded and heroic 15-year career; middle son Peyton, the first choice in the 1998 draft and the 2004 league MVP; and youngest son Eli, the second-most popular player in Ole Miss history behind—who else?—his dad.

Every one a quarterback—all gifted, intelligent and, dare we say in this era of hard edges and bad-boy personas, nice. Their father could be the best-liked person to ever play the game, and his sons are a mixture of politeness and respect that masks a marked determination that characterizes seemingly everything a Manning undertakes.

They get it in a way so many of their peers don't.

Think about it. Name another son of a former NFL star who has been as successful as Peyton—and consider this family now boasts of two players selected first in the draft. These Mannings are a refreshingly grand and classy bunch, close and loving and happy, devoid of psychological scars and blood feuds, strong enough to remain grounded amid ungodly fame and, yes, fortune. "They are the DiMaggios of the NFL," said Ole Miss chancellor Robert Khayat, once a kicker with the

A Manning reunion was enjoyed by all in 2004 when Eli (holding the jersey) was drafted first overall by San Diego and traded to the New York Giants. Lending support were (left to right) Peyton, mother Olivia and father Archie.

Redskins.

"It's mind-boggling, almost unfathomable," said former Packers general manager Ron Wolf, who scouted Archie at Ole Miss and Peyton at Tennessee. "Just consider how hard it is to play quarterback in this league, and you have two brothers this talented. And Archie—he was a really terrific player who got stuck on some really bad teams."

It is also a family that is not blind to reality. When Archie and Eli looked at the 2004 draft, they saw the Chargers at No. 1 and balked. This was a loser of a franchise, with a history of bad personnel decisions and too many coaching

changes. They knew the Giants were extremely interested. New York or San Diego? In their mind, it was a no-brainer. It had to be the Giants. So Archie told Chargers general manager A.J. Smith that Eli did not want to play in San Diego. His confession churned a storm of controversy that possibly only the Manning family could have survived.

Eli and his dad were criticized severely for trying to maneuver the draft, as if they had surrendered their right to seek work in the environment of their choice. They were called greedy and self-centered, but they never wavered.

And neither did Smith. He chose Eli with the first pick, then quickly traded him to the Giants. Everyone wound up happy, just as Archie had hoped.

t was Eli's private pro day. NFL personnel men and head coaches gathered within the Saints' indoor facility. In many ways, what they saw was a clone of Peyton—nearly the same height, at 222 just eight or so pounds lighter, with strikingly similar mechanics and mannerisms. On that day, his passes were crisp and tight, accurate and consistent. But it was an unnecessary exercise; teams like the Chargers, Raiders and Giants, all possessing top-five picks, would learn much more in private meetings with Eli and by watching tapes of his development at Ole Miss, particularly his senior season, when the Rebels, with less-than-elite talent, won 10 games—and a New Year's Day bowl game for the first time in 34 years—and Eli became Peyton-like in his effective use of check-offs and audibles. "He's more athletic than Peyton," said John Dorsey, the Packers' director

'The family is undefeated ... Look what they already have done for college and pro football; they represent everything good about the sport.' –Ernie Accorsi

of college scouting who watched the workout with coach Mike Sherman. "He has better feet, but he is not as cerebral coming to the line as Peyton. But Eli can make all the throws; his arm is alive; he is smart, and he is a Manning."

And something else, too. "The family is undefeated," said Giants general manager Ernie Accorsi. "He comes from a wonderful family of achievers. Everything they do is excellent. Look what they already have done for college and pro football; they represent everything good about our sport. And their humility in this era is so refreshing."

Peyton attended the workout. He was in town for older brother Cooper's 30th birthday party. The quick-witted Cooper, now a successful institutional broker in New Orleans, was an Ole Miss wide receiver with pro potential before a congenital back condition forced him to give up football. The injury hit the family hard, particularly Peyton, who is almost two years younger and still idolizes Cooper. Peyton was in high school when Cooper stopped playing and immediately began wearing his brother's old number, 18, which also was his dad's at Ole Miss. Eli, five years younger than Peyton, also wore the uniform number in high school. All three brothers, who are strikingly similar Huck Finns with varying shades of red hair, attended

Newman, a private high school in New Orleans, and all three played quarterback there (Cooper only briefly); the school retired No. 18 as part of its 100th anniversary celebration.

Eli is not Peyton. It's an inevitable comparison, one they understand but don't particularly enjoy. Nor is it fair. If fans expect another Peyton, they'll be sorely disappointed, and not because Eli is incapable of becoming an NFL star. But Peyton has one of the most intriguing personalities in sports. He is consumed with football to the point of obsession and always has been. When he was being recruited in high school, he would study media guides and talk to college coaches about their staffs and returning players. He always is on, deadly serious, analytical and detailed, so gregarious and focused.

That's not Eli. One family friend, Bo Ball, said it was years before Eli "finished a sentence." Once painfully shy and introverted, Eli dryly blames his brothers. "I could never get a word in," he said. During his time at Ole Miss, he emerged and blossomed to a point where he could give a speech before a sports gathering in Memphis and, when asked about his college recruiting, reply: "I had a great visit to Colorado." When the laughter stopped, he quickly added: "Just kidding." But he still keeps his own counsel. He

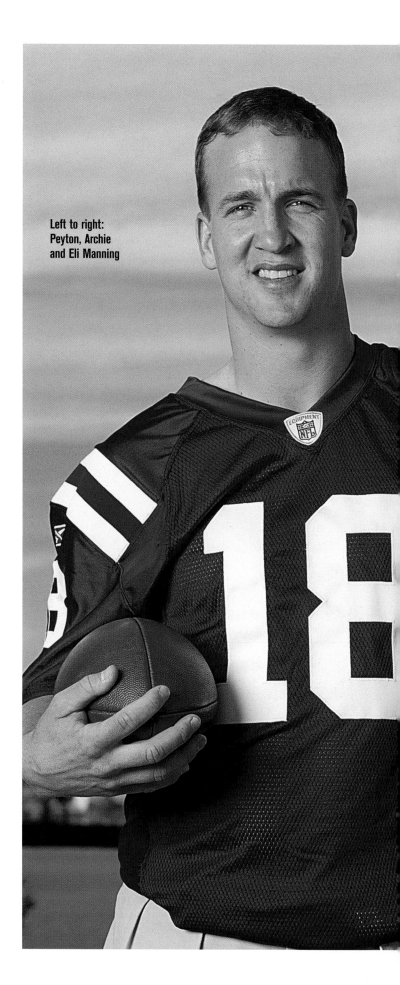

Left to right:
Peyton, Archie
and Eli Manning

is observant, smart, loose, unassuming, but he doesn't readily share his thoughts— even with his parents—and is unwilling to take himself too seriously.

David Cutcliffe, who was Peyton's offensive coordinator at Tennessee and Eli's head coach at Ole Miss, knows the brothers better than anyone outside the immediate family. "Here's the difference," he said. "I would walk into a stadium on a Friday with Peyton, and he would tell me all the great players who had played there. If I tried to talk to Eli about the same thing, he would look at me as if I was crazy." When Eli was young, the only reason he knew the schools in the SEC was because Peyton would hold him down and pound him on the chest until he could name them all.

But Cutcliffe said something else. "He is every bit Peyton when it comes to game preparation," he said. "They both work as hard. They have great minds and a fast-twitch thinking ability that allows them to absorb things very quickly." Eli is passionate, just in a more quiet way. "I love everything about football," he said. "The games, the practices, the preparation, the smells, everything." Anyway, Eli always has developed more slowly than Peyton.

Unfortunately, neither son inherited Archie's mobility.

"Archie had absolutely great feet," said Wolf. Archie's sons are elusive in the pocket but not particularly quick. Instead, they are classic drop-back passers at a moment when Michael Vick-like movement is favored. That's one reason the buzz around Eli did not equal the clamor that surrounded Peyton. Any criticism would nag Peyton. But Eli? "I can't change who I am," he said.

magine how difficult it could have been, growing up in New Orleans with Archie Manning as your father. He last played with the Saints in 1981, yet he remains, by far, the city's most revered sports figure. He still lives in the same classic manor home along splendid St. Charles Avenue. Still works in the city, too, in his own marketing and public relations business. He immersed himself in community affairs and befriended seemingly the entire population. He is instantly charming and warm; no one can remember anyone saying one bad thing about him. But when his sons leaped into

Miss., marries a former Ole Miss homecoming queen. They raise three intelligent, energetic, athletic sons, all of whom also excel academically (Peyton, who graduated cum laude in three years, and Eli both won NCAA scholarship/academic awards, including an $18,000 postgraduate scholarship by Eli).

Archie was fearful of being a Todd Marinovich father, so he never pressured them to play sports or most certainly quarterback. He instructs them only if they ask. But they are smart enough to do just that; he teaches them proper mechanics, his love of sports. It shows. Cooper proudly would have 3-year-old Peyton demonstrate to friends his five-step drop; Eli

Archie instructs his sons only if they ask. But they are smart enough to do just that.

football and then gravitated immediately to quarterback, it seemed like a formula for eventual rebellion—or for offspring so full of themselves to be obnoxious. Maybe because Archie and Olivia feared those possibilities is why none occurred.

"They gave their children a proper Mississippi upbringing," said Billy Van Devender, who roomed with Archie at Ole Miss, was his best man and now is a prosperous businessman in that state. "They were taught to respect adults and have the right manners. All Archie and Olivia wanted was for their kids to be normal. You don't see them flaunting their success. The whole family is warm and generous, a joy to be around."

Some of this seems almost too Hollywood to be true.

Archie, the All-American quarterback from tiny Drew,

would sleep with Nerf baseballs and footballs in his bed, not stuffed animals. But Archie refrained from coaching their youth teams. It has been troubling enough when his sons have been singled out by rival parents who encouraged their kids "to stop that Manning." He vowed to stay in the background, supportive but quiet. To this day, he still is.

n the most simplistic terms, Peyton is Archie, Eli is Olivia and Cooper is everyone. Cooper is the family star, really; its optimist, its energy, its funny bone. "I'm just as proud of what Cooper has done in business as I am of anything Peyton and Eli have accomplished," said Archie. Cooper also produced the first grandchildren. The family is impressively protective

of Cooper's feelings and his role. Eli understands.

When Cooper was at Ole Miss, Eli remembers fondly the time spent in his apartment. So when Eli went there, he was determined to rent the same place. He eventually did.

Archie is detailed, determined, organized, living off lists, making only well-researched and analytical decisions. Peyton always has had lists, too; Eli just got himself his first organizer. His sons love to mess with Archie's habits. At Ole Miss, Archie would straighten up Eli's apartment. When he left the room, Eli would create some clutter, just to see his dad clean that up, too. When Peyton was in college, one of his first roommates was messy. Peyton not only tidied up the room, he made his friend's bed. He thinks it makes perfect sense to map out his life after his dad's.

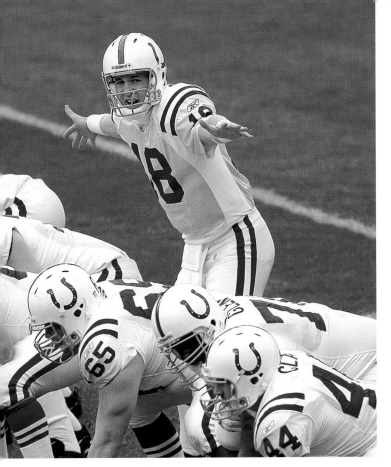

Peyton Manning is at his best when he approaches the line of scrimmage, the point at which he transforms into a masterful field general.

Cooper and Peyton were inseparable; even today, no one laughs harder at Cooper's jokes than Peyton. But Eli was too young to pal around with them; too young to attend his dad's workouts as they did; too young to remember his dad playing in the pros. He would try to play catch with Peyton, but he dropped too many balls, so Peyton took pillows off the couch and taped them to Eli's arms. He looked like a big marshmallow, but at least he could smother the passes.

When Eli was 13, Peyton left for college. Archie was traveling a lot, and Eli and Olivia became best friends. "He's his mama's boy," said Ball, the family friend. Olivia is soft, gentle, quiet, same as Eli, who has the nickname "Easy." Archie calls her "my great equalizer." Their friends credit her with creating the family's solid foundation. "My mom knows how to do everything," said Eli. "My dad is clueless. I don't think he knows how to wash clothes."

Olivia rarely gets upset over anything, even when she had to watch her sons play 17 basketball games in one weekend. One day, she let her men eat in the den so they could watch a game. When they left their plates, she erupted. "I think the least you could do is show me some respect by taking your plates to the kitchen," she told them. She walked away but came back seconds later. "And another thing. I am tired of washing jock straps."

Eli and Peyton have become closer as they have grown older. They talk briefly each weekend about their respective games; every Thursday, they would have lengthy discussions, sometimes about their next opponents. A month before the draft, just after Peyton signed his record $98 million contract with the Colts, he was in Bradenton, Fla., at the training facility run by IMG agency, which represents both brothers. Eli had been training there for his pre-draft workouts, and Peyton spent four days living in Eli's room.

"I don't want to be his coach or mentor," said Peyton, sitting next to the IMG swimming pool. "I just want to be his brother." They watched Peyton's pro workout tape together. It was not very impressive; lots of passes hit the ground. "I'm not as nervous now," said Eli, "seeing how badly he did." Peyton laughed. "It was pretty ugly."

Archie and Olivia understand how special it is that all their boys call them virtually every day, tell them they love them before they hang up and seek their advice. "My wife thinks I talk to my dad too much, but it's hard; he has such an influence on me," said Peyton. Archie has told them the one thing they could do to really hurt their parents "is to not get along. We see families fussing all the time; we don't want to be like that."

There's something else, too. When Archie was at Ole Miss, his father took his own life. In the middle of an interview, Peyton brings up his grandfather and father. "Dad and I haven't talked much about him losing his father," he volunteered. "He was a lot older than my dad, and they never had this super close relationship. I just sensed he was going to be super close to us and hug us."

But the kids aren't perfect, thank God. Cooper strove to have a good time in high school and not always have his parents know it. Peyton was so intense in high school—once quitting the basketball team after disagreeing with the coach over playing time—that his parents had to sternly remind him it is more important to be a great person than a great player. Later, an assistant trainer at Tennessee accused

him of mooning her in the training room. Eli was arrested for being drunk in public his freshman year at Ole Miss. "It was the best thing that happened to him," said his dad. "It taught him he couldn't do stuff like that and not have it reported. It embarrassed him."

He had forgotten what his parents had preached for years. Because of Archie and his fame, the public always would be watching. The boys had to be careful how they behaved.

"It really hasn't been that hard," said Peyton. "We didn't resent being a Manning. We haven't known anything else, but we've never said, 'This isn't fair.' We wouldn't have wanted it any other way." Well, almost. "We just wondered why we didn't get our dad's speed," said Eli.

But quarterback? "I couldn't play anywhere else," said Eli. "I was tall, skinny and slow. Same with Peyton." So much of what you see is natural, of course. When Peyton was in second grade, Archie attended a school function in the cafeteria while the kids played outside. A pass soared past the window and disappeared; it was his son, throwing. "Did you see that?" asked another dad excitedly. Archie just nodded. But he cringes when folks attribute his sons' success to genes. His point is correct; they haven't wasted their gifts. Instead, their admirable work ethic developed their talents into what we see today. It is another Manning commandment: Once you commit to something, you put everything into the obligation. No halfhearted efforts accepted, thank you. It's not the Manning way.

CRUCIAL CO

Not all were things of beauty or game winners. One even was made by

o some, a great pass is a tightly rotating 60-yard arc, the kind that Warren Moon and Jeff George routinely heaved, so picturesque in grainy slow motion. Others would argue a great pass is one completed in the crucial moment of a big game, when a single play can secure or undo a championship. Some will tell you a great pass is one delivered under pressure, with defensive linemen abusing the quarterback and a defensive back shadowing the receiver.

Or maybe it can be all three.

Perhaps the definitive "great pass" is the one Pittsburgh quarterback Terry Bradshaw threw to Lynn Swann with three minutes left in Super Bowl 10. Bradshaw's miraculous offering sailed across the three-way intersection of context, drama and physical excellence, earning a place atop the list of great NFL passes—a list constructed after consulting with former NFL players and

BRADSHAW TO SWANN
SUPER BOWL 10

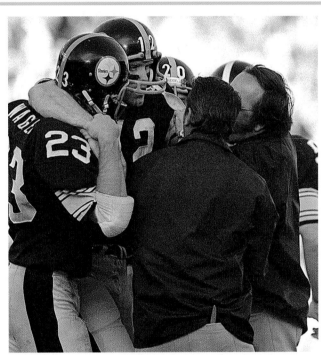

MPLETIONS

a backup quarterback. But they are the 10 best passes in NFL history.

coaches, broadcasters and *Sporting News* writers and editors.

The Steelers and Dallas Cowboys were the dominant teams of the 1970s, which in so many ways represented the golden age of NFL football. The Steelers, with nine future Hall of Famers on their roster, won all four of their Super Bowl appearances in the decade; a solid core of budding Hall of Famers also sparked the Cowboys, who played in five Super Bowls and won two. The teams were coached by Hall of Famers Chuck Noll and Tom Landry.

Their confrontation in Super Bowl 10 was everything the game is supposed to be. Preceded by plenty of trash talk, it was close and hard-fought, a defensive struggle punctuated by big plays.

Dallas led 10-7 at halftime, but Pittsburgh slowly began to assert control in the fourth quarter. With less than four minutes left, the Steelers were up 15-10. Hoping to run the ball down the Cowboys' throats for an insurance touchdown, the Steelers faced a critical third-and-4 from their 36-yard line. Bradshaw called "69 maximum flanker post"—a pass to Swann, who already had distinguished himself with a gravity-defying catch to set up Pittsburgh's first TD.

The Cowboys called a maximum blitz, sending weakside linebacker D.D. Lewis and safety Cliff Harris after Bradshaw. "I loved to blitz," said Harris. "I would try to send the signal to Ernie (Stautner, the Dallas defensive coach) from the field that I wanted to run the safety blitz."

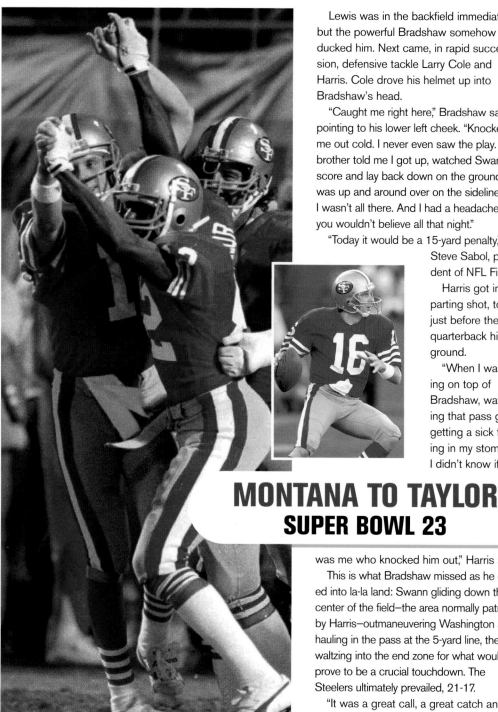

Lewis was in the backfield immediately, but the powerful Bradshaw somehow ducked him. Next came, in rapid succession, defensive tackle Larry Cole and Harris. Cole drove his helmet up into Bradshaw's head.

"Caught me right here," Bradshaw says, pointing to his lower left cheek. "Knocked me out cold. I never even saw the play. My brother told me I got up, watched Swann score and lay back down on the ground. I was up and around over on the sideline, but I wasn't all there. And I had a headache like you wouldn't believe all that night."

"Today it would be a 15-yard penalty," said Steve Sabol, president of NFL Films.

Harris got in a parting shot, too, just before the quarterback hit the ground.

"When I was laying on top of Bradshaw, watching that pass go, getting a sick feeling in my stomach, I didn't know if it

MONTANA TO TAYLOR
SUPER BOWL 23

was me who knocked him out," Harris said.

This is what Bradshaw missed as he drifted into la-la land: Swann gliding down the center of the field—the area normally patrolled by Harris—outmaneuvering Washington and hauling in the pass at the 5-yard line, then waltzing into the end zone for what would prove to be a crucial touchdown. The Steelers ultimately prevailed, 21-17.

"It was a great call, a great catch and … a pretty good throw," Bradshaw said.

But that's overly modest. "Of all the catches I made that day," Swann said, "it was probably the most routine."

"We were supposed to make adjustments if it was a blitz," said Swann. "We called them 'blitz controls.' The routes would adjust to what was called—like an out cut, or an in cut, or a post-flag. I had the post pattern, and (Cowboys cornerback Mark Washington) came up. My job was to get inside for the slant route."

Bradshaw saw it all developing, and he knew where Swann would be. "What he did was kind of go this way, then back out this way," Bradshaw said, gesticulating a gentle zigzag.

The blitz nearly wrecked the play.

"We were able to get away with a lot of that during the season," Washington said of the max blitz. "But we didn't face anyone with an arm like Bradshaw's. Usually you'd have time to recover, even though you weren't in the best position. In this game, the guy put the ball out there."

Three decades later, the play still riles Harris. His Cowboys lost two close Super Bowls to the Steelers in four years. He knows if they had managed to win those two games, the Cowboys, not the Steelers, would have been anointed the Team of the '70s.

"He beat me in two Super Bowls," Harris said of Bradshaw. "I could never take away his talent or his grit. When it's the Super Bowl, it takes that little tiny bit extra something that other players don't have. That's what Bradshaw had that day."

Bradshaw played 14 pro seasons, passed for 27,989 yards and 212 touchdowns and played in 19 postseason games. But the pass to Swann is as special for him as it is for any football fan old enough to have seen it.

"It was for a championship," Bradshaw said. "And really, that's the only thing that matters."

As distant as 1951 or as recent as 2003, a few passes stand out from the countless thousands thrown in NFL games, whether because of difficulty or importance. The rest of our all-time Top 10:

2. Joe Montana to John Taylor, Super Bowl 23.

It always appeared everything came so easily for Montana, and the 49ers' final offensive play of Super Bowl 23 was no different. What most remember is that it came at the culmination of a methodical 92-yard drive, with Cincinnati leading by three points in what was the last game of Bill Walsh's coaching career.

But the pass itself, a straightforward 10-yard slant to Taylor with 34 seconds on the clock, symbolized Montana's career. It wasn't just

the magnitude of the moment. It was the fact Taylor was at least the third option on the play—"20 halfback curl, X up"—and was, in fact, lined up in the wrong position. Running back Roger Craig was the primary receiver, and star receiver Jerry Rice—the MVP of the game—was secondary.

Montana, cool as ever, checked down in a matter of seconds and delivered a perfect pass to Taylor

3. Steve Young to Terrell Owens, 1998 NFC playoffs.

As usual, Young is right behind Montana in the historical hierarchy. There were only three seconds left when the 49ers, trailing by four points, lined up on the Packers' 25-yard line in a 1998 NFC wild-card game. Brett Favre (surprisingly, not on our list of greatest passes)

YOUNG TO OWENS
1998 NFC PLAYOFFS

had put the two-time defending NFC champions ahead with a touch-down pass to Antonio Freeman with 1:56 remaining. But Young did him one better.

Young completed 7 of 9 passes on the ensuing drive, including the absurd clincher to Owens, who had dropped several passes in the game and who was bracketed by Green Bay safeties Darren Sharper and Pat Terrell down the middle of the field. Young's pass was on the money, and Owens hauled it in as he crossed the goal line, ending the Packers' reign.

4. John Elway to Mark Jackson, 1986 AFC championship.

Most people remember Elway's low, well-placed scoring toss to Jackson, the one that capped "The Drive," a 98-yard march that sent this game into overtime. More impressive was the pass that happened five plays earlier, with the Broncos staring at third-and-18 and the Cleveland Dawg Pound foaming at the mouth.

Elway first made it hard on himself by signaling wide receiver Steve Watson's motion at the wrong time; the shotgun snap grazed Watson's butt, and Elway had to pick it off the ground. Elway then backpedaled several yards and fired a sizzling strike to Jackson for a crucial 20-yard first down. Elway and the Broncos ultimately would crush the Browns' Super Bowl hopes in overtime.

5. Montana to Dwight Clark, 1981 NFC championship game.

Yes, they call this one "The Catch," not "The Throw," and it's true Clark seemingly leaped higher than he possibly could to snare Montana's pass in front of Dallas cornerback Everson Walls. But there aren't many quarterbacks who could have gotten the ball there.

As Montana took the snap and drifted right, he was immediately hounded by a trio of Cowboys, led by 6-9 defensive end Ed "Too Tall" Jones. Montana scrambled toward the sideline and threw off his back foot to a deep spot in the end zone that he knew would result either in an incompletion or a touchdown to Clark.

With Montana in trouble, Clark broke off his route and doubled back from left to right, in front of the end line—just as he and Montana had practiced hundreds of times. Clark's catch helped the 49ers launch their dynasty and helped bring the Cowboys' decade of dominance to an end.

6. Joe Namath to Don Maynard, 1968 AFL championship game.

Facing an ornery Oakland defense, nursing multiple injuries (dislocated finger, bruised tailbone, chronically deteriorating knees)

McNABB TO MITCHELL
2003 NFC PLAYOFFS

and throwing into a stiff wind in New York, Namath made a throw that would help cement his Hall of Fame reputation. Actually, he made a couple, both to Maynard. The first took the Jets to the Raiders' 6 inside of eight minutes. The next one was even bigger. Namath looked for halfback Bill Mathis … then wide receiver George Sauer … then tight end Pete Lammons … and finally for Maynard, who caught the low liner that Namath sidearmed across the field.

7. Norm Van Brocklin to Tom Fears, 1951 NFL championship game.

In a battle of two of the most potent offenses of the era, the Browns tied the score, 17-17, with 7:50 left. The Rams struck back immediately. Van Brocklin, who shared quarterbacking duties with Bob Waterfield, dropped back from his 27 and found Fears over the middle. Van Brocklin's pass split Cleveland defenders Cliff Lewis and Tom James, and Fears was gone. His 73-yard touchdown proved to be the game- and title-winner (the Rams' last for 48 years). "It was the best-thrown pass I've ever caught," Fears said later. "He laid it right in there full stride."

8. Clint Longley to Drew Pearson, 1974 Thanksgiving Day.

The Dallas Cowboys seemingly never were out of a game during the Roger Staubach era. Curiously, Staubach was on the bench for what might have been their most amazing finish. The Cowboys had a 6-5 record and were on the brink of playoff elimination when the hated Redskins came to town for Thanksgiving. The Cowboys' chances looked bleak when a dazed Staubach headed to the sideline at 9:57 of the third quarter. But his replacement, Longley, came on for his first NFL snap and played the only great game of his abbreviated career. With 35 seconds left and Dallas down 23-17, Longley sent Pearson deep down the middle. The ball was on the money, and Pearson found his way into the end zone for a 24-23 upset.

9. Ken Stabler to Dave Casper, 1977 AFC playoffs.

Even after he had caught two touchdown passes and set up a game-tying field goal with a spectacular catch, Casper still received man-to-man coverage in the second overtime. So, on second-and-goal from the Baltimore 7, Stabler, one of the great touch passers of all time, went to his tight end again.

Stabler froze cornerback Nelson Munsey with a play-action fake, and Casper ran past his man to the corner of the end zone. Stabler's pass was perfect, a fitting end to an epic game that included eight lead changes and two ties.

10. Donovan McNabb to Freddie Mitchell, 2003 NFC playoffs.

"You would have thought fourth down-and-26 was pretty good odds," Packers defensive backs coach Bob Slowik said afterward. Not good enough. McNabb used his arm to convert that fourth-and-26 from the Philadelphia 26 with 1:12 remaining.

Trailing 17-14, the Eagles lined up in a four-receiver set. Green Bay countered with a four-across dime defense. Mitchell took off from the slot position, veered inside of Darren Sharper and nestled into a seam down the middle. McNabb's throw was exactly where it had to be, just over the fingers of nickel back Bhawoh Jue, and it had enough zip to beat strong safety Marques Anderson, who had raced over in a futile attempt to break up the play. It went for 28 yards and a first down across midfield. The Eagles' David Akers tied the game with a field goal seven plays later and then kicked another to win it in overtime.

THE RIGHT PLACE AT THE RIGHT TIME

Some of the most memorable pass plays in pro football history had almost everything going for them—tension, acrobatic catches, controversy, craziness. All they lacked, really, was a good throw. Six plays on which it was better to be lucky than good:

1. Terry Bradshaw to Frenchy Fuqua, 1972 AFC playoffs. It might be the greatest single play in the annals of the NFL—and the pass was screwy. With the seconds ticking away in frigid Pittsburgh, Bradshaw desperately threw to Fuqua over the middle on fourth-and-10. But the ball had too much loft. It arrived at the same time as Oakland safety Jack Tatum and hit the helmet of either Tatum or Fuqua. As the Raiders began to celebrate what they thought was an incompletion, rookie Franco Harris alertly plucked the ball off his shoe tops—the Immaculate Reception—and streaked down the left sideline for a touchdown and a victory that helped launch a dynasty.

2. Roger Staubach to Drew Pearson, 1975 NFC playoffs. This was the original Hail Mary pass. With 32 seconds left, Staubach's pass was short and a bit wobbly. Pearson adjusted—and maybe pushed Vikings cornerback Nate Wright—to catch the ball at the 5 and stroll in for a game-winning 50-yard touchdown. Staubach said: "After the game, they said, 'What were you thinking about?' I said, 'I closed my eyes and said a Hail Mary.'"

3. Dan Fouts to James Brooks, 1981 AFC playoffs. This 9-yard touchdown pass tied a dizzying game (Chargers 38, Dolphins 38) with 58 seconds to play. The only problem: It was intended for tight end Kellen Winslow, who was too exhausted to leap for the overthrown ball. Fouts hadn't even seen Brooks.

4. Kurt Warner to Isaac Bruce, Super Bowl 34. Hit by a Titan as he released, Warner underthrew. But Bruce slowed to make the catch, broke a tackle and sped off for a 74-yard touchdown, regaining the lead for the Rams.

5. Bart Starr to Max McGee, Super Bowl 1. The first touchdown in the history of the NFL's biggest game was all McGee, a little-used backup. He reached behind him for Starr's off-target pass and outran Kansas City cornerback Fred Williamson to the end zone.

6. Joe Theismann to Charlie Brown, Super Bowl 17. Theismann barely had released the ball when Dolphins defensive end Kim Bokamper stepped in and deflected it. Bokamper had reached for the ball and had the interception in his hands, but Theismann stripped him, preventing a touchdown that might have sunk the Redskins.

RUNNI

When some of the game's most athletic passers become runners, the result is free-form art—and going with the flow can be pure poetry

Otto Graham

*Did everything for the Browns in leading
    them to 7 crowns;
Whether it was a Cleveland rout or
    the game's outcome was in doubt;
An equal threat to run and pass,
    he always was up to the task;
Used his legs to change fates,
    and marched as one of the all-time greats.*

John Elway

*He left you worried about that gun,
    but boy could this Bronco run;
He was ready to go the extra yard,
    even if they hit him extra hard;
Bucking ahead for a first down,
    became the toast of Mile High town;
Diving past the Pack in that big game
    vaulted him into the Hall of Fame.*

Steve McNair

*"Air" McNair also does it on the ground,
few can match him pound for pound;
Gritty and gutty, strong and tough,
tacklers beware: the going is rough;
Even though he plays through pain,
he still is a threat to break contain;
A mighty Titan standing tall,
big as he is, he rarely does fall.*

Randall Cunningham

As leader of the Eagles' fleet,
he dazzled with his amazing feet;
His moves bordered on cunning
and never were short of stunning;
You had to catch him early
to keep him from getting whirly;
Rambling Randall's contorts and twists
were a sight that most defenders missed.

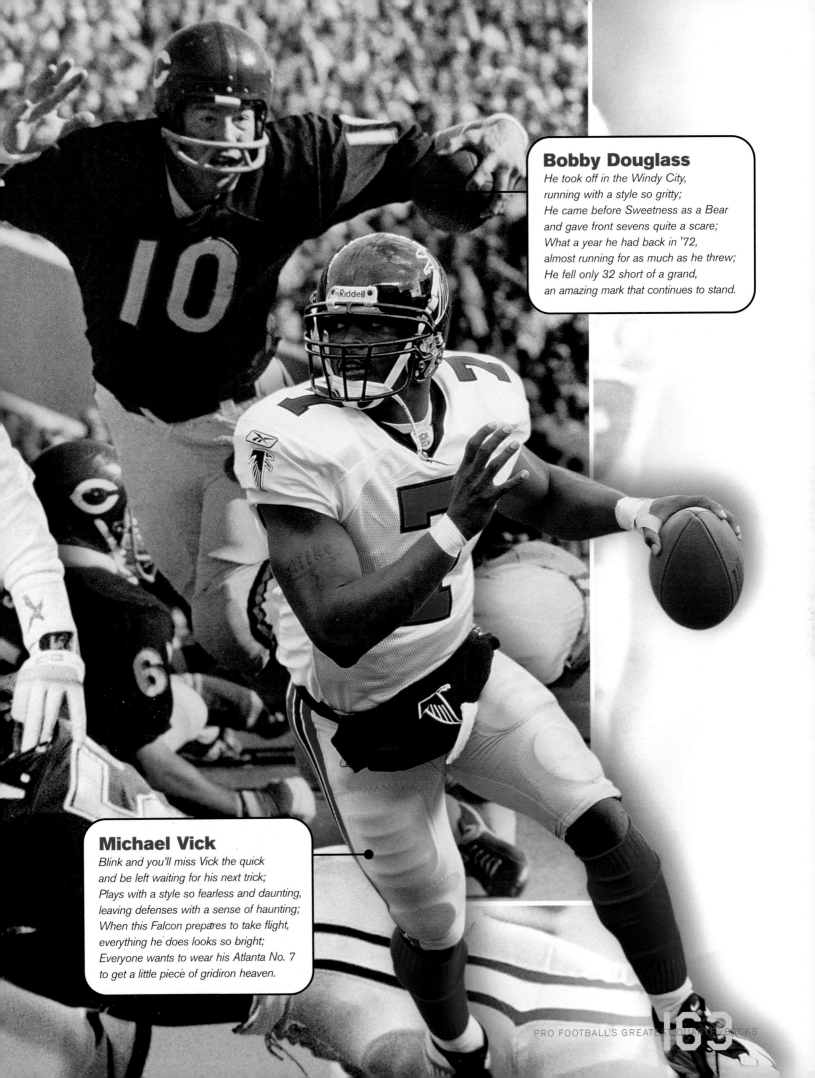

Bobby Douglass

He took off in the Windy City,
running with a style so gritty;
He came before Sweetness as a Bear
and gave front sevens quite a scare;
What a year he had back in '72,
almost running for as much as he threw;
He fell only 32 short of a grand,
an amazing mark that continues to stand.

Michael Vick

Blink and you'll miss Vick the quick
and be left waiting for his next trick;
Plays with a style so fearless and daunting,
leaving defenses with a sense of haunting;
When this Falcon prepares to take flight,
everything he does looks so bright;
Everyone wants to wear his Atlanta No. 7
to get a little piece of gridiron heaven.

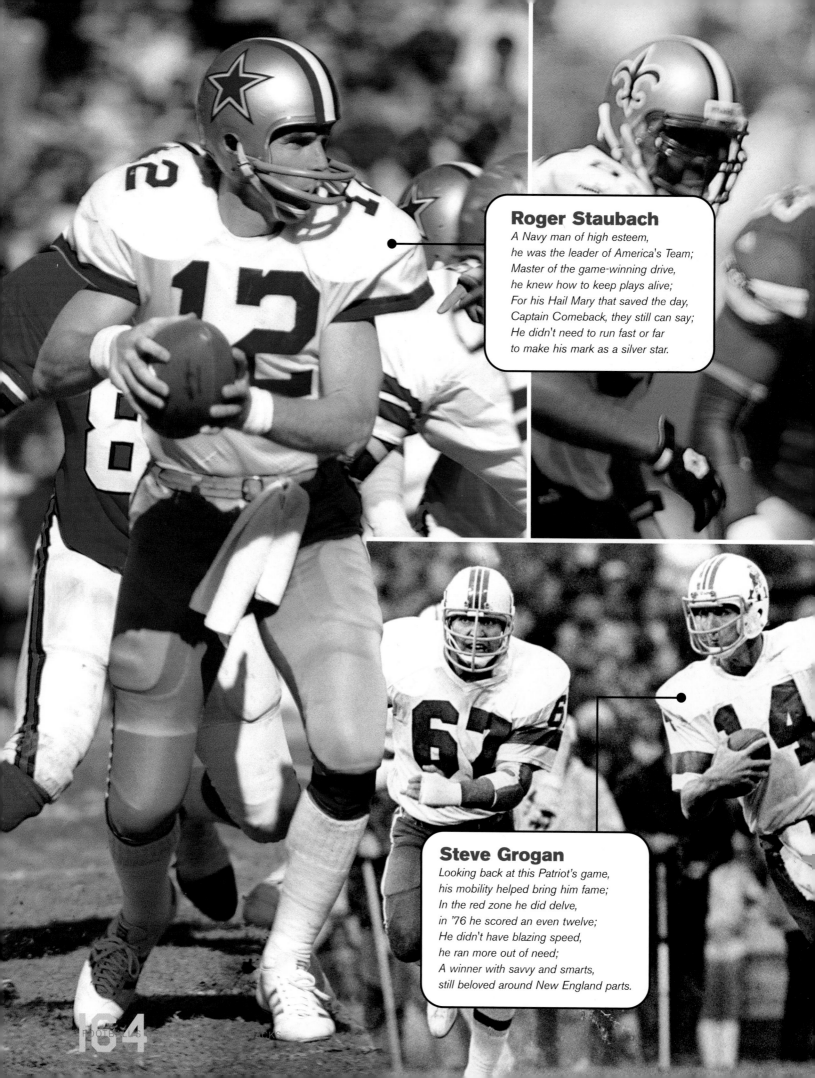

Roger Staubach

A Navy man of high esteem,
he was the leader of America's Team;
Master of the game-winning drive,
he knew how to keep plays alive;
For his Hail Mary that saved the day,
Captain Comeback, they still can say;
He didn't need to run fast or far
to make his mark as a silver star.

Steve Grogan

Looking back at this Patriot's game,
his mobility helped bring him fame;
In the red zone he did delve,
in '76 he scored an even twelve;
He didn't have blazing speed,
he ran more out of need;
A winner with savvy and smarts,
still beloved around New England parts.

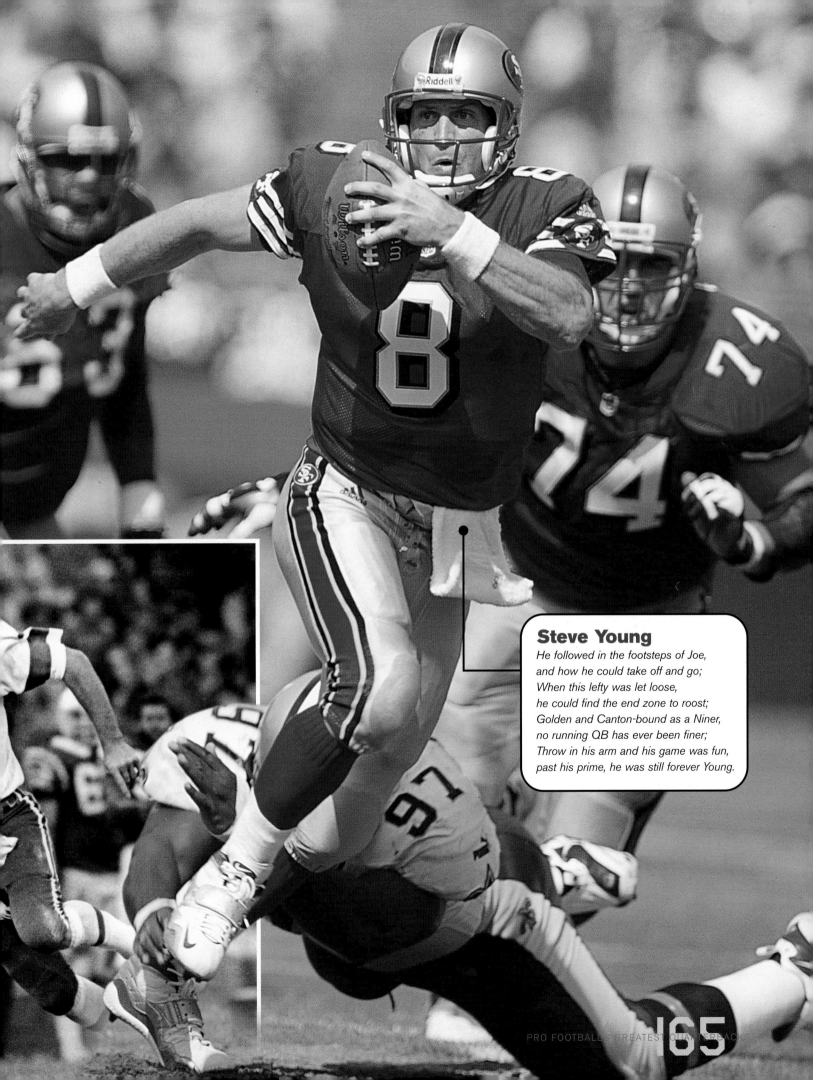

Steve Young

He followed in the footsteps of Joe,
and how he could take off and go;
When this lefty was let loose,
he could find the end zone to roost;
Golden and Canton-bound as a Niner,
no running QB has ever been finer;
Throw in his arm and his game was fun,
past his prime, he was still forever Young.

Fran Tarkenton

*Right here's the skinny
on the running Fran in Minny;
Many would give him good chase,
many would lose this futile race;
That's incredible, they would say,
on how this Viking would make hay;
Rolling out and buying time,
scrambling he made so sublime.*

Donovan McNabb

An Eagle strong like a bull,
he's always running on full;
It's not so easy to pin
a heavyweight with so much spin;
He's all "Thriller," no filler,
his long runs are a killer;
Better think twice before you gamble
as he's the master of the scramble.

Kordell Stewart

Shined as the Steelers' wheels,
making weekly highlight reels;
Simply known as "Slash,"
he could be gone in a dash;
He also liked to slide
and would even line up wide;
Often made opponents fold
as a blur in black and gold.

Kurt
Warner

Jeff
Blake

Jim
McMahon

THE QUARTE

A historical breakdown of the top five signal-callers for each NFL franchise

oger Staubach or Troy Aikman? Dan Marino or Bob Griese? Bart or Brett? Compiling and ranking the top five quarterbacks in each NFL franchise's history is a fun but difficult task.

We even contradicted ourselves in a couple of places, shifting players on *Sporting News*' Top 50 below another of lower ranking on this list or below an unranked player because of longevity with that franchise. We also considered career statistics with the particular franchise, number of trips to the playoffs, tenure and honors.

The hardest team rankings to assemble? No question, the Eagles. Imagine having to leave off Davey O'Brien, an All-Pro selection in one of his only two NFL seasons, and Hall of Famer Sonny Jurgensen. The next toughest? The Rams, where no room remained for Billy Wade, Vince Ferragamo or Pat Haden. Jeff Garcia didn't make the Niners' list, and the Redskins' list is without Super Bowl 22 MVP Doug Williams and 1950s great Eddie LeBaron.

BEARS

1. Sid Luckman (1939-50). His team introduced the modern T-formation to the NFL. Was MVP in 1943 and led the Bears to four league championships. First quarterback to toss seven touchdown passes in a game.

2. Jim McMahon (1982-88). Led the Bears to a commanding victory in Super Bowl 20. His outlaw antics might outlive his on-field accomplishments.

3. Billy Wade (1961-66). Came to the Bears after seven seasons with the L.A. Rams and guided them to the 1963 NFL championship, scoring both touchdowns on short plunges in the 14–10 win over the Giants.

4. Ed Brown (1954-61). Led the NFL in passing in 1956, the same year he took the Bears to the NFL championship game, a 47–7 blowout loss to the Giants.

5. George Blanda (1949, 1950-58). Gained most of his fame for his rocking chair exploits with Oakland but earns a spot here for quarterbacking the Bears on and off for 10 seasons. Led the NFL in completions and attempts in 1953.

BENGALS

1. Ken Anderson (1971-86). Is the top passer in Bengals history and No. 36 in TSN's Top 50, one spot below Boomer Esiason. Takes the top spot because of his lengthy tenure in the Queen City. Both

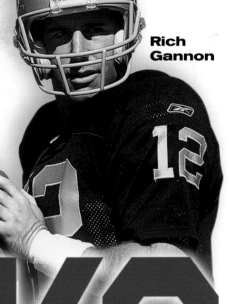

Rich Gannon

RBACKS

TEAM BY TEAM

took teams to the Super Bowl and lost.

2. Boomer Esiason (1984-92, 1997). Spent 10 of his 14 seasons in Cincinnati and was the No. 2 all-time passer in team history. Led the Bengals to three playoff victories, including the 1988 AFC title game.

3. Jeff Blake (1994-99). Was a Pro Bowl player in '95 and will be best remembered for tossing long scoring passes to Darnay Scott and Carl Pickens that year.

4. Greg Cook (1969-74). Was *United Press International* Rookie of the Year in '69. Arm troubles shackled his potential. When Anderson came in '71, Cook was cooked.

5. Carson Palmer (2003-present). Was the No. 1 overall pick in the 2003 draft. Has a cannon arm and already ranks among the best downfield passers in the league. Appears poised to lead an explosive offense for a long, long time.

BILLS

1. Jim Kelly (1986-96). Played two record-breaking seasons in the USFL before coming to Buffalo. Didn't win a Super Bowl in four tries but rewrote the Bills' record book.

2. Joe Ferguson (1973-84). Is the longest-tenured quarterback in Bills history. Held virtually every Bills passing mark in the pre-Kelly era.

3. Jack Kemp (1962-69). The well-known Republican congressman was one of the AFL's outstanding passers. After being cast aside by San Diego, led the Bills to back-to-back AFL titles in 1964 and '65.

4. Dennis Shaw (1970-73). Was the AFC Rookie of the Year in '70 and still ranks sixth in team passing yardage.

5. Frank Reich (1985-94). Was Kelly's superlative backup for nine seasons and was lionized for leading the greatest comeback in NFL history—the Bills' 41-38 overtime win over Houston in a wild-card playoff game after the 1992 season.

BRONCOS

1. John Elway (1983-98). Gained immortality by closing out his Hall of Fame career with back-to-back Super Bowl victories. Is the NFL's No. 2 all-time passer and tops all quarterbacks with 47 fourth-quarter comebacks.

2. Craig Morton (1977-82). Is No. 2 behind Elway in virtually every team passing record. Led the Broncos to their first championship game, a 27-10 loss to Dallas in Super Bowl 12.

3. Brian Griese (1998-2002). Played in Denver just five seasons but owns the team's highest career passer rating (84.1). Will be remembered

as Elway's failed successor.

4. Frank Tripucka (1960-63). The franchise's first quarterback. Threw the second-longest touchdown pass in Denver history—96 yards to Al Frazier against Buffalo in '62.

5. Jake Plummer (2003-present). Is elusive and has big-play flair. In his first two Denver seasons, he posted the two best passer ratings of his career, 91.2 and 84.5, while throwing 42 TD passes. Threw for a franchise-record 4,089 yards in 2004, and his 27 TD passes tied another Elway mark.

BROWNS

1. Otto Graham (1946-55). Set the standard for championship quarterbacks—seven titles in 10 years. He and Elway are the only quarterbacks to conclude their careers with consecutive league championships.

2. Bernie Kosar (1985-93). Led the team to three AFC championship game losses—all against Denver. Still holds the NFL mark for most consecutive attempts without an interception (308).

3. Brian Sipe (1974-83). The Browns' all-time passing leader guided Cleveland to the playoffs twice and was the NFL's MVP in 1980.

4. Frank Ryan (1962-68). Had a Ph.D. in mathematics and brought brains to the position. Career high point was leading the team to its last NFL championship in 1964.

5. Milt Plum (1957-61). Eventually became Graham's successor. As a rookie in '57, teamed with Tommy O'Connell to lead the Browns to their seventh NFL championship game in eight years.

BUCCANEERS

1. Doug Williams (1978-82). Guided Tampa Bay to its first three playoff appearances, including the 1979 NFC championship game.

2. Vinny Testaverde (1987-92). The team was 24-48 when he started, but he still is the franchise's all-time leading passer.

3. Trent Dilfer (1994-99). Garnered a hard-earned Pro Bowl appearance in '97 and had a higher Bucs' career passer rating than Testaverde and Williams.

4. Brad Johnson (2001-04). Was the starting quarterback for Bucs' 2002 Super Bowl season. His unspectacular style has netted the best passer rating in Bucs history.

5. Steve DeBerg (1984-87, 1992-93). Persevered through a 24-71 record during his Tampa Bay stops. Played on six NFL teams and has the third-highest Bucs passer rating (73.9) all-time.

CARDINALS

1. Jim Hart (1966-83). Was a four-time Pro Bowl player and the team's No. 1 all-time passer. Was UPI NFC Player of the Year in '74 and ranks in the Top 20 all-time in career passing yardage.

2. Paddy Driscoll (1920-25). Was a Hall of Fame force in pro football's early days. Was a talented tailback/punter/kicker who led the Cardinals for six seasons, including to the team's first-ever crown in 1925.

3. Paul Christman (1945-49). The team's first passing star guided the club to its second NFL title, in 1947. Was the first passer in franchise history to throw for 300-plus yards in a game (320 vs. Detroit on September 28, 1947).

4. Neil Lomax (1981-89). Early retirement because of an arthritic hip ended a bright career. Still wound up No. 2 on the Cardinals' all-time passing yardage list.

5. Charley Johnson (1961-69). Knee injuries and military service interrupted his career, but he still is No. 4 on the Cardinals' career passing yardage list. Threw a touchdown pass in 16 consecutive games in 1964-65.

CHARGERS

1. Dan Fouts (1973-87). Passed the Chargers into two AFC championship games and became the third quarterback in league history to pass for more than 40,000 yards.

2. John Hadl (1962-72). Guided the Chargers to the AFL championship game in 1964 and '65 and ranks second to Fouts in club passing yards.

3. Jack Kemp (1960-62). Led the team to consecutive AFL championship games in the franchise's first two years. Still ranks fourth all-time in Chargers passing yards.

4. Stan Humphries (1992-97). Had a 47-29 record as a starter, the second-highest winning percentage (.618) of any San Diego quarterback with 20-plus starts. Took the Chargers to the postseason three times, including Super Bowl 29.

5. Tobin Rote (1963-64). Led the Chargers to their only championship, the AFL title in '63.

CHIEFS

1. Len Dawson (1962-75). Took the franchise to its only two world championships, first as the Dallas Texans in the 1962 AFL title game double-overtime thriller and then the Chiefs' big upset in Super Bowl 4.

2. Trent Green (2001-present). Despite lacking a true No. 1 receiver, Green has become the leader of one of the NFL's most potent offenses. Made his first trip to the Pro Bowl after the 2003 season.

3. Bill Kenney (1979-88). Kansas City fielded only two teams with winning records during his decade, but he ranks No. 2 in passing yards.

4. Steve DeBerg (1988-91). The NFL's grand journeyman made a four-year stop in Kansas City, taking it to the playoffs in 1990 and '91. Ranks fourth behind Green in team passing yards.

5. Mike Livingston (1968-79). Spent much of his Kansas City career as a backup but still ranks fifth in team passing yards. Finished in the league's top 10 in passing yards in '76.

COLTS

1. Johnny Unitas (1956-72). Achieved immortal status in the 1958 title game and solidified it the following year, when he again led the Colts to the NFL title.

2. Peyton Manning (1998-present). Broke Dan Marino's long-standing season touchdown pass record with 49 and set a passer rating mark of 121.1 in a phenomenal 2004 season. A five-time Pro Bowl player who topped the 4,000-yard passing barrier in six of his first seven seasons. The 2003 NFL co-MVP and 2004 MVP should surpass all of Unitas' passing marks in time.

3. Bert Jones (1973-81). The '76 NFL MVP. Led the Colts to three consecutive AFC divisional playoff games in the mid-'70s. Is No. 3 in club passing yards behind Unitas and Manning.

4. Earl Morrall (1968-71). A lifetime backup and journeyman who lacks the career numbers of other Colts quarterbacks. Was league MVP in '68, though, when he guided the Colts to Super Bowl 3.

5. George Shaw (1955-58). Always will be known as the injured quarterback who made way for Johnny U. Was the No. 1 overall pick in the '55 draft and helped the Colts' climb to respectability in the immediate pre-Unitas years.

COWBOYS

1. Roger Staubach (1969-79). An artful scrambler and big-play maker. Served four years of military duty before morphing into a Hall of Fame quarterback. Guided the Cowboys to victory in Super Bowl 6 (MVP) and Super Bowl 12.

2. Troy Aikman (1989-2000). Took the Cowboys from the cellar to stellar, directing three Super Bowl victories. Is the Cowboys' all-time leading passer and MVP of Super Bowl 27.

3. Don Meredith (1960-68). The Cowboys' fourth all-time leader in passing yards. Saw the franchise from its inception through the classic Ice Bowl, leading Dallas to consecutive NFL title games. Few quarterbacks were tougher.

4. Danny White (1976-88). Had a longer tenure than any other Dallas quarterback, thanks in part to his skillful punting. Was a great athlete who still ranks No. 3 on Cowboys' passing yardage list. Had more touchdown passes (155) than Staubach (153).

5. Craig Morton (1965-74). Was the quarterback between Meredith and Staubach. Helped the Cowboys to eight consecutive playoff appearances, including a pair of Super Bowls.

DOLPHINS

1. Dan Marino (1983-99). Marino or Griese? Stats vs. rings. To some it might be a tossup, but Marino's exhaustive passel of NFL passing records is extraordinary. Also, a great team surrounded Griese.

2. Bob Griese (1967-80). Is a Hall of Famer, wears two Super Bowl rings and co-quarterbacked the only perfect team in NFL history. Regardless, he still must stand second on the Dolphins' list.

3. Earl Morrall (1972-76). In '72, subbing for injured Griese, he guided Miami to the AFC championship game before handing the reins back to Griese at halftime to land the final two wins. Was the '72 NFL Comeback Player of the Year.

4. Don Strock (1974-87). Produced a memorable performance in a 41-38 overtime playoff loss to San Diego during the 1981 season, in which he passed for 403 yards and four touchdowns.

5. David Woodley (1980-83). Though his career numbers are poor, he led the '82 Dolphins to three playoff victories, including a 14-0 AFC title game win over the Jets.

DON MEREDITH, Cowboys (1960-68)

EAGLES

1. Tommy Thompson (1941-42, 1945-50). Perhaps he was unsung in his time, but the one-eyed Thompson brought the franchise its first two NFL titles, in '48 and '49, leading the league in passing in '48.

2. Donovan McNabb (1999-present). Has guided the Eagles to four consecutive NFC championship games and to a berth in Super Bowl 39. Is a five-time Pro Bowl player. A Super Bowl ring would catapult him to No. 1 on this list.

3. Randall Cunningham (1985-95). Arguably the finest running quarterback in NFL history. Was a three-time Pro Bowler who guided the Eagles to five postseason appearances. Ranks No. 2 all-time in team passing yards.

4. Ron Jaworski (1977-86). Is the leading passer in club history and led the team to its first Super Bowl appearance (1980). Owns the longest touchdown pass in Eagles history, 99 yards to Mike Quick (1985).

5. Norm Van Brocklin (1958-60). Spent the bulk of his career with the Rams but immortalized himself in Philadelphia by leading the team to the 1960 NFL crown in his final game.

FALCONS

1. Steve Bartkowski (1975-85). The Falcons' No. 1 all-time passer. Led the team to three playoff appearances during Atlanta's down years and twice was selected to the Pro Bowl.

2. Chris Miller (1987-93). Only an early retirement-inducing series of concussions kept him from achieving a significant NFL career. Still ranks No. 2 all-time in Atlanta passing yards.

3. Michael Vick (2001-present). Might be the fastest player in the league and has been called the most electrifying performer in NFL history. Can beat opponents with both his arm and legs. Has led the team to the playoffs in each of his two healthy seasons and was named both times to the Pro Bowl.

4. Chris Chandler (1997-2001). A journeyman who took the Falcons to Super Bowl 33. Played for seven NFL teams but hung around Atlanta long enough to rank third all-time in club passing yards.

5. Bob Berry (1968-72). Brought the Falcons their first measure of respectability with a pair of .500 seasons in the early 1970s. Led the team in passing in each of his Atlanta seasons.

49ERS

1. Joe Montana (1979-92). A three-time Super Bowl MVP, a four-time Super Bowl winner, a Hall of Famer and San Francisco's No. 1 passer all-time.

2. Steve Young (1987-99). A seven-time Pro Bowler who might have surpassed all of Montana's and John Brodie's marks had he not succumbed to concussions. Was a two-time NFL MVP and Super Bowl 29 MVP.

3. John Brodie (1957-73). The longest-tenured player in team history and the Niners' No. 2 career passer. Toiled on average teams yet led San Francisco to two NFC title game appearances and was the 1970 league MVP.

4. Y.A. Tittle (1951-60). Was UPI's 1957 league MVP with San Francisco (also twice with the Giants). Was part of the 49ers' famed "Million Dollar Backfield" with Hugh McElhenny, Joe Perry and John Henry Johnson.

5. Frankie Albert (1946-52). The franchise's first quarterback, back in the All-America Football Conference days. Was a stellar but undersized performer. Was the co-MVP of the AAFC in '48 and was the Niners' head coach from 1956-58.

GIANTS

1. Phil Simms (1979-93). Is the Giants' all-time passing yardage leader. Was MVP of Super Bowl 21 and one of only eight quarterbacks to throw for more than 500 yards in an NFL game.

2. Charlie Conerly (1948-61). Also known as Chuckin' Charlie and the Marlboro Man. Drove New York to three NFL title games, winning in '56. Was the NFL co-MVP in '59 and is the Giants' No. 2 all-time passer.

3. Y.A. Tittle (1961-64). Enjoyed four Blanda-like years to cap a Hall of Fame career that included 10 years with San Francisco. Led New York to the NFL championship game three consecutive times but didn't win.

4. Jeff Hostetler (1985-92). A rugged passer/runner, he was Simms' backup until '90, when he came on in relief late in the season and took the Giants to victory in Super Bowl 25.

5. Benny Friedman (1929-31). Was the last player to lead the NFL in rushing touchdowns and touchdown passes in the same year (1928). Led the NFL in touchdown passes two of his three seasons with New York.

JAGUARS

1. Mark Brunell (1995-2003). Was the team's quarterback its first eight seasons. Guided Jacksonville to two AFC championship games. The drafting of Byron Leftwich in '03 made Brunell expendable.

2. Byron Leftwich (2003-present). A traditional pocket passer with great leadership skills and toughness. One of the NFL's rising stars.

JETS

1. Joe Namath (1965-76). Broadway Joe brought more to pro football than the improbable Super Bowl 3 victory over Baltimore. Successfully blended lifestyle, talent and glamour into unrivaled stardom not seen since Red Grange.

2. Ken O'Brien (1983-92). Was an

RON JAWORSKI, Eagles (1977-86)

unsung member of the quarterback draft class of '83. Was a two-time Pro Bowl player. Ended up No. 2 all-time in club passing yards and guided the Jets to three postseason appearances.

3. Richard Todd (1976-83). Followed Namath from Alabama to New York. Is No. 3 all-time in Jets passing yards and took New York to the AFC title game in '82.

4. Vinny Testaverde (1998-2003). Became the Jets' fourth all-time passing yards leader in just six seasons in New York and twice led them to the playoffs.

5. Chad Pennington (2000-present). A consistent thrower who seldom makes mistakes in the red zone; he has 38 TD passes and no interceptions inside the opponents' 20-yard line. Has led the Jets to the playoffs in each season he was healthy enough to start at least 12 games.

LIONS

1. Bobby Layne (1950-58). The cantankerous Hall of Famer, a renowned party hound, led the Lions to three NFL titles (jointly with Tobin Rote in '57). Still is the Lions' all-time leader in passing yards.

2. Dutch Clark (1931-32, 1934-38). The league's last true dropkicker. Was a triple-threat tailback and a six-time All-Pro. Led Detroit to its first NFL championship in '35.

3. Scott Mitchell (1994-98). Detroit's No. 2 leader in passing yards also owns the highest career passer rating (79.2) in team history for quarterbacks with more than 300 attempts. Is the only Detroit quarterback to throw for more than 4,000 yards in a season (4,338 in '95).

4. Greg Landry (1968-78). Logged 11 seasons with Detroit, four as a starter and several as a co-starter with Bill Munson. Was a Pro Bowl quarterback in '71.

5. Bill Munson (1968-75). His numbers for career touchdown passes and interceptions, along with his passer rating, are better than some of the Detroit quarterbacks listed ahead of him.

PACKERS

1. Brett Favre (1992-present). His stats are twice Bart Starr's numbers and he finished the 2004

season ranked No. 2 all-time in touchdown passes (376) and third all-time in passing yards (49,734).

2. Bart Starr (1956-71). Has more world championships (five), Super Bowl victories (two) and Super Bowl MVPs (two) than Favre.

3. Arnie Herber (1930-40). The Hall of Famer led the Packers to four NFL championships in the '30s and is considered the game's first great downfield passer.

4. Cecil Isbell (1938-42). A tailback, like Herber, in Green Bay's single-wing attack became the first passer in NFL history to throw for more than 2,000 yards in a season (1942).

5. Lynn Dickey (1976-77, 1979-85). Threw most of the passes that Hall of Famer James Lofton caught as a Packer. Led the NFL in passing yards in '83. Overcame a debilitating hip dislocation with Houston early in his career.

PANTHERS

1. Steve Beuerlein (1996-2000). The Panthers' all-time leader in passing yards went to the Pro Bowl in '99. After three seasons with Denver, he signed with Carolina in July of '04 so he could retire as a Panther.

2. Jake Delhomme (2003-present). Shows a flare for fourth-quarterback comebacks. Guided the Panthers to Super Bowl 38. Almost led the team to the 2004 playoffs with an offense missing its top five running backs and No. 1 receiver.

3. Kerry Collins (1995-98). The franchise's first draft choice and starting quarterback in its first three years. Led Carolina to the '96 NFC championship game, earning Pro Bowl honors that year.

PATRIOTS

1. Tom Brady (2000-present). After four seasons as New England's starting quarterback, he ranked among the most successful field generals in NFL history. The Brady-led Pats had won three Super Bowls and he had earned two Super Bowl MVP trophies.

2. Drew Bledsoe (1993-2001). Was the No. 1 overall pick in the '93 draft. Tops all Patriots passers in career statistics. Is a four-time Pro Bowl player. Was the youngest quarterback in history to reach 10,000 yards passing and led New England to Super Bowl 31.

3. Steve Grogan (1975-90). The gritty player has the longest tenure in club history. Ranks second all-time behind Bledsoe in team passing records and guided the Pats to three postseason appearances.

4. Babe Parilli (1961-67). Was the franchise's first star quarterback. Was a three-time AFL All-Star Game selection and took the then-Boston Patriots to the AFL Eastern Division title in '63.

5. Tony Eason (1983-89). Was a member of the famed quarterback draft Class of 1983. Best known for leading New England to Super Bowl 20.

RAIDERS

1. Ken Stabler (1970-79). The Snake. The No. 1 passer in Raiders history was NFL MVP in '74 and directed the team to five consecutive AFC championship games and a victory in Super Bowl 11.

2. Jim Plunkett (1978-86). Was the NFL Comeback Player of the Year in '80. His career was all but buried before Al Davis rescued him. Repaid Davis with victories in Super Bowl 15 (he was the MVP) and 18.

3. Daryle Lamonica (1967-74). Was a great downfield passer. Took

VINNY TESTAVERDE, Jets (1998-2003)

the Raiders to four consecutive AFL/AFC championship games. Won the AFL title in '67 and appeared in Super Bowl 2.

4. George Blanda (1967-75). To appreciate Blanda's longevity, understand that he's the Raiders' all-time leading scorer–but he didn't register his first point with them until his 18th season in pro football.

5. Rich Gannon (1999-present). The four-time Oakland Pro Bowl player became the NFL MVP in 2002, when he guided the Raiders to the AFC championship. Threw for a career-high 4,689 yards in his 14th NFL season.

RAMS

1. Bob Waterfield (1945-52). Led the league in passing twice and was NFL MVP in 1945. The five-time All-Pro helped the Rams reach four NFL title games and win two championships.

2. Norm Van Brocklin (1949-57). One of the great pure passers. Led the NFL three times in passing and helped guide Los Angeles to the NFL title in '51. Was named to six consecutive Pro Bowls with the Rams.

3. Roman Gabriel (1962-72). Took the Rams to two division titles ('67, '69). Was NFL Player of the Year in '69 and a three-time Pro Bowl selection.

4. Kurt Warner (1998-2003). His rags-to-riches-to-rags tale features two league MVP awards, two Super Bowl appearances, one Super Bowl ring and one Super Bowl MVP award.

5. Jim Everett (1986-93). Is the Rams' career leader in passing yards and completions. Led the team to the playoffs three times and reached the NFC championship game in '89.

RAVENS

1. Vinny Testaverde (1996-97). Is the club's all-time leading passer with 7,148 yards and 51 touchdown passes. Was named to his first Pro Bowl in '96 after 10 seasons in the NFL.

2. Kyle Boller (2003-present). A healthy 2005 season could give him status as the first quarterback to start three seasons for the Ravens.

3. Tony Banks (1999-2000). Logged about half of Testaverde's career totals in yards, touchdowns and interceptions.

REDSKINS

1. Sammy Baugh (1937-52). Slingin' Sammy–with Herber, Isbell and Luckman–pioneered the modern pro passing game. Was a six-time NFL passing leader. Led the club to championships in '37 and '42.

2. Joe Theismann (1974-85). Is the all-time leading passer in Redskins history and led Washington to consecutive Super Bowls, winning 17.

3. Sonny Jurgensen (1964-74). Carved Hall of Fame credentials with a shotgun arm that amassed enough statistics to rate No. 2 on the Redskins' career passing yardage list.

4. Mark Rypien (1988-93). Was the MVP of Super Bowl 26. Led Washington in passing five consecutive seasons, gaining Pro Bowl honors twice. Ranks fourth all-time in Redskins passing yards.

ROMAN GABRIEL, Rams

5. Billy Kilmer (1971-78). Survived a near-fatal car wreck in 1962 to play 14 additional seasons and spent the last eight with Washington. Is No. 5 all-time in team passing yards. Guided the Redskins to Super Bowl 7.

SAINTS

1. Archie Manning (1971-75, 1977-82). The famous Manning bloodline began here. Was the NFC Player of the Year in 1978. Is the Saints' No. 1 career passer. Never played on a team with a winning record over 11 seasons.

2. Aaron Brooks (2000-present). Moved into second on Saints' career passing yardage list in 2004. Threw for more than 3,500 yards in each of the four seasons from 2001-04.

3. Bobby Hebert (1985-89, 1991-92). In 1987, he guided New Orleans to its first winning record and first postseason appearance.

4. Billy Kilmer (1967-70). A Bobby Layne replica who ranks fifth in career passing yards for Saints. Completed the longest pass in Saints history–a 96-yarder to Walt Roberts in '67.

5. Jim Everett (1994-96). Performed brilliantly in just three seasons and posted the highest career passing percentage in club history (61.0).

SEAHAWKS

1. Dave Krieg (1980-91). Is No. 1 in career passing yards for Seattle and among the NFL's top 10 quarterbacks all-time statistically. Led Seattle to four of its first seven playoff appearances and to a franchise-best mark of 12-4 in '84.

2. Jim Zorn (1976-84). The franchise's inaugural quarterback was a southpaw who still ranks No. 2 on the team's passing yardage list. Helped quarterback team to its only AFC championship game appearance in '83.

3. Matt Hasselbeck (2001-present). The No. 3 man in franchise passing yards earned his first Pro Bowl selection in 2003. Led the 2003 and 2004 Seahawks to their first playoff appearances since 1999.

4. Jon Kitna (1997-2000). Had his finest season as a Seahawk in '99, passing for 3,346 yards and 23 touchdowns, and took Seattle to its first playoff appearance in 11 years.

5. Rick Mirer (1993-96). Selected No. 2 overall in the '93 draft, he was cast as the franchise savior but failed to deliver.

STEELERS

1. Terry Bradshaw (1970-83). Directed arguably the strongest dynasty in NFL history to four Super Bowl victories in six seasons during the '70s. Was MVP of

DAVID CARR, Texans (2002-present)

Super Bowls 13 and 14.

2. Neil O'Donnell (1990-95). Is No. 1 all-time in Pittsburgh passer ratings (81.6). Took the Steelers to the AFC championship game in '94 and Super Bowl 30 a year later.

3. Bobby Layne (1958-62). After a prolific career in Detroit, he lifted the Steelers of the late '50s and early '60s. Took the team to the 1962 Playoff Bowl.

4. Jim Finks (1949-55). Before there was Jim Finks, the Hall of Fame front office executive, there was Jim Finks, the quarterback for the Steelers. Led the NFL in touchdown passes in '52 and in attempts, completions and yards in '55.

5. Kordell Stewart (1995-2002). Versatile and athletic, Stewart ranks No. 2 all-time in Steelers career passing yards. Guided Pittsburgh to AFC championship games in 1997 and 2001 and earned Pro Bowl recognition in '01.

TEXANS

1. David Carr (2002-present). The first draft pick in Texans' history has prospered as the talent has improved around him. Started 43 of 48 possible games as the Texans' No. 1 quarterback through their first three seasons.

TITANS/OILERS

1. Warren Moon (1984-93). Is NFL's No. 4 all-time leader in pass attempts, completions and yards. Was the triggerman of the Oilers' run-and-shoot offense, guiding Houston to the playoffs seven consecutive seasons.

2. George Blanda (1960-66). Had his best years with Houston, taking the team to AFL championships in 1960 and '61.

3. Steve McNair (1995-present). The NFL's 2003 co-MVP is regarded as one of the toughest quarterbacks ever to play the game. Led Tennessee to five playoff victories and an appearance in Super Bowl 34.

4. Dan Pastorini (1971-79). Was the third overall pick in the '71 draft. Took the Oilers to two playoff appearances, including classic AFC championship game losses to Pittsburgh in '78 and '79.

5. Pete Beathard (1967-69). The 10-year NFL quarterback spent three seasons in Houston, guiding it to the '67 AFL championship game and a '69 AFL playoff game, both losses to Oakland.

VIKINGS

1. Fran Tarkenton (1961-66, 1972-78). An uncanny scrambler, he's the franchise's No. 1 all-time passer. Guided the Vikes to three Super Bowl losses in the mid-'70s.

2. Daunte Culpepper (1999-present). Threw 39 touchdown passes in 2004, tied for fifth most in a season, and only 11 interceptions for an amazing 110.9 passer rating. Has an outstanding 93.2 career passer rating and 129 TD passes. Is a dual threat who has run for 28 career TDs.

3. Tommy Kramer (1977-89). Was Tarkenton's successor and the No. 2 career passer in Minnesota history. Owns the club record for most passing yards in a game (490) and took the Vikings to the postseason twice.

4. Wade Wilson (1981-91). Replaced Kramer in '87. Directed the Vikings to three consecutive postseasons, including the NFC title game in '87. Led the NFL in completion percentage (61.4) in '88.

5. Joe Kapp (1967-69). The swashbuckling former CFL passer was in Minnesota for just three seasons but will be remembered for leading the '69 team to Super Bowl 4, where it was upset by AFL champion Kansas City.

SELECT COMPANY

How we did it A quarterback's greatness, as Paul Attner explains in the book's opening essay, is difficult to measure. And yet that was the task accepted by a panel of experts when asked to rank the top 50 quarterbacks in pro football history.

The ranking process began with the collection of names of quarterbacks worthy of consideration. Quarterbacks in the Pro Football Hall of Fame, league MVPs, Super Bowl MVPs and so on—all those names and more were gathered. Statistics revealed dozens of career and season leaders in various categories. Pro Bowl rosters were scanned to ensure that no deserving candidates were overlooked.

A list of 144 quarterbacks, from Aikman to Zorn, was presented to a dozen *Sporting News* writers and editors who are, or have been, involved with NFL coverage and have extensive knowledge of pro football history. The voters were instructed to consider numerous criteria, including statistical achievements relative to each quarterback's era, team success, leadership ability and performance in big games. The voters then dived into the research materials in preparation for the balloting.

The voting went through several stages, beginning with the selection of a top 50. Armed with those 50 names, the panel was asked to vote again on just the top 10. A third ballot produced the order of the top 10. This process was repeated for subsequent groupings of players until all 50 quarterbacks were ranked.

Though the top 50 reflects the voting of 12 experts, the resulting list generated some in-house debate after the fact—this guy is too high, that guy is too low. But that's the nature of the beast when trying to measure greatness. We can only imagine the discussion our top 50 will provoke among those who weren't involved in its production.

Let the debate begin.